Male Rape is a Feminist Issue

Critical Criminological Perspectives

The Palgrave *Critical Criminological Perspectives* book series aims to showcase the importance of critical criminological thinking when examining problems of crime, social harm and criminal and social justice. Critical perspectives have been instrumental in creating new research agendas and areas of criminological interest. By challenging state defined concepts of crime and rejecting positive analyses of criminality, critical criminological approaches continually push the boundaries and scope of criminology, creating new areas of focus and developing new ways of thinking about, and responding to, issues of social concern at local, national and global levels. Recent years have witnessed a flourishing of critical criminological narratives and this series seeks to capture the original and innovative ways that these discourses are engaging with contemporary issues of crime and justice.

Series editors:
Professor Reece Walters
Faculty of Law, Queensland University of Technology, Australia

Dr. Deborah Drake
Department of Social Policy and Criminology, The Open University, UK

Titles include:

Claire Cohen
MALE RAPE IS A FEMINIST ISSUE
Feminism, Governmentality and Male Rape

Deborah Drake
PRISONS, PUNISHMENT AND THE PURSUIT OF SECURITY

Maggie O'Neill and Lizzie Seal (*editors*)
TRANSGRESSIVE IMAGINATIONS
Crime, Deviance and Culture

Critical Criminological Perspectives
Series Standing Order ISBN 978–0–230–36045–7 hardback
(*outside North America only*)

You can receive future titles in this series as they are published by placing a standing order. Please contact your bookseller or, in case of difficulty, write to us at the address below with your name and address, the title of the series and the ISBN quoted above.

Customer Services Department, Macmillan Distribution Ltd, Houndmills, Basingstoke, Hampshire RG21 6XS, England

Male Rape is a Feminist Issue

Feminism, Governmentality and Male Rape

Claire Cohen
Senior Lecturer in Criminology, Division of Sociology, Nottingham Trent University, UK

First published 2014 by
PALGRAVE MACMILLAN

Palgrave Macmillan in the UK is an imprint of Macmillan Publishers Limited, registered in England, company number 785998, of Houndmills, Basingstoke, Hampshire RG21 6XS.

Palgrave Macmillan in the US is a division of St Martin's Press LLC, 175 Fifth Avenue, New York, NY 10010.

Palgrave Macmillan is the global academic imprint of the above companies and has companies and representatives throughout the world.

Palgrave® and Macmillan® are registered trademarks in the United States, the United Kingdom, Europe and other countries.

ISBN 978–0–230–22396–7

This book is printed on paper suitable for recycling and made from fully managed and sustained forest sources. Logging, pulping and manufacturing processes are expected to conform to the environmental regulations of the country of origin.

A catalogue record for this book is available from the British Library.

A catalog record for this book is available from the Library of Congress.

Typeset by MPS Limited, Chennai, India.

*To Susan and Phillip, my beloved
and inspirational parents*

Contents

Acknowledgements

The majority of this project was undertaken whilst I was in post as Senior Lecturer in Applied Criminology and Programme Director for Crime and Policing at Canterbury Christ Church University, UK. I would like to thank staff and students at my former institution for their interest and encouragement; I am particularly grateful for the award of three months study leave – it simply would not have been possible to complete this project within three years without it.

My sincere thanks to Senior Commissioning Editor Philippa Grand, for giving me the opportunity and encouragement to bring this project to fruition – I am forever indebted. Thanks also to the Palgrave team: Commisioning Editor Julia Willan, and Assistant Editors Harriet Barker, Olivia Middleton, Andrew James and Ellie Shillito, for their endless support, patience and kindness; to Senior Production Editors Matthew Aldridge and Jonathan Lewis; and to editors Alec McAulay and Laurie McAulay. My appreciation also goes to the Series Editor Professor Reece Walters for his enthusiasm and feedback. Thank you to my PhD supervisor Dr Colin Wright for his kind words of encouragement, constant faith in this thesis and for reading and commenting on early draft chapters; to Professor Roger Bromley for generously looking through and commenting on an early complete draft; and to Dr Robin Bryant for his helpful observations and questions in relation to an early draft of the introduction.

A project of this scope takes a toll on family. To that end I must express my gratitude to my mother, Sue, and to my sisters Samantha and Cheryl – thank you all for lending me your boundless strength and determination; to my grandmother, Joan, I could not have achieved this without you; and finally, to my wonderful husband Alan Lee, my best friend and staunch ally for 20 years, whose unwavering belief in me and endless emotional support made it possible to see this project through: I owe you far more than I can ever express. Thank you.

Part I
Contextualizing Chapters –
Thinking Differently

1
Introduction – Feminism, Governmentality and 'Male' Rape

1.1 Preliminary reflections

Rape has long been a feminist issue.[1,2] So apparently uncontentious is this statement that it is often held as a truism. However, one must attend to the assumptions inherent within this construct.[3] Just as feminists highlighted gender bias in language, whereby certain gender-neutral terms were imbued with assumptions of masculinity, so it can be noted that the rise of feminism and its proliferation within victimology has imbued certain categories of victimization as intrinsically female – this is especially the case with rape. Hence the need to denote the male in this 'gender-neutral' crime.

Thus, whilst it is now some 20 years since the Criminal Justice and Public Order Act (1994) first recognized the male rape victim in law,[4] and 19 years[5] since the first conviction for this crime, we are still far from regarding rape as gender-neutral in terms of victimization – in fact it is vehemently (and erroneously) preserved as gendered. Consider the following statements highlighted in, and seemingly endorsed by, a 1997 jurisprudence text that was published subsequent to the legislative change: 'rape is still the most gender specific of all crimes' (Temkin, 1987, cited in Barnett, 1997, p. 387), 'only a man ... can be the actual perpetrator, *only a woman the victim*' (Sexual Offences Amendment Act, 1976, cited in Barnett, 1997, p. 387 (italics added)).[6] Consider also the official recorded statistics that show an enormous disparity between the incidence of male rape reported to the police and that of female rape.[7] How might these phenomena be explained? For some, the statistics might be construed as legitimizing the popular misperceptions, enabling us to state that rape is still a disproportionately gendered crime; for others, perhaps the misperceptions can be regarded as generating the statistics – that is, our gendered misperceptions inhibit reporting and recording practices and result in rape merely appearing to be disproportionately gendered. I can certainly see value in each of these explanations, but neither is one I seek to endorse.

A little caution needs to be exercised here. As Foucault (1984, cited in Gordon, 2001, p. xxxiv) states: 'the work of an intellectual is ... to bring assumptions and things taken for granted again into question, to shake habits, ways of acting and thinking, to dispel the familiarity of the accepted'. It is incumbent on those of us engaged in 'knowledge production' to stop and question logics that are taken for granted, common sense, or supposedly obvious. Shared, popular or common knowledge[8] is essentially what everyone knows to be true, and furthermore 'what everyone knows everyone knows' (Graham, 2006, cited in Hassan and Thomas, 2006, p. 64). In many ways the implications and reach of this is far greater than that of the specialist and exclusive realm of the academy – given that it 'is essential to public debate in democracies' (Hassan and Thomas, 2006, p. 64). In this sense it is central to civil society, and to social control – to knowing others and one's self. This caution is doubly so for those of us informed by Foucault, as he urges us to step outside those well-worn conceptual grooves that function both in forming and delimiting our enquiry. We must therefore impel ourselves to 'think differently',[9] or at least attempt to do so.

Thus I do not seek to explain the phenomenon of male rape in respect of either position outlined above, not least because it can readily be observed that British Crime Survey (self-report) data – which seeks to present a more accurate picture of crime and victimization – reveals far less disparity;[10] but also, and more importantly, because each position described above represents a polarized stance that is not reconcilable, and hence serves merely to consume and deflect energies in zero-sum arguments. Most significantly, the above positions are frequently allied to populist rhetoric in defence of feminism versus castigation of feminism respectively. It is in fact this supposedly futile exchange that I find to be compelling and significant.

In line with my peers, the initial inclination I had when first investigating the issue of 'male' rape was to place my enquiry squarely within the established debate. Specifically, I sought to attribute this trend to the primacy of feminism in victimology. Or rather, to conceive of feminism as something akin to a paradigm that regulated discourse through the construction of the 'legitimate' victim in reference to gendered hierarchies relating to patriarchal oppression. This would function, therefore, to effectively gender the debate in victimology in general and that relating to sexual victimization in particular. Consequently, I saw my objective quite clearly as in line with many of my contemporaries: to assert the normalcy and hence significance of male rape; to rail against the injustices faced by victims; and, moreover, to explicate precisely 'who' is to blame for those injustices – where, of course, 'who' was already conveniently populated by the supposedly culpable figure of feminism.

These rationales, and facets thereof, are routinely invoked and are explored and elucidated in existing texts in various forms and at various levels, for example, from innocuous bias discussed by Graham (2006) to outright allegations of sexual discrimination in the form of misandry as outlined by Nathanson and Young (2006). Although I will admit all are both plausible and persuasive, they are rationales I have come to be increasingly dissatisfied with for precisely these reasons.

Instead of pursuing an enquiry in relation to substantive 'truth' or 'justice' then, or orienting my discussion to the influence of feminism, I move my discussion beyond these concepts and issues. I argue instead that we ought to focus on the specific construct of the rape of the male, to its particularization, transformations and consensus that contribute to a discursive regularity; and thus to its potential significance within governmentality. In doing so I recognize that oppositional polemics – and indeed the 'evidence' upon which these are based – are necessarily implicated in this process, rather than existing outside of it.

In pursuing this agenda and its line of enquiry, I have deliberately revolted against the siren song emanating from the established debate and from its well-worn path of least resistance. However, can that original thesis simply be dismissed as a marker of what should not be? Retained here merely as a sketch of an abandoned or failed project? Not at all. That thesis has influenced my work pervasively in that I have felt it necessary to sustain a clear rejection of it – not because it was readily abandoned or clearly failing, but precisely because it was neither. I have constantly struggled to free my work from its persistent murmurings and its temptation. In this sense, the contours of that thesis, and the debate of which it was so comfortably a part, have been enormously influential – and so it is a problematization of that debate that I specifically explore.

Consequently, that original thesis has been complexified to query how and why male rape is presented as a feminist issue. My interest therefore is not a rights- or justice-based agenda, but recognition that the male victim of rape is constructed at present in reluctant and stilted conversation with feminism and, outside of rape crisis activism, as a product – at least in part – of a circumspect and defensive positioning that may be attributed to fear of backlash, such as can be noted in analyses by Gillespie (1996), Gavey (2005) and Bourke (2007). I acknowledge and respect such concerns, but propose that 'male rape' in its current form functions far more effectively as part of backlash by virtue of such protectionism, not despite it.

The conclusion I have reached is that male rape is indeed a political (and politicized) issue – just not in the way that I first thought. The 'feminism as a paradigm' rationale is seductive, appealing and simplistic. This in itself should be a cause for concern. Foucault conceptualizes power as operating on subjects via a 'polyhedron'[11] of technologies – dynamic, multifarious, complex and confounding – to enable governance. Most significantly, for the purpose of this work, he notes the utility of counter-discourse as assimilated and affirming,[12] implicitly suggesting therefore that we should not seek the 'truth' but the 'irony'[13] in order to divest ourselves of the progressive illusion.

Hence, my interest in this area concerns the ways that current constructs of male rape – especially feminist, pro-feminist and pseudo-feminist constructs – function 'ironically', for example, being self-defeating and conformist despite appearing to be empowering and subversive. The ultimate example of which I argue to be the phenomenon of recursion or 'writing back'.[14] In this sense, I posit that the supposedly competing knowledges around rape, especially gendered knowledges regarding a particularization of male versus female rape, can actually be said to comprise a single archive that runs along several corresponding registers; and that, therefore, constructs relating to the supposed specificity of male rape draw from and in effect resuscitate previously discredited (ostensibly female oriented) rape myths[15] that are in themselves recognized as having a concrete impact on all victims of sexual violence.[16] I speculate that this functions to reinforce, support and perpetuate hegemonic masculinities[17] and patriarchal power relations; and that our understanding of rape then is not so much gendered as it is gendering – coming to constitute the subject[18] in line with patriarchal gender norms.

Suffice to say that feminist discourse, and indeed faux-feminist(ish) discourse, in relation to male rape can plausibly be claimed to operate as a 'regime of truth',[19] but as a Foucauldian, one must necessarily question whether this runs counter to patriarchy.[20] This is my attempt to 'think differently' about the discourse around male rape and feminism.

1.2   Overview

Above all, this work is an experiment in, and conversation with, Foucauldian thought. Situated ostensibly at the interface between feminism and victimology,[21] this book is divided into three discrete but interrelated parts. Part I contextualizes the forthcoming triangulation and consists of: Chapter 1, the introduction; Chapter 2, 'Problematization: A Critical Ontology of the Present', which presents the case for the need to 'think differently' in relation to the phenomenon of male rape as a problematic. In so doing, it re-examines the historical and thematic trajectories of academic knowledge in this area, contributes a genealogy of male rape to the field, and provides the justification and context for the following discussion; and Chapter 3, 'A Foucauldian Triangulation?', which explores methodological and epistemological considerations for thinking and investigating through Foucault, and therefore focuses on clarifying and substantiating my particular method and its contribution to the field which includes, but is not limited to, the concept of recursion. Part II deals with the application of my method and presents new data and original analysis. Part III summarizes the key findings in this work, presents new analysis and critique and articulates the theoretical implications of these for the continuing dialogue between Foucauldian thought and feminism; and of Foucauldian theory to criminology.

Chapter 2 traces the contours and transformations of 'knowledge' produced in respect of male rape within the academy. In doing so it performs two functions: it serves as a cursory literature review, whilst in itself comprising a contingent aspect of the first stage of the triangulation by highlighting trends, consensus and transformations in accepted 'truths', which in the subsequent chapters will then be tracked across the dimensions that are taken to comprise governmentality. In essence, this is intended to vindicate the need to 'think differently' in respect of this problem and expressly explicates my resultant problematization of this issue.

The aim of Chapter 3 is twofold: to clarify my interpretation of Foucauldian thought and to justify the application of that to this issue. In essence, it explores how one might investigate differently by thinking through Foucault. I am sensitive to the resistance to and denigration of a (stereotyped) notion of Foucauldian thought within certain sectors of criminology, particularly those that regard themselves as 'crime science', and to the exploitation of a simplified and perhaps even erroneous adaptation within others.[22] Consequently, in this chapter I highlight relevant debate around the defining of Foucault's concepts, the extent to which these concepts might be operationalized as methods and indeed the issues surrounding whether in fact they should be.[23] Chapter 3 explicitly addresses such concerns, delineates core concepts for the purpose of this book and explores guiding assumptions. In so doing it establishes the overarching method for this work, provides an example of how other criminologists might go about 'doing' Foucault, and extends an invitation to them.

Part II is concerned with the application of my method, and addresses three separate, albeit interrelated, areas of concern: representations, bio-politics and individuation, which together comprise governmentality – or, more accurately, come to constitute the individual or subject as the site of and vehicle for governmentality. The aim here is not only to apply my particular Foucauldian 'method', but also to reflexively evaluate and modify it. It is enough to say at this point that Foucault's power/knowledge is not a nexus as such, rather it is a complex and mul-tifaceted process[24] that has been incisively abridged by authors such as Mendieta (2002) as Foucault's 'triangulation' – a beautifully simple dis-tillation of Foucault's oeuvre that provided the impetus for the creation of my own methodological approach, briefly described below.

Foucault (1997, p. 24) simplified governmentality as discernible by two limits: 'on the one hand, the rules of right that formally delineate power, and on the other hand, at the opposite extreme, the other limit might be the truth-effects that power produces, that this power conducts and which in their turn, reproduce power. So we have the triangle: power, right, truth.' Mendieta (2002, p. 6) sketches this as lying 'between the discourses of the production of truth, the power that these discourses enact and make available to social agents, and the constitution of a political rationality that is linked to the invention and creation of its horizon of activity and surveillance'. In my method these limits have been disaggregated to contrive three social 'realms' that co-constitute the subject – this is intended to illustrate governmentality in action whilst comprising what Nadeson (2008, p. 12) termed a 'geneal-ogy without history'.

I have allowed this to guide and divide my areas of interest thus: the production of the truth of male rape and sexual victimization located in the media; the power that these enact, arguably located at the level of the individual and in institutional practice and 'expertise'; and the hori-zon of activity and surveillance concerned with what Mendieta, (2002, p. 6) calls the 'regulation of life', which – in this instance – I argue is enabled through the guiding rationalities that promote and facilitate the inevitability and primacy of the conflations of sex/sexuality/gender that enable the discourse on male rape to function as a biopolitic in its deployment of gender. This for me is the crux of male rape when understood through governmentality. Thus, the triangulation chapter as a whole is intended to excavate present homologies in the area of male rape and to counter and problematize the current knowledge and practices that reify[25] the male rape victim in accordance with these.

The preceding chapters all involve a discussion of feminist theories and activism, but to a degree that is necessarily tentative and simplified. However, Part III is an explicit reflection on the significance of male rape to feminism(s) and indeed on the significance of feminism to male rape. It involves a sketching of the reflexive opportunities for feminist thought – not least of which compels a reappraisal of what is currently termed Foucauldian feminism, but which I posit might more accurately be regarded as feminist Foucauldianism. At the very least, this will elucidate why my research should not be read as either feminist, anti-feminist or post-feminist.

2
Problematization – A Critical Ontology of the Present

Regimes of truth both prescribe and proscribe the conceptualization of a given 'problem' and the parameters for its solution; in advocating particular ways of seeing and doing, they necessarily abjure others. In this sense they are key to the formation of what Foucault (1997, p. 7) termed 'subjugated knowledges', which he explains means two things: 'On the one hand I am referring to historical contents that have been buried or masked in functional coherences and systemizations ... I am also referring to a whole series of knowledges that have been disqualified' (ibid., p. 7). Not only are regimes of truth key to the creation of subjugated knowledges, but they are also key to the insurrection of subjugated knowledges – as when one destabilizes a regime of truth, one enables the emancipation of those knowledges disqualified by its internal conventions. This is problematization, and it underscores Foucault's imperative for us to 'think differently'.

This effort to think differently necessitates a critical grasp of both where we 'are' and how we 'got' here. The tool that Foucault gives us through which to achieve this, which I employ in this chapter, is genealogy.[1] Foucault employs genealogies to expose knowledge as situated and present it as problematized, rather than to regard it as progressive and absolute. The historical specificity of knowledge in this sense can be said to 'reveal' power. In this vein Foucault attends to the superficial constancies that belie a struggle over meaning and, conversely, the superficial discontinuities that mask constancies in operation. In both instances the resultant 'truths' are recognized to serve as part of the regime of knowledge. Thus genealogy is a vital tool in disrupting truth claims.

In the course of my genealogy, I identify three discrete phases in the rhetorical journey of knowledge construction around male rape: the 'forgotten history' of the male rape victim, the 'discovery' of the male rape victim, and the 'battle' over the male rape victim. These phases were excavated in the course of a literature review and a critical analysis of that literature,[2] performed in order to sketch the current discourse, drawing out recurrent themes and issues, and clusters and contradictions in the first instance.

This chapter both draws from and adds to the literature reviews that exist at present (Poropot and Rosevear, 1992; Rentoul and Applebloom, 1997; Davies, 2002; Davies and Rogers, 2006; Graham, 2006; Rumney and Jamel, 2009), but I note that whilst these reviews recognize various trends and limitations in the published research, they do so in a fashion that is embedded in a search for truth. They prefer to focus on ascertaining the size and nature or incidence and impact of the problem, and seek to examine the weight of empirical research, rather than reflexively engaging with the messages and assumptions such research espouses. My genealogy of male rape thus remedies a gap in the literature and, as a genealogy – sensitized therefore to excavating the situated nature of knowledge construction, not least of which is in regards to socio-historical context and shifts in consensus – it contributes a new dimension.

My inquiry reveals that the issue of male rape, in its earliest modern constructions within the academy, was very much a marginalized and pathologized phenomenon. It was situated outside of the mainstream heterosexual masculine experience and acknowledged by victimology only when it could be regarded as part of a general misogynistic continuum. Such constructions that are visible are informed by and, in turn, reinforce hegemonic masculinity,[3] generating and sustaining myths based on such stereotypes, and resulting in continued invisibility – most notably regarding heterosexual male victims and female offenders. Whilst recently assimilated by feminists within a masculinities frame for the offender, and marginalized minorities frame for the assumed homosexual or assumed 'effeminate'[4] victim, these skews are a clear attempt to make the male 'rape-able',[5] and to facilitate his tentative inclusion within a feminized rape paradigm. But I note that such inclusion, and the means by which it is achieved, ultimately serves to lend credence to essentialized notions of gender and resuscitate previously discredited rape myths. I argue that this should be a concern.

Besides this, the single most consistent trend noted is that this issue is readily oriented to feminism – either to castigate or defend; but I found that doing so requires a selective history of both rape and feminism, as not only does the construct of rape pre-date feminism, but in its earliest forms, sexual violence pre-dates our modern notions of gender. Rape, in antiquity, was not gendered. Our understanding of it became gendered. What can be noted in those earliest forms, applicable to all, is the construct of the *ideal victim*.[6] Thus, we have both our discontinuity and our continuity in the trajectory of rape.

This chapter is divided into four sections, three of which reflect the broad trajectories of the construct described above and which, chronologically speaking, are presented in reverse order – but it must be noted that they represent thematics to be discussed rather than neat time periods. This counter-intuitive presentation is intended to facilitate reflexive engagement with, and disruption of, those logics and guiding assumptions that have become conventions in this area. Thus, we commence with 'battle'.

2.1   Battle over the male rape victim

Current contours of knowledge construction in regards to 'male rape' are characterized by polemical engagement amongst invested participants. Hence, 'male' rape has become a political and politicized issue, set up in relation to the normative female – and by extension the champion of the female rape victim: feminism. The current context for debate about male rape is mired in the issues of justice and parity for the male victim in relation to the female victim – or rather the allegations of injustice and disparity, and rationalizations of those states. This comprises the present 'battle' over male rape.

In privileging one truth over another, present research in this area fuels combative and polemical academic engagement of the ilk denounced by Bhattacharyya (2000). This combativeness is clearly seen in the works of Graham (2006) versus Rumney and Jamel (2009), where these authors struggle over a denouncement of feminism versus its vindication. This type of positioning is recurrent in the literature, where dialogue about male rape frequently invokes a discussion of feminism – polarized as either denounce or defend – such as can be noted in some of the earliest specialist texts, for example, Scarce (1997) and of the more recent, for example, Abdullah-Khan (2008). The pertinent question for me, though, is not who is right – it is how did we arrive at this point? Under what circumstances, in what contexts, and moreover why might the competing 'truths' espoused by such authors be supported?

Yes, male rape victims now have recognition and redress in law alongside their female counterparts, but their inclusion in statute has not resulted in equality. This simple observation is surprisingly inflammatory, and is what has produced and continues to fuel those antagonistic camps. Positioning themselves within the aforementioned established or indeed orthodox debate, there are those who champion the male rape victim's 'cause' versus those who belittle and assail it. Concomitantly there are those who use the male rape victim to attack feminism and those who use him to defend it. Time and again I have found my enquiry interpreted by colleagues and students as steadfastly within this combative arena and with this same agenda. As a consequence, my project has been both denigrated as anti-feminist and lauded as pro-feminist – neither of which I am particularly comfortable with. Also of concern have been responses to what is misperceived as the target of my research: the male rape victim himself. I have been told that male rape is interesting but unimportant, that male rape is not really relevant and that male rape is not as bad as rape for women, as well as that it is worse. Of course, this is merely anecdotal, but it is surprising the extent to which these attitudes are borne out as themes in the literature. The issue is not that such opinions are uninformed, but rather that they can be readily supported through reference to enquiry and critique.

In recent research, there persists a perceived need to explicitly render the male as a victim. What implicitly underscores these approaches is the issue of masculinity and sexuality. In essence, it is deemed necessary to make the male 'rape-able' despite his masculinity. This is especially so where that male is heterosexual. Rather than turning the gaze onto the precarious validity of that perceived necessity, many proceed to compare and contrast male rape with that of the assumed norm – female rape – which then results in supposed evidence to support '*more than/ less than/same as*' declaratives. This seems logical within the context of existing enquiry, but it is particularly damaging in its consequences – both in attempting to quantify harm and in fuelling continued polarization of debate.

At present, many elements of conventional wisdom in the understanding of female rape become contentious when it is attempted to apply these to men. For example: authors accept that rape is a women's issue, but struggle to conceptualize it as a men's issue; they accept that women suffer trauma and other serious harms, but debate this for males; they accept that rape is not sex when women are assaulted, but query this for men; they denounce the relevance of victim culpability for women, but consider it for men; they accept that for female victims the number and frequency of offences are much greater than official statistics show, but discuss whether this is likely for males. Thus male rape is presented as a discrete area, and is frequently interpreted as at odds with or incongruous to female victimhood.

In part, this might be explained by difficulty in incorporating the male victim within the feminist model of rape,[7] a model which polarizes men as aggressors and women as victims and is based on the notion 'that such criminal behavior is most fundamentally the result of traditions of male domination in most sociopolitical and economic affairs' (Ellis and Beattie, 1983, p. 74), 'an act of male domination and demonstration of power and aggression' (Barnett, 1997, p. 426), or simply an expression of sexism (Bart, 1979). The female victim, being normative within feminist models that foreground patriarchal power, subtly continues to gender our understanding of sexual violence as a phenomenon.

The allegation that research into male rape is not abundant is itself ubiquitous, and it can be readily upheld. The area of male rape is particularly notable for its absence from current social science research and texts. This observation can clearly be made in respect of criminology's silence about this offence and its perpetrators, but it is arguably most damning in its omission from victimology, given the supposed egalitarian ethos and activism in this field. Such invisibility has been attributed to the incompatibility of male (sexual) victimization with the prevailing (essentialized) feminist theory (Mezey and King, 2000). Indeed, using the feminist rationale against itself, such silences have been decried as oppressive (Jones, 2009). In victimology this contributes to the derogation of the discipline as biased,[8] and thus exacerbates existing concerns about stagnation and irrelevancy.[9] Much of the existing research, with its lacunas and obfuscation, has already become fodder for a seemingly re-essentialized identity politics between those castigated as proponents of the men's rights movement,[10] post-feminist detractors[11] and 'activist' feminism.[12]

However, in routinely relaying that allegation, such authors erroneously dismiss the activity in this area. It is imperative to recognize that male rape is a growing field of contemporary interest that crosses disciplinary boundaries. The review performed by Graham in 2001 (published 2006) identified only 50 specialist articles, whilst Rumney and Jamel (2009), amongst the most recent reviews of the literature, cite around 100 relevant sources. Furthermore, where earlier authors were largely dependent on research oriented towards male rape in institutional settings,[13] there is now a clear move towards exploration of this phenomenon in community settings. Thus whilst not a burgeoning or rapidly growing area, it is evidently receiving more attention and is most certainly not static.

Whilst this can be regarded as a growing field in its own right, it is often scantly represented in research and scholarship within the traditional disciplinary boundaries. As a consequence, this is an issue or area often marginalized within individual disciplines. This is evidenced in popular criminology, psychology, sociology and victimology textbooks, many of which reveal the conspicuous absence of the male rape victim. Using a quasi-random technique (in line with Landrum's 1993 review of introductory psychology texts),[14] I noted omissions in core texts in forensic and generalist psychology (for example in texts by: Ainsworth, 2000; McGuire, 2004; Hansell and Damour, 2005; Bartol and Bartol, 2006; Memon et al., 2006); omissions in sociological and generalist criminology (such as: Maguire, Morgan and Reiner, 2002; Hopkins-Burke, 2003; Carrabine et al., 2004; Williams, 2004; Barkan, 2006; Watts et al., 2008); I found that it was even routinely overlooked in the specialist textbooks relating to sexual violence in general and rape in particular (for example in: Sielke, 2002; Bumiller, 2008; Horvath and Brown, 2009). This is important, as inclusion of an issue or area in textbooks can be taken not only as an as indicator of whether or not it is likely to be widely taught, and so how students and future academics are being instructed (Blumberg, 2007), but also of how they are being inducted into the conventions of their respective disciplines (Lynch and Bogen, 1997), and indeed their prejudice and biases (Peterson and Kroner, 2006).

However, whilst omission is certainly a core issue of contention and undoubtedly an indefensible practice, I would argue that the most pressing concern is not so much the academy's reluctance to engage with this issue, but rather precisely how those within academia are presently engaging, and what the repercussions of this might be. After all, the boundaries of knowledge might be marked by absence, but they are policed by inclusion. Thus it is not so much sites of resistance or limited engagement per se that are of urgent concern, but rather the manifestation of convention and consensus, obfuscation and deflection amongst those scholars who are addressing this phenomenon – irrespective of their agenda, politics or impetus.

I note that where male rape is included in the literature, it is done so in quite particular ways. I found that material regarding male rape found in current texts, tends to share certain features: the trend is to either include the subject within specialist texts with limited or no theoretical context (for example: Scacco, 1982; McMullen, 1990; Koss and Harvey, 1991; Scarce, 1997; Van de Veer, 1998; Gregory and Lees, 1999; Mezey and King, 2000; Bourke, 2007; Abdullah-Khan, 2008); or within texts that are far too generalist, being basic textbooks that deal with male victimization to some extent but only to a very limited degree with male sexual victimization (for example: Newburn and Stanko, 2002; Sgarzi and McDevitt, 2003; Goodey, 2005; Walklate, 2007a, b; Wallace, 2007); it is often the case that it is either dismissed in footnotes, asides, assertions, afterthoughts and addenda (as seen in: Koss and Harvey, 1991; Sgarzi and McDevitt, 2003; Goodey, 2005; Howitt, 2006; Meadows, 2007); or situated erroneously within chapters on, or overtly expressed as, homosexual victimization or homophobic crime (a trend that can be seen in Shively, 2003 and Wallace, 2007). Furthermore, the male rape victim is also routinely given far less textual space than the female victim (this can be noted in Lees, 1999; Sgarzi and McDevitt, 2003; Goodey, 2005; Howitt, 2006; Conklin, 2007; Davies, Francis and Greer, 2007; Gregory and Meadows, 2007; Oltmans et al., 2007; Wallace, 2007). In this sense, the message is clear: male rape victims are marginal at best, an aberration at worst. This must be regarded as a significant indictment of the academy.

In an effort to briefly illustrate the trend of dismissal, consider that Koss and Harvey (1991, p. 56) deal with male rape under a subheading, as a brief aside: 'treatment of male victims is hampered by lack of knowledge about their experiences and male support groups'; Sgarzi and McDevitt's (2003, p. 37) work contains only a brief assertion regarding acknowledgement of male rape; whilst Goodey (2005, p. 123) includes, at the end of a chapter, just four lines relating to male rape.

In regards to situating this erroneously as 'homosexual', consider Wallace's (2007) textbook, where rape is mainly addressed in a chapter entitled 'Females as Victims', a chapter pervaded by gendered assumptions underlying a victim/offender dichotomy, whilst – despite the statement that 'male rape is rarely, if ever, a homosexual problem' (ibid., p. 252) – men as victims of sexual violence are curiously only acknowledged in a chapter on special victim populations, specifically designated as 'gays and lesbians as victims of crime' (ibid., p. 251). In Meadows (2007), male rape is dealt with in the chapter 'Victims of Intimate Violence'. But despite a gender-neutral title, and a statement making neutrality explicit – 'both males and females commit such crimes and are victims' (ibid., p. 38) – the overall focus is female, with the male victim quickly redacted. Hence, when dealing specifically with marital rape the focus is solely female, as is his dealing with rape in general. Indeed, despite the overt acknowledgement that men can be victims, there are no statistics or examples apart from a bemusing statement that 'males may be victims of either heterosexual or homosexual rape' (ibid., p. 74). A further example can be found in Shively's (2003, p. 37) work, which is likewise pervaded by gendered assumptions underlying a gendered binary, enabling him to dismissively state that:

> research shows that both victims and offenders can be of either gender ... however the research described in this paper examined date rape with men as offenders and women as victims ... The main reason was that the vast majority of rapes ... are committed against women by men. Another was that college students were studied (the majority of whom identify themselves as heterosexual).

Shively's (ibid.) assumptions are that male rape is not prevalent overall, and that where it does occur, it only concerns homosexual communities.

In the textbooks I examined, I found an obvious disparity in quantity and focus, and use of gendered redaction and sexualized rationalizations – such trends as were previously criticized as significant in respect of the sidelining and marginalizing of the female in criminology[15] and criticized in relation to lack of diversity in psychology.[16]

I hoped the specialist literature that is dedicated to male rape in its own right would resolve this. Unfortunately, I found that there are very few books specializing in male rape,[17] many of which are neither readily obtainable in university libraries (because they do not generally hold them)[18] or via electronic databases[19] nor easily sourced through bookshops;[20] and that one[21] is out of print. Furthermore, on examining these specialist texts, I discovered that none challenge the established frame or seek to expressly apply or develop theory – either in the area of sexual violence or feminism itself.

Instead, specialist research and scholarship in the area of male rape is also a site for conventions. As Poropat and Rosevear (1992) assert, almost invariably an observation is made about the lack of research in this area – this is ubiquitous and is widely acknowledged as such. But I also found that this is frequently followed by an acceptance that: this crime is under-reported (as illustrated in Groth and Burgess, 1980; Kaufman et al., 1980; McMullen, 1990; Stanko and Hobdell, 1993; Pino and Meier, 1999; Mitchell et al., 1999); that myths and stereotypes abound[22] (see Struckman-Johnson and Struckman-Johnson, 1992; Davies, 2002; Stermac et al., 2004); that the impact on the victim and harm caused is substantial (see Groth and Burgess, 1980; Goyer and Eddleman, 1984; Mezey and King, 1989; Lacey and Roberts, 1991; King, 1992; Frazier, 1993; Struckman-Johnson and Struckman Johnson, 1994; Huckle, 1995; Isely and Gehrenbeck-Shim, 1997; Pino and Mier, 1999; Walker et al., 2005; Tewkesbury, 2007); and long-standing (Anderson, 1982; Coxell et al., 1999); and that prevalence, incidence and risk are significant (Kaufman et al., 1980; Forman, 1982; Sorenson et al., 1987; Coxell et al., 1999; Larimer, 1999; King et al., 2000; Kershaw et al., 2008; Light and Monk-Turner, 2009; White and Kurpius, 2002).

Such conventions are then compounded by the discernible trend to posit the male 'experience' in contrast to the female, as can be observed in recent literature reviews (Poropot and Rosevear, 1992; Rentoul and Applebloom, 1997; Davies et al., 2006; Davies and Rogers, 2006; Graham, 2006; Rumney and Jamel, 2009); and monographs (for example, Scacco, 1982; McMullen, 1990; Koss and Harvey, 1991; Scarce, 1997; Van de Veer, 1998; Gregory and Lees, 1999; Mezey and King, 2000; Bourke, 2007; Abdullah-Khan, 2008); be that implicitly (in the case of Struckman-Johnson, 1988; Stermac et al., 1996; Canter and Hodge, 1998; Rogers, 1998; Crome et al., 1999; Coxell et al., 1999; Stermac et al., 2004; Walker et al., 2005; Crome, 2006; Tewkesbury, 2007; Light and Monk-Turner, 2008), or overtly – for example, comparing and contrasting males with females in relation to prevalence (Larimer, 1999), attribution of blame (Anderson, 1999; Wakelin and Long, 2003; Davies et al., 2006), perceived motivation of the rapist by victim gender (Anderson and Swainson, 2001); reporting practices (Pino and Meier, 1999), and even in regards to emotional and behavioural reactions by gender (Seigal et al., 1990). Such trends are particularly problematic when constructed as quantifiable in comparison with female victims of rape, especially in relation to measures of 'harm' – where there emerges the articulation of rape for the male as 'more than/less than' in comparison with the female.

But such trends should not be surprising given that many researchers have as their goals the very pragmatic aim to influence criminal justice policy and practice. The provision of comparisons between rape of the male and that of the female is strategically placed to enable visibility, and is succeeding in this goal. For those researchers – diligently working within the existing boundaries of debate that have been scored for them – their inevitable agenda is a focus on rights, fairness, justice and equality. Hence, after noting limited provision for the male victim (for example, Mezey and King, 1989), their express aim is to promote understanding and recognition of this crime and its victims, in order to: raise the profile of this crime (Brochman, 1991; *Dispatches*, 1995, cited in Gregory and Lees, 1999; Davies, 2002), to improve reporting, recording and prosecution rates, and to provide the impetus for specialist provision (Perrott and Webber, 1996), as well as to stimulate further research (Pino and Meier, 1999). All of which are undoubtedly well-meaning, but regrettably insidious.

As a consequence of these otherwise noble intentions and practical agendas, what is being surreptitiously produced here is what Graham (2006, p. 187) terms the construction of the 'credible' male rape victim, but what victimologists, particularly feminist victimologists, should recognize as an 'ideal victim', or rather an ideal victim binary that creates on the one hand 'a person or category of individuals who, when hit by crime, are given most readily the complete and legitimate status of being a victim' (Christie, 1986, cited in Carrabine et al., 2004, p. 115) and so deemed worthy or deserving of recognition as a victim; and, on the other hand, creates the converse – the person or category who is deemed unworthy, undeserving and to whom legitimate status as a victim is therefore denied. Victimhood being an ascribed status, that is conditional, contingent and partisan – determined by factors other than the behaviour/offence itself.

Unsurprisingly, I found that advocates for the neglected male rape victim often promote claims that reside in the 'more than' bracket. These include that: male rape is more serious because it involves a greater level of violence and/or threats of violence through the presence of weapons and/or multiple assailants (Kaufman et al, 1980; Hillman et al., 1990; Frazier, 1993; Pino and Meier, 1999; Tewkesbury, 2007); that it is more stigmatizing and psychologically damaging than for women given these scenarios; and that such victimization carries the 'taint' (Sivakumaran, 2005, p. 1274) of homosexuality; and of a feminized vulnerability. Such rationales are a concern not only because they fail to question why men's rape scripts in relation to the male victim necessitate a high level of violence, weaponry and/or multiple assailants, but also because they become prescriptive – influencing reporting, recording and prosecution practices.

There is a rape script in effect here. This can be inferred from existing studies. For example, the study by Kaufman et al. (1980) concluded that male victims are more likely to seek medical support (and thus be referred to the police) if the crime caused serious injury. This same study found that if there is no serious injury, the victim is more likely to deny victimization occurred and thus fail to report or seek support. Therefore male rape seemingly 'must' be a crime of extreme violence in order to categorically exonerate the victim from suspicion of precipitation and willing participation; significant trauma must be exhibited or else victimhood becomes questionable; and the victim must identify himself as heterosexual or risk suspicion of culpability.[23] What is interesting in works that espouse these rationales is the persistence of the underlying conflations of rape/sex/sexuality and gender/victimhood that continue to pervade this construct of the male rape victim. In particular this profile continues to be oriented around sexuality and masculinity – invoking and re-fixing old essentialisms around biology as destiny or sexuality as identity – rather than violence per se.

Consequently, far from liberating the male from rape myths, such well-meaning analyses actually bolster them. They legitimate the assumption that men in general are not sexually violable and hence sexual victimization must involve clear physical constraint or coercion to vindicate the victim from his perceived breach of gender and of sexual orientation. Ironically, even advocates for the male victim deem it necessary to render him rape-able despite his masculinity and/or his heterosexuality. Paradoxically, such advocates bolster the core myths that are supportive of rape and minimize harm involved, namely the general conflations of rape/sex/sexuality and the specific construct of hegemonic masculinity.

Whilst implicitly drawing on such conflations in constructing male rape, I found that specialist monographs and journal articles often then choose to either forgo any attempt at theoretical explication or look to 'blame feminism'. The latter is a response that is common in non-feminist explications of this phenomenon and is a trend that has been noted and decried as 'backlash' by feminist authors (for example, Gillespie, 1996). Such explications as are available are grossly unsatisfactory as to the level of theorizing – attributing the phenomenon variously as: situated within same-sex relationships (see Hickson et al., 1994; Donnelly and Kenyon, 1996; Wallace, 2007); indicative of psychoanalytic conflict regarding sexuality on the part of either the offender or victim (Groth and Burgess, 1980; Stermac et al., 1996); a hate crime attributed to homophobia (Berrill, 1990; Toolis, 1995; Canter and Hodge, 1998); or as an extension of misogyny (Funk, 1997). Such cursory explanations have thus far served to circumvent the need to theorize the rape of the male as a phenomenon in its own right, instead conveniently subjugating it within existing frames, which is stymieing.

It is also often the case that very broad-brush feminist theory is applied (for example, Davies and Rogers, 2006) in order to simplistically assimilate male rape into the prevailing frame that predominates in the sexual violence literature; alternatively it is otherwise set up outside of this frame and used instead to detract from feminism (for example, Davies, 2002).[24] It is certainly recognized that the theorizations of this phenomenon that use the existing models oriented around female victimization is contentious (Rentoul and Applebloom, 1997). At the very least, such works propose that the problematic of male sexual victimization constitutes a question for feminism to answer.

Indeed, the invisibility of male sexual victimization is often steadfastly attributed to the primacy of feminism in the area of sexual violence, for example, Mezey and King (2000, p. vi) assert that 'in becoming a "women's issue" the debate about rape and sexual violence polarized women as victims and men as perpetrators ... in contrast, there has been no "men's movement" to raise awareness of the plight of victims and demand effective services'. It is rare indeed for feminism to be omitted. This is important, as whilst authors engaging with male rape are mindful of feminism, feminism is not mindful of male rape – this inevitably results in a rather stilted conversation with feminist theory, which is at best apologetic, and at worst, denigrating.

Overall, in my examination of the recent literature concerned with male rape, I was neither overly surprised at the tendency of those constructing knowledge from outside the feminist stances to scapegoat feminism nor particularly surprised by the subjugation of male rape by those espousing feminist theory. I was however very surprised by the trend for some within the feminist school of thought to lend credence to responsibilization by rejecting the significance of this victim group; and I was particularly concerned by the framing of male rape as part of a perceived conspiratorial backlash.

In order to negotiate such conflicting and hostile terrain, I turned to the proliferating body of work identified as 'Foucauldian feminism' as I was confident that this would lead the way in the insurrection of such knowledge – if only to liberate sexual violence from its sexualized and gendered forms. Unfortunately, I was to be sorely disappointed, as even in this body of works the same oppositional polemics are in evidence, the same frame is resurrected time and again, and the same trends towards minimization, obfuscation and deflection in respect of male rape victims recur. This being the case, Foucauldian feminism falls far short of its aspirations, and existing work bearing this mantle might more accurately be described as 'feminist Foucauldianism'.[25] At present any claim to the contrary seems disingenuous, to say the least. This issue will be revisited in Part III, however, the trends within this body of work, which contribute to the current 'battle' over the male rape victim, will now be sketched.

Examples of feminists drawing on Foucault in their analyses of rape – and including male rape to varying extents – include Diamond and Quinby (1988), Nicholson (1990), Sawicki (1991), McNay (1992), Ramazanoglu (1993), Bevacqua (2000), Allen (2002), Taylor and Vintges (2004) and Gavey (2005). Without fail, such works as I have been able to uncover follow a troubling pattern in their handling of the male rape 'problem' – such authors acknowledge male victims of rape, but do so in a way that either trivializes, minimizes, obfuscates or ultimately redacts this group. Common techniques here mirror those already noted in the wider academic literature: by rendering this group superfluous (for example by regarding male rape as a homosexual phenomenon where their analysis is concerned with heterosexuality, à la Gavey, 2005), by asserting that this group is a statistical anomaly (that is, therefore, insignificant compared with the far greater statistical incidence of the victimization of women – this can be seen in all the works listed above), and even by simply asserting that the impact of rape on men is less (and therefore that the greater harm is to women, this can be noted in Bevacqua, 2000 and Gavey, 2005). Certainly this is by no means unique in the literature in general, but those identifying as feminist should have a particular concern to avoid what are in essence techniques of 'invisibilization', likewise those feminists utilizing Foucault should endeavour to avoid techniques of 'subjugation' – given that each of which were so rightly decried when used by our forebears in respect of the female. Startlingly, such criticism is recognized in various forms by many of the authors mentioned, but is then widely derided as mere academic equivalency or denigrated as politicized gender-neutrality – thus the criticism is postulated as commensurate itself with backlash, a denouncement that serves as a rather nifty intellectual straightjacket, stifling analyses in this area.

It is important to note that I struggled to find relevant feminist Foucauldian works – not least because any inclusion of the male is frequently fleeting and/or obfuscated. For example, whilst the male rape victim may be included to some extent in a discussion, he is rarely included in the contents, index or back jacket, or even in reviews of the work. This makes locating him a rather onerous task. He is there, but it appears that he is disavowed even by those authors who see fit to include him. This obfuscation also means that many of the authors in this field are prevented from recognizing the contributions of their peers; for example, Bevacqua (2000), Allen (2002), Gavey (2005), Graham (2006), Bourke (2007), Abdullah-Khan (2008) and Anderson and Doherty (2008) go largely unacknowledged in the wider field, and even by each other – a regrettable state of affairs that in itself illustrates the successful subjugation of the male victim. Furthermore, in later works that do cite these publications, the mainstay remains the female victim rather than the male. This elision can be readily discerned in numerous examples, for instance, focussing on subsequent works that draw on Gavey (2005), authors such as Gilchrist et al. (2012) nevertheless expressly focus solely on the female rape victim, neglecting the male entirely; whilst Lea (2007), Das (2008) and O'Neill (2012) might mistakenly be interpreted as adopting a neutrality in scope that is not borne out in practice. Thus later works render effacement of the male complete.

Two particularly important examples that I did unearth are Gavey's (2005) psychology monograph *Just Sex? The Cultural Scaffolding of Rape* and Bourke's (2007) history monograph, *Rape: A History from 1860 to the Present*.[26] Each goes to far greater lengths to include the male rape victim than any of the others I consulted, although their modalities of inclusion remain largely in line with established convention around gender specificity, including hierarchies of harm; and techniques of invisibility, including marginalization and redaction.

However, neither book integrates the male victim of rape and sexual violence within its general thesis, but instead includes him via sporadic asides and in separate chapters specifically about male rape – albeit specifically concerned with male victims of female assailants, where the main focus of discussion is assuredly the female assailant rather than the male victim.[27] Both books cynically rest their thesis on an uncritical acceptance of official statistics (and even official estimates) to justify female rape as their priority, and both express concerns regarding the recognition of the male as facilitating backlash; and reject gender-neutrality. In addition, both draw on a notion of heterosexual versus homosexual rape. As a corollary, both therefore effectively draw on and credibilize contingent rape myths, such as male rape is of low incidence, low harm, driven by or in accordance with sexuality, etc.; and both are seemingly unaware that these resonate with and revalidate the logics around the ideal victim.[28]

Interestingly, each of these authors credibilize male rape myths within chapters where these selfsame myths have already been expressly problematized (albeit to varying degrees) in respect of female victims. What is truly fascinating is that these myths then are given credence that is in effect beyond any consideration of facticity – and as a consequence they can be simultaneously deconstructed (for female victims) and shored back up (for males).

A superficial distinction between these two works is that Gavey (2005) appears to reject any significance of male rape beyond the merely theoretical, whereas Bourke (2007) accedes that there may indeed be far more male rape victims than presently acknowledged. Unfortunately, they both concur that analyses that incorporate the male victim as an equal victim are guilty of 'equivalency' and are therefore dangerous for feminism and activism in respect of backlash. For Gavey

(2005), equivalency arguments simply are backlash; for Bourke (2007), equivalency arguments are co-opted by backlash. Ultimately, both defend rationales of gendered particularization and, in doing so, readily fall back on the notion of men as fundamentally advantaged and rape as overwhelmingly gendered – despite the fact that, of course, the very existence of male rape victims refutes both these assertions.

What is particularly concerning is that such techniques of invisibilization are employed by these authors with insight rather than in ignorance and are deployed consciously and explicitly by an imperative to preserve the feminist model that postulates rape as male oppression of women. This cannot be characterized as the result of a struggle to comprehend or as difficulty in inclusion – this is more a distinct effort to obviate and excoriate that is frequently presented by those enacting it as a principled and pre-emptive defence. In the battle around male rape, this is the frontline.

Thus, at present, male rape is the site of struggle by those acting for versus those acting against recognition and inclusion – stances that tally with or are oriented to feminism and the feminist (gendered) model of rape in particular, with both pro- and anti-feminist authors claiming fact and justice on their side. The construct of the male rape victim bears the scars of this tactical engagement, and results in the generation of an ideal victim binary that is championed even – and perhaps especially – by those striving to overcome male rape myths. This is where we are, but how did we get here? I seek to answer this question in the remainder of this chapter.

2.2   Discovery of the male rape victim

In the previous section, I highlighted various trends and conventions in the current literature around male rape. Whilst engaging with that body of literature, I was struck by a consistent omission in critique that has tacitly become an accepted practice in framing analyses: the pre-legislative history of male rape. With the best of intentions, many working in this field are producing an orthodox 'story' of male rape in the UK that for them begins with the 1994 Criminal Justice and Public Order Act, which 'recognized male victims of rape for the first time' (Mezey and King, 2000, p. vii) by covering both anal and vaginal penile penetration,[29] and continues with the subsequent 2003 Sexual Offences Act that expanded the definition of rape to include non-consensual oral penile penetration. For many researchers in this area, this is where it all begins, and as a consequence this is where their analysis begins;

and indeed it is precisely what their analysis is usually oriented to – the official 'discovery' of male rape.

But in being oriented to this official acknowledgement, many analyses miss a large and significant part of the discursive construction of male rape and the male rape victim, as whilst these recent legislative developments are important, it is both erroneous and disingenuous to present them as the first constructions of male rape. It is easy to be distracted by the semantics involved here, so it must be clarified that for the purpose of this work I recognize that the harm of rape and/or sexual violence can exist even where a formalized legal crime recognizing the same does not. Neither a material nor discursive reality is simply legislated into existence.[30]

What is interesting for me is that in omitting the pre-legislative rhetorical journey of male rape, the significant role that feminism played in highlighting, supporting and leading research and activism in relation to the male rape victim is obscured. We are also misled into divorcing the knowledge construction outlined above from its impetus and origins in academic study, thereby sanctioning ignorance in respect of the legacy this has and the influence it continues to exert.

A solely legislative focus also overlooks the role that non-statutory agencies have played in the landscape of male sexual victimization. The voluntary or third sector – in the form of support services and pressure groups – played a significant role in UK and US experiences. As Mezey and King (2000) observe, the first support service dealing solely with male victims of sexual violence –'Survivors' – opened in the late 1980s, mirroring rape crisis and feminism, and was the result of gay rights activism. However, they note that it quickly had to adapt beyond this initial remit to include all male victims, irrespective of sexuality, in direct response to demand.[31] Activism and awareness-raising in the early stages were also allied to the gay rights movement – in fact it was once almost their sole preserve. Thus Scarce's (1997) and McMullen's (1990) classic texts were, unsurprisingly, printed and distributed by independent presses allied to the gay men's movement – Perseus and The Gay Men's Press (respectively).

Scarce (1997, p. 12) notes that 'academic research on male rape has been conducted only since the late 1970s with any regularity', whilst we must note that the forms of that earliest research are problematic and have a lasting legacy. Male rape was first 'known' through the gaze of the academy in four contexts: homosexual populations, institutional populations, children and clinical samples (for example work by Lockwood, 1980; Scacco, 1982; Etherington, 1995, Stermac et al., 2004) – a framing that arguably serves to make male rape explicable or legitimized via the apparent absence of female victims or the self-evident vulnerability of that particular male population. This is how the male rape victim was first given credence and legitimized.

I am not pursuing engagement in any of these areas, but I note that their influence continues; for example, a recent move that can be noted as informed by this is towards credibilizing a model for male victims, a model that bears a striking resemblance to the discredited date-rape paradigm (as can be seen in Mezey and King, 1989; Waterman et al., 1989; Island and Letellier, 1991; Struckman-Johnson, 1991; Hickson et al., 1994; Stermac et al., 1996; Krahe, 2000; Ratner et al., 2002). This is a shift that both responsibilizes and Others by drawing on supposed sex/rape conflations that can be argued to have arisen as a consequence of the overt failure of psychopathologizing, and serves a similar function in terms of placing this phenomenon as distinctly outside of 'normal' heterosexual masculinity, as well as in legitimizing a hierarchy of harm for male rape through categories not dissimilar to 'rapettes' – terminology trivializing the assault as 'mini-rapes' or 'not-really-rapes' – previously decried by feminist researchers in relation to women.[32]

Goodey (2005) notes that it is only since the 1990s that male victimization per se has become of any interest to criminology and victimology. But although it has indeed gained wider recognition, we must note that its inclusion is hardly mainstream, and that the manner of that inclusion remains very much tethered to those early academic origins. Dedicated texts (which numbered only four when I commenced research) highlight and compound the marginalization of this issue.[33] Those by Scarce (1997) and McMullen (1990) are oriented towards homosexual men, Mezey and King's (2000) text is situated within forensic psychology and Scacco's (1982) text deals predominantly with institutionalized populations. Significant trends in modern theorizing and consequent visibility of the issue of male rape outside of institutions – as oriented around either homosexuality or psychopathology – was thus exemplified in these four works.

Much of the research from the mid-1970s onwards has been impacted by the need to repudiate the established 'truth' that male sexual victimization only occurs in the contexts and the populations noted above, whilst the tendency to conceptualize male-on-male rape as 'homosexual', either on the part of the offender or victim, persists in various forms, as does the notion that victims of male rape are in some way 'vulnerable'. A contingent logic that underscores this is that rape of the male is somehow an impoverished relation of the normative model of female sexual victimization, and that it occurs only where female victims are not available, where male victims are assumed effeminate or female proxies, or where their 'selection' might be understood as misogynistic. Irrespective of the validity of any of these explanations, it must at least be noted that the persistent message that endures is that male sexual victimization in general, and male rape in particular, are anomalous to 'normal' female victimhood. Even in those enquiries that do not support this position, this allegation is highlighted and addressed.

These pre-legislative forms of male rape are important because they inevitably contribute to how it is known – not least of which is in providing the impetus and context for academic research, but also in delineating the realm in which that research was concentrated. This in no small part contributes to the present tendency to marginalize this act as the preserve of gay men as a minority population, to concomitantly sexualize this act through reference to homosexuality, and to psychopathologize it, both in terms of precipitation and impact - locating it largely within forensic and clinical psychology (for example work by Kaszniak and Nassbaum, 1988; Hunter, 1990; Gonsiorek et al., 1994; King et al., 2002; Budrionis and Jongsma, 2003), and in self-help literature (such as La Valle, 1996). This is part of the context that has produced the current orthodox understanding of male rape – to blindly attempt to detach it from this is inordinately naive.

It is in direct response to this legacy that researchers' recent critiques in this field – as I describe in the previous section: 'battle' – fall into four broad areas: a call for more research; a criticism of provision; a bemoaning that this crime is under-reported; and a utilization of data to debunk myths and stereotypes. But for me this – albeit principled and important – activity rather misses the point. I argue that male rape in itself warrants our attention on two counts: as both a discursive construct and a material practice, of both significance and of signification; that because of its perceived anomalous and incongruent nature, reveals the current politics of knowledge production in this field. Amongst other researchers who have acknowledged bias in knowledge production around male rape, this is usually the point at which feminism (as a simplified, homogenous and intractable mass) is called into question and frequently hung out to dry.

Scapegoating feminism – overtly or implicitly – is ultimately untenable. The common criticism relayed is that feminist authors have either paid scant attention to this phenomenon or have overlooked it entirely. However, it can be readily noted that it is simply not accurate to allege that feminism has ignored male victimization in general or male sexual victimization in particular.[34] Feminism has engaged with male rape; indeed, it is even mentioned in Brownmiller's (1975) classic *Against Our Will*, albeit not expanded upon therein. The debate about the adoption of gender-neutral rape definitions has been vitriolic and lengthy;[35] concern around the impact of male rape as part of the backlash has been explored;[36] provision and impact have been examined;[37] and attempts have been made to apply and extend feminist analysis.[38] Indeed, feminism has been pivotal in recognizing the constraint of masculinities, pointing out male vulnerabilities and victimization in general.[39] Furthermore, recognition of heterosexual masculinity as hierarchical has also been raised in the literature.[40]

There is a complex interweaving of discursive strands in evidence in the construction of the male rape victim that simplistic scapegoating of feminism conveniently overlooks. It may well be the case that the feminist model of rape is predominant, and certainly it can be said that this model finds it difficult to encompass male-on-male heterosexual rape and sexual assault, and almost impossible to countenance female on male sexual offending, but a degree of caution must be exercised. One cannot move from these observations to responsibilizing feminism,[41] although many influential authors have. Amongst them, Mezey and King (1992) note in their classic text that the widely disseminated message that 'rape is a feminist issue' produced a neglect of the male victim. Even more direct is the critique by Graham (2006, p. 187), who asserts that 'male victims are largely neglected by a predominantly feminist perspective that seeks to highlight the gendered nature of sexual assault as a social phenomenon'. Both works are logical, but they are – nevertheless – unreasonable.

This is not to exculpate feminist theory and activism of any role here – on the contrary – but backlash in its many forms is implicated too. The construct of the male rape victim is not just a product of feminism, but of pre-, post- and anti-feminism. As a consequence, it must be made explicit that this is a phenomenon for which any singular responsibilization and sticking-plaster solutions simply will not suffice.

Scarce (1997, p. 104) insightfully commented in a very brief aside that 'the treatment of male rape as an emergent form of criminal victimization has been so consistent for more than a decade that one must wonder if male rape will ever be popularly regarded as a violence with a history'. Unfortunately, almost two decades on, it appears that we have our answer: male rape seems stuck in a persistent state of 'emergence' and its lengthy history, alongside that of the female, and struggle for formal recognition is readily obscured. Indeed, one of the most recent specialist texts in this area is entitled *Male Rape: The Emergence of a Social and Legal Issue* (Abdullah-Khan, 2008). But to conceive of it in this way requires that we orient our analyses to the legal construct only – forgoing, therefore, critical consideration of its pre-legislative forms and struggles, and thus enabling these to persist in their influence.

Scarce (1997, p. 104) criticized this perpetual state of newness as 'treading water', preventing a true understanding of this phenomenon. I disagree. It is not so much that it stops us understanding, rather that it colours our understanding. The forgotten history of male rape is key to its construction. Omission of pre-legislative forms are however not the whole 'story'. The following section presents a lengthier sight line cast down the annals.

2.3   Forgotten history of the male rape victim

I found that there is a preference in existing works to keep male rape divorced from both its immediate and its lengthy history. This can be readily contrasted with the wealth of works dedicated to examining the history of female rape. I am concerned not to denounce the omission, but to question what purpose it serves. Why is the lengthy history of male rape actively disavowed in favour of that pertaining to the female?

Authors such as Scarce (1997), Jones (2000) and Brownmiller (1975) have noted historical examples of male rape. However, the significance of these in the discursive trajectory of rape has not been explored, and the analyses that these examples of the male rape victim have incurred bear the scars of the embattled delimitation that I have described.

Representations of male rape have been noted (Jones, 2000),[42] in Ancient China (Ng, 1987),[43] the legends of the Maya's (Sigal, 2002)[44] and in Ancient Greece, including forms enshrined in Athenian law (Guettel-Cole, 1984).[45] Numerous examples can be found in Greek myths and Ancient Roman legends; the culture of North American Native peoples; the *Malleus Mallificarum*; and indeed various religious texts, including the Bible.

Interestingly, and of distinct relevance to feminist understandings of rape, many of those early depictions illustrate the significance of this practice as aggression, not sex, in its use as a weapon of war. Scarce (1997, p. 83) raises this point when noting the North American berdaches – a third gender status that was ascribed to and enforced upon 'defeated enemies', a fate that effectively stripped the loser of his status as a warrior and made the conquest complete.

Both male and female 'sexual molesters' are noted in various Latin–Christian texts, such as the Acts of Thomas, writings relating to the lives of saints such as St Anthony and St Bernard, and commentaries by Martyr, Isadore and Strabo (see Kiessling, 1975). Assailants and victims are recognized as being both male and female in texts from Pagan–Celtic Britain, for example, the Morrigan (ibid.), and the Middle Ages, for example, the *Malleus Mallificarum* details female demons – *succubi* – who molest sleeping men.

Present in Christian, Jewish and Islamic religious texts (the Protestant Bible, the Catholic Bible, the Torah and the Qur'an), in various forms, is the parable of Sodom and Gomorrah. The citizens of those towns are reputed to have practised (amongst other unrepentant sins) indiscriminate rape against outsiders. It is their attempted rape of male strangers in their midst – angels that were sent to save Lot – that is the pivotal moment that epitomizes the base and bestial nature of those peoples and puts them beyond redemption and deserving of God's wrath.

What I find interesting is how these examples are interpreted. These historical examples are often utilized as examples to demonstrate the 'normality' of male rape, by illustrating that it has a history as lengthy as that of female rape (as in the work of Scarce, 1997; Jones, 2000). Many of these examples have been interpreted as 'homosexual' for precisely the same reason – either inferred as 'homosexual rape' if the lack of consent is sustained in the reader's interpretation or as 'homosexual sex' rather than rape if it is not.[46] But there is another dynamic here that deserves attention – it is also interesting to see how these examples fail to be utilized.

The classic feminist work by Brownmiller (1975) includes some interesting limitations in both selection and analyses of historical examples – principally I found that, despite engaging with Greek and Roman history, she does not note accounts pertaining to adult male victims, or to female perpetrators. The oversight is significant, but also of pertinence is that she does note Poseidon's rape of Kainis,[47] but does so in relation to the supposed invulnerability of males – given that Kainis, the young girl, asks Poseidon to change her into a man 'to avoid future violations' (ibid., p. 284). Meanwhile she configures female-perpetrated assaults as seductions – giving the example of Aphrodite as 'a champion seducer in her own right' (ibid., p. 283) and thus neglecting her part in orchestrating abduction, procuring incest, and rape of both women and men. She also makes no mention of Goddesses who are themselves reputed to have made a sport of abducting and raping mortal men, such as

Eos.[48] Such bias and omission inadvertently demonstrate a subscription to hegemonic masculinity in her analysis.

For me, these historical examples illustrate that the ideal victim binary in respect of male rape is not new. Indeed, with the ideal victim construct firmly in mind, neglected examples from Greek and Roman myths and legends – Zeus's rape of Ganymede and Laius's rape of Chrysippus – will be discussed. Both of these myths begin with the abduction of a male mortal, but there are pertinent differences that resonate with current rape myths and thus bear closer scrutiny. The ideal victim construct can be seen as operating in both.

Ganymede's rape is explained in a manner akin to victim precipitation as his forced abduction is reputedly invited by his beauty. He is later made culpable for his fate by supposedly transforming into the willing lover of Zeus, a development that is intended to cast doubt as to his overall level of complicity. As a consequence, this scenario is often interpreted as seduction, and one must note that in the tale he is implicitly responsibilized as no punishment or retribution is visited on Zeus. For Chrysippus, however, this is certainly not so. His abduction and violation is explained as motivated in no small part by the aggressor's (Laius) desire for revenge. He is not and does not become a willing partner. Chrysippus is wholly cast as innocent, bearing no 'blameworthy' behaviour – in fact, Ross (1982) draws specifically on evidence of violence in the abduction and rape of Chrysippus to explain why punishment is incurred. For Ross (Ibid.) it is this that enables recognition of clear transgressions deserving of punitive consequence.[49]

Look again at the example of Sodom and Gomorrah, and it can be noted that as the intended victims were angels, they were of course the epitome of innocence and hence their own behaviour was beyond question – they are utterly blameless and are quintessentially rendered ideal victims, enabling their recognition.

Rather than ask why male rape took so long to become recognized then, I would far rather query why it was that male victims of sexual violence stopped being recognized, a cessation which might best be regarded as apocryphal; and also query why, when female rape became a legislative and political concern, male victims of sexual violence become cast outside the feminized crime of rape, and were effectively demoted as victims of the lesser offence of buggery. Thereafter the underlying reason for the continued marginalization of male rape, and its configuration as somehow 'different' to that of the female, demands attention.

Ancient peoples regarded offences of this nature as undifferentiated by gender, but over time, understanding of this has become disassembled along a gendered fault line; and thereafter tethered steadfastly to rationales around the logics of sexuality and gender – and, moreover, the sex/gender/sexuality conflation. In more recent times this gendered division of rape has become politically expedient – subsumed within a binaristic identity politics that, in so appropriating, seeks to garner legitimacy for, and to revalidate, itself.

The fixity of conflated notions of sex/gender/sexuality is key to identity and to legitimizing stratification – best epitomized in the maxim 'biology is destiny'. Given that the scientific 'discovery' of gender enabled the constitution of populations along patriarchal lines, it is conceivable that male rape became subsumed within the history of homosexuality to preserve that hierarchical ideology of heterosexual masculine supremacy. We should recall that 'for Foucault, sex was constructed as the secret of our being in the nineteenth century ... [by the rise of the experts] who represented it as prediscursive even as they were producing it through discourse' (Mardorossian, 2002, p. 762).

The example of Gilles de Rais or Bluebeard, who is documented as abducting, raping and murdering male children and young men during the sixteenth century, is of importance here. Brownmiller (1975) makes reference to this case, noting that male victims are not simply overlooked or actively 'forgotten', but are replaced with female substitutes whom she argues are more 'acceptable' (ibid., p. 292). What she does not consider is the significance in itself of this transposition. I would argue that such examples illustrate the effacing of the male in accordance with the rise of patriarchy and its necessity for naturalized and normalized gendered divisions, which plausibly such examples of male violability and vulnerability belie.

Foucault (2001, p. 226) cautions that changes in articulation mask an underlying constancy, thus, 'to recognise a discontinuity is never anything more than to register a problem that needs to be solved'. Hence, the process of 'silencing' male rape victims and rendering the phenomenon invisible is precisely what indicates male rape as key to governmentality. This process, of necessity, draws on the old, formally discredited, myths relating to victim precipitation and culpability – and surreptitiously re-legitimizes them. Furthermore it reinforces the gendered script that fosters and necessitates this imperative: hegemonic masculinity.

Consequently, rather than taking historic examples to illustrate the normality of male rape, or indeed current examples to problematize rape myths, I argue that what we should attend to is the discursive regularity here – over time – in terms of our understanding of male rape (or more accurately those situated historical forms of sexual/ized violence against the male that are the forerunners of the male rape construct). Principally, I argue that this is delimited by an ideal victim binary that pre-dates any legislative recognition and that has re-emerged in response to a misperceived 'need' to make the male rape-able – a need that only makes sense through the distorted lens of hegemonic masculinity, and thus reifies it.

2.4 Conclusion

The history of male rape is significant for feminism as the discursive journey indicates this phenomenon is intrinsically intertwined with the creation and policing of hierarchies of masculinity and more generalist reproduction of gender roles, and sex/gender conflation. In this way rape – or at least our understanding of it – can be argued to be gendering rather than gendered. If research commences only from the time of inclusion of male rape in legislative forms, one might be tempted to consider resistance to the assimilation, inclusion and recognition of male rape as explicated by its supposed invisibility prior to its inclusion in law. It might also be assumed that male rape is simply following the same or similar struggle for recognition and understanding that inhibited female rape – that, to paraphrase Foucault (2001, p. 300), it is 'trapped by its history'. However, as the examples discussed in this chapter illustrate, these forms have a lengthy history of their own alongside that of female rape, and were obfuscated or rendered invisible – subjugated in respect of the formalized and feminized constructs of the gendered binary of sexual violence which posits female victim versus male offender. If analysis begins from the position of defending feminism or castigating feminism, one validates the assumption that feminism has a case to answer. This would entail a disregard that the phenomenon of male rape pre-exists feminism and that feminist understanding of female rape is just as much a product of this discursive trajectory as is male rape.

What should be questioned then is this discontinuity – not of male rape struggling to become recognized, but of it ceasing to be so in the first place. The issue of significance then is not the subjugation of knowledge, which might adequately comprise our present state, but rather the apocrypha of knowledge – this more aptly describes that historic transformation, with a subtle yet pervasive process of redaction arguably its current form. Whilst feminism may have become caught up in this process, this merely illustrates just one aspect of its transformation and discursive trajectory.

It is not whether feminism is or is not to blame that is important, but rather that feminism is commonly implicated at all that is interesting. One should step back and problematize what can be regarded as the orthodox parameters of debate – not merely because these can be regarded as short-sighted in the face of conflicting historical evidence, but because this very process and its present forms are of import. I argue that not only does current discourse in the area of male sexual victimization serve to limit our understanding by occluding and Othering the male, but it also successfully delimits debate around a crude and essentialized notion of gender and of identity politics. Orienting this around gender and feminism serves to reproduce gendered discourse in our rejection of it, and in doing so 'writes-back' to frame sexual violence in general, thus ironically undermining feminist contributions full stop – significantly, it also serves to deflect from this very function.

It can be accepted that there are limitations to present modalities of acknowledgement and inclusion. For sure, authors have highlighted the importance of masculinity to male rape and of male rape to feminist thought in this area, though this is usually in very general terms – a vague call to arms, rather than clear exposition or analysis. Feminist masculinities research has highlighted men as victims, and men as victims of rape, but overwhelmingly lacks a clear and coherent theoretical framework for conceptualizing male rape as an assuredly feminist issue. Instead, this phenomenon is frequently presented either as contrasting with feminism (Graham, 2006) or according with feminism in respect of a continuum of misogynies (Kimmel, 1994; Funk, 1997) explained in reference to a feminist understanding of the power/aggression thesis (Nicholson and Bibbings, 2000) or related to feminism via masculinities (Groth and Burgess, 1980; Lees, 1997). Inclusion of the male rape victim then is conditional and precarious. Aside from brief, tenuous assertions, the theoretical implications of male rape have not been explicated and explored in depth. Nor has male rape been situated clearly and soundly within feminist theory or feminist activism. Indeed it has provoked staunch and vitriolic resistance.[50]

But this is not the whole story. The present 'neglect' of the male is not just the preserve of those operating within a feminist paradigm. To responsibilize feminism in this way requires that we assume this preference for the female rape victim as particular to them and therefore that there is a wealth of research and debate going on outside of the supposedly insular and insulated feminist frame that is in some way being resisted. But there is not. Neglect of the male rape victim is sustained over disciplinary, political and theoretical boundaries. Thus the great weight of the literature, across the various disciplines that engage with sexual violence, remains skewed towards female victimhood in general, whilst the bulk of literature regarding male victims is limited to institutionalized settings, such as prisons. Male rape in community settings remains a largely neglected area.

Even in research by those operating outside the feminist paradigm, the male rape victim is still tentatively oriented towards feminism – be this as evidence denouncing feminism, as faithful application of feminist theory or as benevolent inclusion by feminism – whilst feminist theory itself is routinely presented as homogenous and amorphous, and by implication intransigent and inexorable. Certainly the trend is to present feminism as activist and second wave only, obscuring the complexity in feminisms and thus to invite popular conflation with what has been decried as 'rape crisis feminism' (Roiphe, 1994) or 'victim feminism' (Atmore, 1999, p. 183).

But why should male rape continually be presented as an issue oriented to or around feminism? Of course the histories of feminism, of rape and of victimology are all inextricably interlinked.[51] Feminism has a long and productive alliance with victimology and victim rights in respect of rape, but the social construction of rape is no more a product of feminism than feminism is a product of the social construction of rape. There is something of a selective history in effect in the analyses that suggest otherwise.

What is frequently overlooked is that this problematic existed before feminism full stop. Rape as a construct was revised to achieve gender specificity for both victim and offender – it was not originally thus. It is a gendered revision that pre-dates feminism. Hence, whilst it may well be the case that feminism is caught up in perpetuating the particularization of 'male' rape, the gendering of rape and the subjugation of knowledge pertaining to the male in respect of this phenomenon must be recognized as historic and preceding even early movements that might later be regarded as the forerunners of feminism. Those authors who seek to defend or blame feminism are really missing the point – that the debate itself is contrived as part of the existing regime of knowledge.

In closing this chapter, let me simply say that for me, insurrecting such knowledge serves as a reminder of the tenuous nature of our gendered truth claims on the one hand, and the troubling persistence of the construct of the ideal victim binary on the other. It also points to the significance of a gendered understanding of rape to a process of gendering or, to be blunt, the importance of the feminist (feminized) model of rape to patriarchy.

Thus, the title of this work – *Male Rape is a Feminist Issue* – is deliberately oblique. It can – rightly – be read on several levels. The first: that 'male rape' is an issue deserving of feminism's attention; the second: that 'male' rape is a product of feminism. These two readings can be summarized as reflecting existing concerns that male rape is both a problem for feminism and a problem of feminism. But there is also a third reading – a quizzical one. Why has male rape been posited as a question for feminism to answer? Why is male rape regarded as a political issue in relation to feminism and, moreover, why is male rape emerging as a separate concern anyway? These are the aspects that are significant in seeking to understand male rape, feminism and governmentality; or rather, in seeking to understand the significance of the gendering of 'rape' – and the concomitant appropriation of feminism – to governmentality. This is my problematization of 'male' rape.

3
Investigation – A Foucauldian Triangulation?

My investigation, which arises from my observations and resultant problematization, is concerned with the gendering of rape, and the concomitant appropriation of feminism, in service of governmentality. Specifically, I explore how the present construction of male rape is a highly particularized form, with its own stereotypes and myths, disciplinary niches, and policy and provision – the hallmark of what Foucault terms 'subjugated knowledge'. I argue that this particularization, enshrined in discursive regularities, impacts to create and sustain an 'ideal victim' for visibility and that this itself is key to the deployment of gender in respect of governmentality. Consequently it is this ideal victim construct, pertaining to the male rape victim, which I trace over the course of my triangulation. This chapter explicates precisely how I proceed in this regard. In my initial discussion, I will clarify several concepts, amongst them the ideal victim and governmentality, highlight contingent aspects of my thesis, and describe – in broad terms – my overarching method. Subsequent chapters will apply and develop that method; and discuss the findings.

The construct of the ideal victim, as described and discussed in Chapter 2, is key to my examination and to my thesis, both for how it is composed and what it incurs. Its binaristic delineation of categories or individuals as 'deserving' of the victim mantle versus 'undeserving' of it; imbued with culturally situated notions of innocence versus guilt, is irrevocably tied to victim exoneration versus victim blame which are discriminatory in their application. Where tied to gendered notions of rape, it serves a social control function. In this sense, it is a construct that is readily recognized as key to 'governing through crime' (Crawford, 1997 and Coleman, 2004, cited in Walklate, 2007b). But as was illustrated in 'the forgotten history' of male rape, the ideal victim pre-dates legislative rape constructs, gendered or otherwise; and pre-dates the construction of modern sex/gender conflation. Its roots are historically entwined in both the historical construction of rape (or rather the gendering of rape) and that of gender (or rather the sexing of genders, and the gendering of sex). As such it points to a significance for power relations predicated on that, and to the mechanism by which those relations are perpetuated: patriarchy and governmentality.

The construct of the ideal victim achieves on the one hand the idealizing of some victims, and the simultaneous denigration of others. Whilst superficially antagonistic, these are fundamentally symbiotic – one cannot construct the ideal without its anathema. For designates of the former, there is vindication; for the latter only censure. This negative capacity is best known simply as 'victim blame'.

Victim blame, the dark side of the idealized victim, is similar to contributory negligence, a concept outlined by Amir (1967, 1971) in a series of papers.[1] Papers that owed more than a small debt to the works of Von Hentig, whose work, along with that of Mendelsohn, was pivotal to the development of early victimology,[2] a victimology that was most assuredly pre-victims' rights, and in fact rather more concerned with offender exculpation.[3] Indeed, Mendelsohn proposed that rape victims were predisposed to victimhood – a justification and rationalization that was in no small part inspired by his role as a defence barrister.

However they are expressed, notions under this victim blaming umbrella – victim predisposition, victim precipitation, or contributory negligence – all serve to shift the focus away from the offender and on to the complainant, in adjudging complainants to be responsible for their experience. In this sense it is inherently underpinned by notions of a 'just-world',[4] a rationalization that one's fate is righteous and that – in essence – people 'get what they deserve and deserve what they get' (Anderson and Doherty, 2008, p. 34). This draws on and reinforces the notion of a moral balance, lending credence to the notion that – if one's fate is both just and deserved – one has ultimate control, and ultimate responsibility. As a rationale, the just world thesis is underscored by Othering, which at its simplest enables populations to be reassuringly divided into: *those to whom bad things happen because they deserve it* (them) and *those to whom nothing bad can happen because they don't deserve it* (us) – thus enabling defensive attribution, and intrinsically (re) validating victim blaming.

Taken as a system of thought then, comprising inherent circular logics that are mutually-affirming, the ideal victim is best understood as a regime of truth; where tied to gender norms, as in the case of male rape versus female rape, a gendered social control function is served – this regime then, perpetuates patriarchy. This observation, related to the female and the feminine, was a significant contribution of second wave feminists. When the legislative construct of rape was solely female, feminists noted that the ideal victim was one who most readily conformed to patriarchal stereotypes about 'good' women. Second-wave feminists carefully dismantled this construct and its various hierarchies and exclusions, as applied to female victims of sexual violence and rape, recognizing this as a barrier to justice and a mechanism of social control that ultimately functions to uphold the gender-normative behaviour that serves patriarchy. The significance of this cannot be overstated. However, this model has not been eradicated in the criminal justice system – indeed it is still regarded as key to attrition for females.[5] Its impact can merely be asserted as mitigated somewhat in respect of reporting, prosecution and provision – although this too is debatable; one can at least state that its explicit articulation is no longer widely tolerated.[6]

However, whilst the ideal victim may be resisted in respect of females, as I illustrated in Chapter 2, the construct of the ideal victim is both implicitly and overtly resurrected in respect of male victims. Moreover, it is readily credibilized in respect of the male – by advocates acting for him, and by advocates (re)acting on behalf of female victims. This serves to create a gendered division of, and hierarchy in, sexual victimization and rape; but that is not all – this validation of the rationale, irrespective of the gender it is ostensibly oriented to, is nevertheless a validation of the rationale: a resuscitation of the ideal victim for all victims of rape. Thus, despite being overtly disavowed, the notion of 'asking for it' can continue to pervert justice for all victims of rape and sexual violence.

Unfortunate then, that this validating strategy is tied to (oriented to, attributed to, if not performed by) the feminist movement. As indicated in my discussion around the present 'battle', this new ideal victim construct is not only tolerated but advocated: by those who use it in seeking to exclude men from recognition and services, for example through a belittling of their experiences; or those seeking to include men, for example by fostering them as victims of some type of misogyny. But one must not be distracted – this is not actually about feminism per se, it is more accurately about the feminist rape model. The core problematic that binds each group's agenda is subscription to the (simplistic) feminist rape model that is popularly understood as explaining rape primarily as male violence against women.

The populist understanding of the feminist rape 'model' is woefully simplified. There are several feminist 'models' proffered to explain rape, inevitably so given differences between various stances within feminist theory. Interesting then that it is the 'traditional' radical feminist model, that can be argued to have achieved populist status and thus – in its appropriation by scholars in the field of sexual violence – something of an orthodoxy.[7] This popularized model finds it difficult, to say the least, to recognize male sexual victimization, and the vulnerability of men in general, to sexual assault.

Indeed, even where seemingly modified beyond gender, the construct of 'victim' itself remains underscored by this model, with 'the assumption that it may only be applied to members of relatively powerless groups, or that it describes a state of being that itself produces powerlessness' (Newburn and Stanko, 2002, p. 263) and that conversely offending behaviours – relating to interpersonal violence – are expressions of power. Thus, a range of caveats seemingly must be imposed on the male victim of rape in order to accommodate him as configured powerless – he must be rendered either a vulnerable 'minority'[8] or otherwise 'innately' vulnerable.[9]

Such simplistic feminist framing, coupled with the persistence of a binaristic and dichotomy between offender and victim, genders certain categories of crime and victimization whilst rendering others inconceivable or improbable. For those influenced by this model, male victims of rape and sexual assault struggle to be considered real victims. Given the understanding of such exclusions as related to governing through crime, one must attend to the function of this delegitimization.

To my mind the very existence of an ideal victim in the area of male rape has the very real impact of lending credence to all those previously discredited constructs in the general area of sexual violence and victimization. At the very simplest level, we have enabled rationalizations that *all rape is real rape except ...* and *all rape victims are real victims apart from ...* – rationalities that are recursive and thus cannot be constrained by gender. But the ramifications go beyond this. I speculate that the discursive construct of male rape appears to have arisen to take the place of female sexual victimization, and I would argue it serves much the same function and is deserving of analysis in this vein.

Current logics around male rape – epitomized in the ideal (male rape) victim, have the capacity to contribute to a post-feminist turn, to the resuscitation by stealth of traditional (patriarchal) rape myths, and to a bolstering of patriarchal power. This demands attention. This is most assuredly not the same thing as asserting that male rape itself – or interest in it – is part of a backlash à la Gillespie (1996). Indeed, denying this phenomenon adequate and sensitive recognition and theorization is a key part of the problem, and at present it is one not only tolerated in the name of feminism, but also supposedly valorized in celebration of it. For all these reasons, male rape is most assuredly a feminist issue.

In seeking to explore this area of concern, I had to identify and make practicable an appropriate Foucauldian 'method' which could be applied to this criminological and victimological 'problem'. Governmentality is the epistemological crux of my methodology. This is a Foucauldian concept that refers to a modality of governance (or control) not confined to the state, but executed through various technologies and agencies of power, the cumulative effect of which is to extend the reach of governance whilst diminishing its appearance - diffusing rather than defusing power. As Rose (1999, p. 5) notes: 'the question of the state that was so central to earlier investigations of political power is now relocated. The state now appears as one element ... in multiple circuits of power' – the influence of which is pervasive, normative and, above all, productive.

Foucault (2001, p. xxiv) talks of power 'from below' and in doing so broadens his conception as beyond the macro institutions of the state to the micro sites, or 'capillary circuits', for example societal interaction. The Gramscian concept of hegemony is key to this as it enables power relations to be perpetuated from 'below' by influencing the supposedly free interactions between individuals through the internalization of normative values and the delimiting of conceptual or psychological schema, thus impacting on the 'conduct of potential conduct' without the overt need to exercise the state's recourse to force. This notion of power explains how the status quo can survive liberalism. This is more than the iron fist in the velvet glove notion of disingenuous liberal facades though, as this conception of power implicates us all in pervasive and normative power transactions.

Governmentality goes further than previous notions of ideology or hegemony. For Foucault, changes in modalities are regarded as disingenuous 'transformation'. This mechanism of social control is effectively articulated and rearticulated to circumvent and deflect resistance. Change in expression thus demonstrates the adaptability of this technology within the social body, as it is not threatened by resistance but evolved through it. As Foucault (1996, cited in Lazzarato, 2002, p. 14) asserts:

> power is not omnipotent or omniscient – quite the contrary! If power relationships have produced forms of investigation, of analysis, of models of knowledge, etc., it is precisely not because power was omniscient, but because it was blind ... if it is true that so many power relationships have been developed, so many systems of control ... it is precisely because power was always impotent.

It is the very 'impotence' of power that drives the mechanisms, technologies and so forth that are necessary to its deployment. This is indicative of a conception of power that adapts and circulates within the social body, rather than one that imposes itself upon it.

These are the broad conceptual foundations for this book. How do I intend to put these to work? As stated above, it is my contention that existing critical engagement in the area of male rape persists in perpetuating discursive regularities. As a consequence, there is an urgent need for an examination of these knowledges as discursive practices[10] and formations[11] that are enabling disciplinary power.[12] This will enable what Foucault termed a (problematized) history of the present – one that is sensitized to contingent and subjugated knowledges. For the sake of clarity and expedience, the various intersecting and interrelated fields of enquiry implicated in this area must be delineated.

My method, in its application, describes a clearly demarcated Foucauldian triangulation, devised explicitly to facilitate the implementation, organization and presentation of this project. In attempting this, I must caution that I recognize this to be a contrivance. In Foucault's (2001, p. 338) own words:

> Power relations, relationships of communication, objective capacities should not ... be confused. This is not to say that there is a question of three separate domains. Nor that there is, on the one hand, the field of things, of perfected technique, work and the transformation of the real, and, on the other, that of signs, communication, reciprocity, and the production of meaning; finally that of the domination of the means of constraint, of inequality and the action of man upon other men. It is a question of all three types of relationships that in fact always overlap one another, support one another reciprocally, and use each other mutually as means to an end.

This is a sophisticated, contingent and complex view of power in the social and metaphysical realm. Foucault himself cautions, though, that these are not neatly compartmentalized areas; that they interact and correspond in complex and paradoxical ways. As a consequence, implementing this triangulation as a methodological technique will simultaneously illustrate and obscure. My triangulation purports to recognize a certain ontology, but it cannot possibly hope to reveal it. I can only hope to achieve a facsimile of what could be, rather than a revelation of what is.

The dimensions of my triangulation, devised for the purpose of tracing discursive regularities in the construct of the male rape victim, are largely in accordance with Mendieta's (2002) essay, which I build on to delineate an approximated and replicable method. This endeavour is motivated in part by my frustration at the continuing predilection in criminology for a false distinction between the administrative, the cultural, and the self. Hence, my method comprises an examination of representations of male rape in the media (or more specifically, an examination of the discursive regularities in media depictions of sexual violence towards men that come to constitute the 'truth' of victimhood, using framing as a constituent part of governmentality); an examination of the biopolitics of audience understanding of male rape (more specifically an examination of the discursive regularities contained within audience artifacts such as slash fiction, where slash is taken to exemplify the 'active' audience, thus using the 'ethics' of the fan as a constituent part of governmentality); and finally, individuation as reflected in the practices around the male rape victim (with a specific focus on government policy and third-sector provision, where 'ethics' can be seen in action and implementation – or indeed, failure to action and to implement in respect of the male rape victim). Particular attention will be paid to tracing those instances where the particularized construct of male rape (epitomized in the ideal victim) traverses the various aspects of the triangulation. What is employed here as a stratagem is a notion of the 'conduct of conduct' in respect of the male rape victim, presented in linear form and as a process – but with the caution that of course it is neither, and with the rider that in all cases the ramifications go beyond the male.

A simplistic reading of this as a process: that gendered representations in the media impact to inhibit reporting practices at the level of the individual, thus skewing official statistics, which then has a knock-on effect in respect of legislative and institutional recognition – whilst plausible – is not satisfying, not least because it implies a primacy and a causality. To accept this implication is to effectively close down this phenomenon as a system in the singular – something that must be avoided, else we become enmeshed in a search for a simplistic scapegoat and a quick-fix solution. It must be recalled that unintended, specifically deleterious, consequences are a concern for Foucault, particularly that such consequences can result in the appropriation of supposed resistance in service of governmentality – as through unintended or ironic consequences, counter-culture can be rendered conformist, disruption can become consolidation, subversion can be made normative. This is not to say that they will, merely that they can.

Precisely because counter-discourse runs in contrast to the orthodox, it necessarily references that which it opposes; therefore knowledges are not simply oppositional, they are tangential. In this sense I argue that ostensibly competing knowledges around rape – particularly gendered knowledge – can be said to comprise a single archive that runs along several corresponding albeit competing registers. Thus what denotes also connotes, where there is clarity there is also conflation, and where there is particularization there is also slippage. It is this fluid process that is important in constructing the subject. Where the subject is understood as the locus for both accepted knowledge and subjugated knowledges, he is constructed somewhere in the struggle that lies between these two registers. Likewise, this duality and transgression means that each register invites simultaneous intertextualization. I suggest that this is where the possibility for recursion lies.

Nor should one overlook concordance which, as a state, can only be known in reference to discord and, furthermore, that the latter does not necessarily preclude the former. In this sense discord might be better conceived of as counterpoints. Instances of discord should not be perceived as operating antagonistically to this process then, or seized upon as evidence of or opportunities for resistance, as this would overlook the broader repertoires that the discursive construct of male sexual victimization draws from and writes back to. Consideration must be given to how male rape both draws from, affirms, challenges and modifies established understanding of female rape and the consequences this may have for all victims, and indeed for the primacy of the gendered model in feminist thought as pivoting on a gendered division in sexual violence and sexual victimization.

I bear in mind Foucault's caution that power is productive, and Zizek's (2002) assertion that in rejecting something we continue our orientation to it. To simplistically conceive of the discourse of male rape as linear and causal then is at best severely limited, but at worst – in isolating fragments of this practice and presenting them out of context – serves to deflect from the complexity at play here and thus becomes an intrinsic part of the problem.

Having broadly carved out my areas of interest, method and rationale, the next stage entails an attempt to 'get at' the discourse that both constitutes and permeates these areas or aspects of my triangulation. Many authors engaging with male rape have sought to do this using varying degrees of discourse analysis (Anderson and Doherty, 2008) or critical discourse analysis (CDA)[13] (Graham, 2006; Gavey, 2005). One of the problems for any researcher seeking to implement CDA is that – as Meyer (2001) cautions – it is not a method, but more an approach within which there are multiple methods, all of which share core underlying assumptions. Thus as Meyer (2001, pp. 23–24) states, CDA is not a method as such, but rather 'a cluster of approaches with a similar theoretical base and similar research questions'.

CDA is therefore best understood as eclectic, multimodal and interdisciplinary. Implementing this (or aspects thereof) as a methodological approach is complicated by the fact that the notion of discourse itself is open to contestation (Jaworski and Pritchard, 2005, p. 4), by dispute within Foucauldian thought on the remit and range of discourse, as well as by the vagaries of and dispute around data collection. As Meyer (2001, p. 23) notes, 'there is no typical CDA way of collecting data. Some authors do not even mention data collection methods and others rely strongly on traditions based outside the sociolinguistic field ... data collection is not [even] considered to be a specific phase that must be completed before analysis begins'.

Consequently, the extent to which any existing research satisfies an expressly Foucauldian notion of discourse is negligible, whilst the extent to which it ever could is at best debatable. Graham's (2006) piece is the most pertinent in terms of the pretensions, for her work certainly has a Foucauldian ethic, and utilizes Foucauldian concepts, but unfortunately her methodology is vague at best and her operationalization of Foucauldian thought is done more as conceptual seasoning, or appeals to authority, rather than as a rigorous application of or engagement with theory and method. This is a problem that Graham (2005) noted in a great many works that claim to be Foucauldian. Subsequently, Graham's (2006) project falls short of its ambition, and indeed its claim; worse still, the lack of rigor in Graham's (ibid.) application has been used to further denigrate the post-modern turn that supposedly threatens the crime sciences, as can be seen in the response piece by Rumney and Jamel (2009).

Although I concur with Graham (2005) in seeing the need to clarify one's own method, whilst cautioning against this as prescriptive for others, where I part company with Graham (ibid.) is in her desire for 'methodological anarchy' to facilitate 'conversation' with Foucault. It seems torturous that the only way for me to be faithful to Foucault is to deny myself use of the very body of work that inspires me. I understand the need for caution in applying Foucauldian concepts as models, and recognize that systematization and conformity is undesirable. However, I can appreciate use of a Foucauldian 'tool-kit'[14] as a way to steer past the methodological cul-de-sac that Graham (ibid.) advocates.

For my own purposes, when adopting a Foucauldian usage, 'discourse' necessarily goes beyond textual and empirical examination. This is not to say that the micro sites are irrelevant – precisely the opposite. This is what Foucault means when he refers to power as coming 'from below'. These micro sites are significant as the foundation for the macro processes of political and politicized societal 'realities'. It is recognition of the latter, of course, that constitutes precisely what it means to be critical when adopting CDA, and is of course why this project's scope must be refracted to engage with the academy itself and popular culture in order to recognize the complexities of reification that occur through societal reaction (the aggregation of collective practices, enshrined in institutions, professions and their technologies). In this sense reification is key to what Foucault calls 'constituting populations', achieved in modern societies through governmentality. Thus, discourse implicates a complex and reciprocal notion of reification in the generation of social facts. It is symptomatic of and indeed integral to governmentality whereby the 'constitution of populations' is the objective of power/knowledge. Indeed, it is important to note that in Foucault's usage it is the productive aspect of power, rather than the repressive, that is arguably of most significance and is often overlooked. In this sense my triangulation comprises a 'genealogy without history' (Nadeson 2008, p. 12).

Now, a caution: Foucault (2001, p. 327) asserts that 'it is not power, but the subject, that is the general theme of my research'; one must not lose sight of this. Too often in governmentality studies, particularly those arising in the political sciences from which many criminologists seem to prefer to draw,[15] the working definition of governmentality is at odds with Foucault's summation and is therefore decidedly problematic. Too often, such works reconfigure Foucauldian theory to satisfy a Marxist, or at least structuralist, agenda. The state and its agencies are foregrounded, and the subject is effectively demoted as merely a target for governance (in its thinnest sense). Attempting to utilize these whilst remaining faithful to Foucault has proven to be difficult. Foucault's notion of power as a transaction, albeit asymmetrical, neither sits well with such top-down configurations, nor does it lend itself easily to analyses that see power as imposed. Finally – and perhaps most significantly – Foucault's major contribution in governmentality – his understanding of power as dispersed throughout the social body, and indeed power as blind – is utterly antithetical to the notion of governmentality as synonymous with state governance and indeed government.[16] Yet, this does tend to be the preferred understanding and usage in that body of work that has come to be known as governmentality studies.

Yet, the very point of investigating governmentality through genealogy is that the distinction between public and private, state and individual, in the circulation of power and forming of power relations, is revealed as erroneous. Transactional notions of power and power relations are important, not institutions or the state per se. These merely reflect cumulative impacts of behaviours and the sedimenting, concretizing or formalizing of beliefs and truths (fears, moral panic and so on). This is not to say that the state and its agencies are unimportant, but it is to move away from their pre-eminence in analyses, and to be sensitized to the minutiae of everyday life and the role that each of us plays in maintaining the status quo or a particular modality of asymmetric power.

One must be mindful that in the criminal justice system we generate data to inform practice, but it is our practice that generates the data. We constitute the population in line with this knowledge, and furthermore they come to constitute themselves. This is the significance of the normalized self as a practice – it becomes reifying. Citing Allen (1998), Moss (1998, p. 3) states that '"[g]overnmentality" was the term Foucault coined to identify both the way in which power guides the conduct of individuals and the modern rationality that demands that everything and everyone be "managed"'. This clearly interlinks the objective measurement of socially constructed and impelled behaviours to become self-legitimating and self-perpetuating through their integration within technologies. Thus the current managerialist[17] concerns with supposedly objective measurement as providing evidence-based policy and intelligence-led practice is revealed as rooted within governmentality.

As Smart (1986, p. 162) argues '[t]he modern state does not constitute a monolith confronting individuals from above, but a "matrix of individualization" which forms, shapes and governs individuality through the exercise of new forms of "pastoral power" over the social'. This inevitably includes agencies, technologies and other dispositifs that are administrative, but this does not mean these should be conflated or that one is ultimately reducible to the other. Rather it concerns the 'individualizing technologies ... it is in this area that natural-social man appears as normal man, the correlate and target of specific kinds of professional expertise' (Burchell, 1991, p. 142) – in this sense, subjectivity can thus be analysed in connection with governmental rationality and legal-political forms.

Bratich (2003) meanwhile begins his analysis with the very clear and simple premise that thought governs action – which we can take to also imply that 'self' governs behaviour. He cites Foucault's exaltation that 'thought is freedom in relation to what one does' (Foucault, 1997, cited in Bratich, 2003, p. 69), but of course one should also invoke Foucault's caution about the nature of 'freedom' in relation to governmentality. Nevertheless, Bratich (ibid.) goes on to draw on Foucault's (ibid., p. 70) statement that '[t]he study of forms of experience can thus proceed from an analysis of "practices" – discursive or not – as long as one qualifies that to mean the different systems of action insofar as they are inhabited by thought', and clarifies that this is because 'thought ... is a condition of possibility for those experiences'.

This is obviously an important condition for the ethical[18] subject, but when not garnered for ethics it is of course exploited by normalization. This is where the action of self-on-self becomes the conduct of conduct, allowing what Rose (1999) termed the governance of 'souls', and ultimately, therefore, governmentality – through the creation of the self in relation to the subject and its aggregation in population. As Burchell (1991, p. 126) states, 'population comes to be seen through the grid of politically or administratively identified regularities in the natural phenomena and processes', thus clearly relating knowledge to biopower. This objectification of the population enables management based on 'the grain of things' (ibid.), a supposedly self-indicating 'natural' condition and need. Such a measure of 'normality' is precisely what enables this disciplinary tautology to be enacted. Above all, for Foucault (1984, cited in Connelly, 1998, p. 117), discourse is fundamentally a 'violence which we do to things' and one that he states is intrinsically linked to 'practices', within which he asserts 'the events of discourse find the principle of their regularity' (ibid.).

Consequently, my inquiry is threefold: to investigate the salience of the particularization of male rape across a Foucauldian triangulation in order to ascertain discursive regularities and concordance that traverse the various sites and realms that constitute the subject; to look specifically at how the construct of the male rape victim intersects with established repertoires of sexual violence, particularly those configured in respect of the female and of feminist thought and activism; and, furthermore, to consider how this construct draws from and reconfigures those repertoires.[19] The last is particularly important. As previously indicated, Foucault implicitly suggested that we should seek not the 'truth', but the irony[20] in order to strip away the progressive illusion. I therefore draw out and discuss several 'ironies' that illustrate how the discourse around male rape, particularly that oriented around 'feminism' (by which I mean both pro- and anti-feminist stances) can be said to have become entangled in the deployment of gender through the resuscitation of rape myths.

Part II
Triangulation Chapters – Deploying the (Male Rape) Subject

4
Representations – Knowing Victimhood

4.1 The production of the 'truth' of male rape: the knowing and known subject

For the purpose of this chapter the 'violence which we do to things' will be examined in reference to instances of discursive regularity around the construct of the male rape victim as depicted in the media, via bias, tropes and framing, both within and across several different mediated forms. These will be informed initially through reference to established male rape myths[1] and established 'truths' discerned from my own review of the academic literature. Through Foucault, one should understand any such instances as 'violence' because of their role in the production and indeed the delimitation of the 'truth' of male rape, a 'truth' through which the subject comes to know himself and others, and indeed through which he is known as a subject.

Despite media depictions being of importance, in the instance of male rape the attention given by the academy is slight by any measure. Notwithstanding Scarce's (1997) classic text that contained a chapter on 'the spectacle' of male rape, with a cursory examination of a variety of forms (albeit oriented to 'homosexuality'), Wlordaz's (2001) essay, 'Rape Fantasies: Hollywood and Homophobia', today remains one of the most thorough treatments and is often cited as almost the sole authority[2] in discussions of media depictions of male rape. This is despite it running to a mere 13 pages and involving a detailed analysis of only one film. Projansky's (2001, pp. 104–106) book *Watching Rape: Film and Television in Post-Feminist Culture* ostensibly seeks to analyse rape in its most general terms, but in actuality does so in highly gendered terms with male-on-male rape and sexual violence mentioned only briefly. Abdullah-Khan's (2008) monograph specifically on male rape includes a chapter on male rape in the news, but this ran to just 13 pages. It seems to be the case that general texts on rape in the media have very little interest in male rape, whilst texts specifically on male rape have very little interest in the media. One cannot help but juxtapose this with the wealth of material generated in respect of depictions of female rape scenarios in analyses of the intersection of sexual violence and the mediated form.[3]

4.2   A focus on reportage and entertainment: framing and governmentality

Male rape appears in many guises – not simply overt, explicit sexual assault. It can also be rather more subtle than that – suggested via symbolism, metaphor, connotation and so on. It can also be implied through sexualized aggression. It might be on screen, off screen; narrated or not; first person or third. Likewise, its function is multifold: it might appear to be relegated, for example, in its use as punctuation, or for comedic effect, or it might appear to be given priority – serving to push the story forward or develop characters. It might be a pivotal point in the text, or apparently no point at all. What is important for us is that it is there – manifest in various narratives and story arcs, and that it has thus far been grossly neglected.[4]

Existing analyses of male rape and the media have thus far situated male-on-male rape as oriented to homosexuality, for example Boyle (2005) cites Wlodarz (2001) who examined films depicting male rape during the 1990s, and reiterates his findings that in male rape revenge film narratives it is invariably gay men who are scapegoated, thus depicting male-on-male rape as inherently deviant; and that furthermore the revenge scenes themselves are painstakingly unerotic and thus desexualized. I disagree with this analysis, and would argue that the very fact that the protagonist's sexual orientation is communicated is to sexualize the act. Moreover the 'revenge' itself usually takes the form of either a literal rape as a revenge scenario or a symbolic rape (including castration or other sexualized aggression). More recently, Demirkan-Martin (2009) has examined male rape in a dedicated chapter, but this too configures it in respect of homosexuality. Male rape understood as motivated by sexual desire, sexual deviance or sexualized aggression, rather than desexualized altogether, inevitably serves to re-inscribe the understanding of rape as primarily a sexual act.

For the purpose of this chapter, I will engage in critical readings of depictions of male rape and sexualized aggression towards males across various forms. For clarity's sake, this is simplistically organized by purported audience impetus or motivation rather than media type, format or technology. Thus, it is crudely divided into only two areas: information and entertainment.[5] The information media section will primarily examine textual data: electronic newspapers (tabloid and broadsheet coverage) and examples from broadcast media; the entertainment media section will primarily address lexical and visual data, including film and television dramatizations, organized by genre (with a focus on horror versus comedy). My aim is to identify the framing at work, including the overt regularities, the underlying constancies and the seemingly contradictory inconstancies – in particular I will seek to ascertain the narratives and tropes in effect in the framing of such depictions and sketch the possibilities for recursion and reification. Male rape forms turn up in disparate genres, but I argue that these draw on the same 'tropes', narratives (be they supported or subverted), and scripts/ schemas – thus contributing to a discursive regularity that is in this sense pervasive. Projansky's (2001) use of 'screwball comedy' in the analysis of comedic depictions of female rape is very dated precisely because contemporary comedy lacks this form of victimization. However, the converse is true of male rape – there is a wealth of current examples from mainstream distributors, and some examples are even located in family films. Consequently this form can be purported as having arisen to replace the female in these genres. This is significant, not least because this form is ostensibly different in all ways, yet in reality operates within the same discursive space to reinforce heterosexual and patriarchal norms.

To examine the media within a Foucauldian triangulation is not simply to examine the dissemination of knowledge – its role and function is rather more complex than that. Said (2003) asserts that historically the role of the academy and its collusion with the state as key to governmentality; and he attributes this pivotal role in contemporary society to the mass media. The mass media is, on one level, simply a medium of communication and mediator of information. So far, so innocuous. But of course, this is not all it is. The media has become far more than its technology. The media has authority, credence and credibility – it legitimates knowledge of the social world whilst simplifying it or even inventing it. It has been regarded as a prime source of learning, of socialization and, indeed, of normalization. It is in this last regard that I am to consider it – within a Foucauldian triangulation – as key to governmentality.

The simplest conceptions of the media's power in this vein draw on notions of propaganda and control. I am sensitive to these, and I do subscribe to certain of them and will acknowledge a debt to them, but I am mindful that governmentality functions not through direct oppression or overt censorship – it is far more diffuse and subtle than such explicit modes can account for. Of primary concern for the purpose of this section is its role in constituting populations – the creation of 'imagined communities' and personal identities that are postulated as a result of shared knowledge, understanding and meaning.

As Hall (1993, cited in Ferrell, 1999, p. 414) has observed, 'there is no escape from the politics of representation'. Whilst Said (1993) asserts that the crucial role of the media is as a 'linchpin' which functions to disseminate partisan and particularized knowledge and manufacture consent for government action. Regularity within media representations functions hegemonically to limit informed discussion and understanding (Williams and Chrisman, 1994); this can be most easily conceived of as 'framing'.

For Scheufele (1999), 'framing' is a vague concept used to loosely define various similar but distinct approaches. He goes on to distinguish two forms, media and audience, cautioning that in research both types must be identified and linked consistently. For the purpose of this endeavour, I will use framing as relating to a focus on the media text. Although I am aware that media framing (in terms of agenda setting, narratives and tropes) and audience framing (in the form of scripts and schemas) are related, and to some extent contingent, I prefer to examine the latter separately and will do so explicitly in Chapter 5, in the section relating to fan fiction.[6] This accords more easily with my levels and aspects of Foucauldian analysis and in my opinion facilitates clarity of examination, especially in terms of ascertaining regularities or consensus across the triangulation. Having said that, the audience cannot be overlooked and aspects of the following discussion necessarily co-implicate media framing and audience framing simultaneously.

'Framing' involves techniques such as discursive regulation, agenda setting and the use of stereotypes that together become consistent and standardized reportage, thereby resulting in consensus. Frames represent 'persistent patterns of selection, emphasis, and exclusion that furnish a coherent interpretation and evaluation of events' (Norris et al., 2003, p. 4). Framing constructs the issue in question and also positions (denoting who you are supposed to identify with, via camera angles/viewpoints) the spectator or audience. The consequences are significant as 'it is not only what we see, but how we are positioned to see it that is important' (Boyle, 2005, p. 127). Framing enables meaning-making for the audience – contributing both to our understanding of the world and our place in it, the importance of which is emphasized by Said (1997, p. 46) who observes that 'no one lives in direct contact either with truth or with reality' everyone lives in a world of 'meanings'. Which, of course, is also to recognize that there can be no such thing as non-constructed knowledge.

On an individual level, media narratives of criminality and victimhood intersect and co-constitute personal scripts and schemas. This does not just impact on understanding, but also on identity. At this point, and for these very reasons, it is important to note that the concept of framing itself 'is embedded in effects research' (Scheufele, 1999, p. 104). Effects research posits that the media has a concrete impact. Whilst the precise influence of the media is contested, and must be accepted as complex and not causal, effects models regarding the societal impact of media representations of crime 'argue that routine portrayals of violence, crime and deviance enhance the power of those with a vested interest in the status quo rather than effecting a breakdown in social order' (Sanders and Lyon, 1995, p. 26). Media representations legitimate authority, promoting social cohesion and social control through the transmission of normative values and the manufacturing of consensus that, together with para-social interaction, function to construct and constrain the population as an 'imagined' community.

Effects research is not without its critics, for example Jewkes (2004, p. 11) is dismissive of effects research as she believes 'much effects research cannot adequately address the subtleties of media meanings, the polysemy of media texts (that is, that they are open to multiple interpretations), the unique characteristics and identity of the audience member, or the social and cultural context within which the encounter between media text and audience member occurs'. Fair comment, but unfortunately this criticism is guilty of precisely what it alleges – oversimplification. This is made explicitly clear when she goes on to critique the majority of current research in media effects as still drawing on the hypodermic syringe model. This is a swift and wholesale denigration of a massive and varied area of study. Such criticism may bear relevance to some research, but I would hesitate to posit this against the majority. It is perfectly possible to appreciate the role and impact of the media whilst being sensitized to complexity and contingency. Effects do not have to be causal, inevitable nor homogenous. As Reiner (1997, p. 191) attests, 'it is of course a non sequitur to move from the denial of a direct influence to the assertion of no influence'.[7] Indeed, it is the very multiplicity of effects that contribute to, rather than erode, the power of the media.

Cultural criminology is proving to be a fruitful site of research into media effects, although the 'effects' label is resisted and the resultant work is assiduously designated otherwise, plausibly because of the very denigration Jewkes (2004) and others have performed. Cultural criminology's work in respect of the media has a legacy that is in no small way a part of the evolution of left realism.[8] Authors within this vein who are at present more wholeheartedly seizing upon critical theory and cultural studies note the 'convergence of cultural and criminal processes in contemporary social life ... highlight[ing] issues of image, meaning, and representation in the interplay of crime and crime control' (Ferrell, 1999, p. 395) and furthermore emphasize the participatory and performative nature of the audience.

Speaking of the complexity at work here, Kern et al. (2003, p. 282) state in their work relating to reportage that 'it is often difficult to disentangle how news frames shape the social construction of reality from the "actual" reality of events. It is like being surrounded by an endless hall of mirrors'. The notion of social constructions in the media and the co-constitution of reality as 'a walk down an infinite hall of mirrors' (Ferrell, 1999, p. 397) is pivotal to the work of cultural criminologists.[9] Whilst Said (cited in Viswanathan, 2004, p. 43) doubts whether we can ever hope to understand the relationship between the media and the social world as 'we have not yet devised the means to deal with a television or film or even a script image, and to criticize the framework in which the image is presented, because it is *given* as a reality, mediated so powerfully, and accepted almost subliminally', he expressly resolves the problem of media influence, regarding the apparent contradiction between a centralized mechanism of control versus a disaggregated audience and how this might result in a homogenous or quasi-homogenous mechanism for the manufacturing of consent, by noting the effect of 'the homogenization of a certain level of consciousness by the media ... I wouldn't call it the system of indoctrination ... but it has some of those elements. It's also, characteristically, I think, an anesthetization of the critical sense' (ibid). For these authors then, 'effects' research is far from redundant.

Whilst effects research might be popularly criticized, one effect of the media that is nevertheless garnering popular credence is 'fear'. It has long been accepted that 'fear ... reproduces the existing social order' (Signorelli in Reiner, 1997, p. 217); indeed, there is a contemporary recognition of moral panic as a mechanism of social control that enables an encroaching governmentality.[10] If moral panic and the climate of fear[11] are widely accepted as mechanisms of social control, surely then so is a state of 'no fear' and, indeed, a climate of complacency. What is interesting to me here is the plausible flipside of this: where male sexual victimization is concerned we have a minimized fear.[12]

Osborne (1995, cited in Jewkes, 2004, p. 28) asserts that 'media discourses about crime now constitute all viewers as equally subject to the fragmented and random danger of criminality, and in so doing provide the preconditions for endless narratives of criminality that rehearse this everpresent danger'. I strongly disagree. Whilst depictions of crime are ubiquitously present in the media, victimhood as a construct is highly differentiated by crime type and victim group. This is never clearer than in respect of sexual violence. Fear of crime – as a formless and dislocated event – may well be pervasive throughout the audience, but fear of sexual assault and rape most certainly is not.

Fear of sexual victimization is highly particularized by gender. Both the promotion of fearful women and fearless men are governed by conformity to gendered ideals of normative behaviour. As Schlesinger et al. (1992, cited in Kidd-Hewitt, 2002, p. 125) state, 'women identify strongly with the dangers of being physically attacked'. This is especially the case where sexual violence is concerned. The same is not true of the male audience. We have often considered the impact of this perpetual state of sensitization to vulnerability in respect of women; what we have not given serious consideration to is the desensitization of men to their own vulnerability. Wholesale female vulnerability is just as much a construct as male invulnerability. Each is a false position, and we must question what each serves. It is this gendered disparity that should be of concern and interest, particularly in terms of 'constituting populations' within that audience. This is especially so when consensus framing is in place within the media, and is compounded by concordance across the triangulation which cumulatively produces discursive regularity and indeed regulation. This is undoubtedly where the media and its gendering of rape become key to governmentality.

4.3   Male rape is not real rape: mediated messages of difference and indifference

Information media

I expected to find a fairly sizable level of reportage around male rape (at least relative to 'official' statistics), and, therefore, anticipated that any analysis of frequency would prove a precarious base on which to try to balance my discussion. Consequently I decided I would confine my analysis to framing within and between pieces. In essence, my express intention was for this discussion to surpass the 'invisibility' debate simply because I had thought it a moot point. Outmoded, archaic, anachronistic and irrelevant, surely? Given the various legislative changes in the Western world that enshrine in law the recognition of male rape victims, I had thought visibility of sorts to be a reasonable assumption. I very quickly found otherwise.

In order to ascertain the framing of male rape, I used online archives of various newspapers,[13] as well as broadcast media. My means of enabling the aggregation of relevant sources will be sketched out in the interests of transparency rather than methodology, but it broadly follows the examples set by Abdullah-Khan (2008) and Poole (2002).

In my preliminary research I sought to determine the nature of coverage rather than the extent of it. The reason for this is twofold: first, my express aim was to produce qualitative research that more readily accords with a Foucauldian analysis and, second, for the reasons outlined above, I had assumed issues relating to quantity to be redundant. My overriding concern was to consider the media 'messages' in the public domain, particularly what validation, if any, a male rape victim might receive from these.

As a consequence I performed a rudimentary conceptual content analysis whereby I identified articles by using a keyword search using the terms 'male rape', and when articles were identified I read these to check the terms in context. This was to allow me to draw out themes and issues salient to their framing, then group articles accordingly. It is important to note that the themes and issues were not determined beforehand and the articles tallied to them, rather it was intended that critical readings of the articles themselves should produce the various themes and issues. To this end, it was necessary to perform a second complete reading of all the articles once the initial grouping was performed in order to check these groupings against one another. Needless to say this was a time consuming process.

For this stage in my research, I consulted nine online newspapers – four from the UK,[14] three from the US,[15] one from Hong Kong[16] and one from Canada[17] – each having national distribution in hard copy in its country of publication and each having an online, searchable archive of news articles from its own database, without the need for registration or subscription. It was important to me that the sources I used be free and accessible for their resident population as well as to the greater online community. In all, I consulted at least 50 articles on each of the aforementioned sites, with each article identified through the relevant site's own search engines. In each case the default search was used first (some databases default to 'most relevant', others to 'most recent'); in some instances a subsequent search was performed using elected options, especially if the default search had errors in returns or produced few hits. In all, a total of 600 individual articles were consulted.[18]

This did not produce the wealth of results I had expected. Of the 600 articles highlighted by the search engines and thereafter read in full, very few were wholly gendered as a male experience, or even mentioned or at least implied males as victims. The initial aim of drawing out groupings of themes and issues salient to their framing was quickly determined to be impracticable. In total, there were 15 articles found that could be said to satisfy the not particularly rigorous test of inclusiveness set out above. Of these 15, the breakdown is as follows: three related to reviews of works of fiction[19] (one stage play, one book, one television episode), one was simply a figure of speech,[20] seven related to overseas incidents, particularly involving war or conflict,[21] and one to child-on-child.[22] Of the three that remained, two related to a single case involving a transgender male to female offender,[23] and one was a general article where only the final statement, made by a police officer urging rape victims to come forward despite a wave of false allegations by women being reported in the press, expressly mentioned male victims.[24] The results here did not lend themselves to 'grouping' per se – they were barely enough to form a 'group' in themselves. For a male rape victim, the examples were of tenuous relevance and I would suggest that their use by such an individual would be fraught with compromise.

Looking again at those results, such as they are, I would point out the following as being pertinent and deserving of further consideration, the presentation of: male-on-male rape in the community where this is child-on-child; rape in war/overseas conflict; rape and transgender perpetrators. These are significant as they variously serve to present male-on-male rape as outside the realm of 'normal' male experience by locating it within particular populations that might be crudely (I am drawing on stereotypes and bigotry here, not validating it) denigrated in popular understanding as they resonate with stereotypical and pejorative discourse around childhood, the Oriental (à la Said), and 'deviant' sexuality respectively. Looking at 'children' as a distinct victim group, for example, allows for the rationalization of male-on-male rape as impacting on those who are perceived as both innocent and powerless/ base and amoral (part of the demonizing of children in the media). Situating male rape as 'foreign' (linking to notions of the 'Oriental') draws on the dual discourse of the effeminate and vulnerable Other/the oversexed and insatiable Other, whilst situating it within transgender populations enables it to be perceived as effeminacy/abnormality, drawing on psychopathology and derogated notions of homosexuality. It is significant that we are not presented with any scenarios relating to adult, heterosexual males in community settings. Instead, each of the above plausibly serves to delegitimize male-on-male rape as outside the realm of 'normal' male experience, and furthermore serves to reinforce notions of a 'just world' – that the world is fair and just and, therefore, people get what they deserve (it can't happen to me, I don't deserve it) – and enables 'defensive attribution' – blaming victims for their own misfortune, pivoting on perceived difference ('it can't happen to me, I'm not like them') – both of which ultimately underscore the notion of the ideal victim by legitimizing victim precipitation.

I returned to the 600 articles and read them again. I chose to repeat interrogation of this sample on the basis that this sample is what would be generated by a person searching for 'male rape'. Having accepted that they might not have many hits directly relating to male rape, I wanted to see what they would be presented with.

Whilst gender-specific articles relating to male rape were few, a greater number of articles (112 in total) could be classed as 'neutral', dealing with rape rather than male rape. This, at least, was a promising indication of a move towards a measure of inclusivity – assimilation if not representation. However, on closer inspection, it became apparent that 'neutral' in this instance does not necessarily mean genuinely non-gender-specific – often it simply denotes gender not specified. This is most assuredly not the same thing. Truly neutral would be genuinely inclusive; unfortunately many of the examples simply are not.

From my sweep of 600 articles, the trend seems to be that 'rape', where used in a seemingly neutral sense, is actually mostly included as either a figure of speech or an example – often amongst a lengthy or disparate list of offences. The term 'rape' is often included as an emotive term, or as an appeal to authority or included in lists of evidence. Furthermore, even where the focus of the piece is neutral, the examples from survivors are not; where content can be said to be genuinely neutral, the illustration often is not. Neutrality in regards to rape is routinely undermined in myriad ways that serve to gender by stealth. Indeed, conversely to what one might assume, I found it to be the case that where articles seek to discuss rape in any depth whatsoever they almost invariably and routinely become gendered, and this is both explicit and implicit – through examples included and context, images, etc. Casual use, therefore, is possibly implicitly gendered – not an indication of gender neutrality therefore, but of an embedded pervasion of gendering in respect of this crime.

At this point it was apparent that any attempt I might make in respect of analysing male rape in reportage, based as it would be on the handful of examples I found, would be redundant. As a consequence, a second and distinct interrogation of online sources was performed. I deliberately contrived to increase my hit rate by searching a specialist portal within one of the UK newspapers, the dedicated Guardian Society Rape archive.[25] This portion of their website functions solely as a repository and reference section dedicated to rape reportage from within their publication.[26] It includes not only articles solely dealing with cases of rape, but also legislation, policy and other government and institutional initiatives, editorials and comment. Therefore, I felt it a reasonable presupposition that the articles aggregated there would at least be inclusive to the lowest standard of 'inclusivity'. I initially decided to select a sample of only the most recent from their total list of 93 articles (as at 1 October 2009) for the purpose of critical readings. It rapidly became clear to me that this simply would not suffice; consequently, all 93 were consulted. Each article was read in full, its themes and issues noted and its level of inclusivity determined as per the previous sample.

In my search on this specialized portal I found only six articles[27] that did at least attempt to be inclusive; unfortunately I have to note that these still fell back on the 'rape as feminized' trope to varying extents. This is most certainly not what I had expected. Even in a specialist archive of news, the male is presented as relegated, as marginalized and as aberrant. I do not doubt that these articles intend to be inclusive; I only note that they remain limited in this respect.

Working through the material in detail, in the order in which it was presented, the first hit came after just two pieces – a very promising start. Halfway through the piece, which details the use of rape as a war crime, the author asserts '[r]ape is used to humiliate, defeat and emasculate the enemy. It is also used against men with the same rationale' (Harvey, 2009), going on to specifically mention the male victim later in the same paragraph. This, at least, is a clear recognition of this victim group. Unfortunately, a closer reading of the piece leaves one less than satisfied. The only cases included concern female victims. The author leads with detailed cases of two assaults involving female victims, and – after the paragraph where male victims are briefly acknowledged as a phenomenon – she rapidly disregards them, citing again the two female examples. Furthermore this piece expressly genders the phenomenon of rape in war itself by framing it as 'human rights violations of women' (ibid.), highlighting 'women's organisations on the ground' (ibid.), and asserting that 'women aren't waiting around for the UN to sort things out' (ibid.) – all of which might be entirely accurate, but it is also skewed.

The piece itself is presented from the outset as non-gender-specific; the headline, after all, is 'Rape: the unprosecuted war crime'. Given both the established research on male sexual victimization within war and the inclusion of men within rape legislation, this plainly should not have been a gendered piece. Yet that first quote reveals the crux of the problem: 'Rape is used to humiliate, defeat and emasculate the enemy. It is also used against men with the same rationale' (ibid.). In this usage, rape is plainly gendered as female; her mention of 'the enemy' is therefore also female – otherwise that second sentence denoting the male would be redundant. This piece is limited by its reliance on the gendered binary of victim status. Unfortunately, from my analysis of the 93 articles on this database, it seems that this slippage of rape as gendered – connoting exclusive female victimization irrespective of any gender-specific denotation – is the norm.

Indeed, the remaining 87 articles were solely female-centric. Whilst this stark disproportionality is an issue, I am sure it can, in certain instances, be justified perfectly soundly by the authors concerned, for example, in terms of their particular polemic, or the angle of the story, or even simply due to available statistics, press releases and detailed cases. Perhaps in these instances it might be said that ensuring that there is room for validation of the male rape victim is more an issue of moral conscience than it is an ethical imperative or factual obligation. As a consequence, what is of more concern for me is the number of articles within this total that clearly should have included either explicit recognition of male victims or conscientious and sustained neutrality, both as a clear duty to the public and to accuracy. For example, those whose focus specifically draws on the phenomenon of rape as a legal construct – thus in its criminal incidence or legislative forms – after all, any discussion of statistics would be remiss to overlook the male experience as it does contribute to the overall incidence of rape; likewise any discussion of legislation, policy and initiatives should also be decidedly inclusive as this victim group is recognized in statute and case law. Any reference to 'fairness' here is irrelevant – in these instances it becomes simply a matter of fact. Reportage, in these instances, must be inclusive to be accurate.

Unfortunately, this is most assuredly not the case. The number of articles that male victims of rape are effectively edited out of – redacted, if you will – is simply astonishing, as is the range of 'professionals' and 'experts' who seemingly collude with this. Where 'experts' were cited as authorities, for example ministers, councillors, lawyers, police officers and charity workers, they also fail to give due recognition to male victims of rape. Logically, these people should have fared far better – not least because we would assume they are better informed and have the public interest at heart, and of course some have an express public duty.

In all, I identified 35 articles[28] that by the standards expressed above clearly should have included men and yet inexplicably did not. These articles have the clearest mandate and hence the most glaring exclusion. I grouped these articles in very broad terms, thematically, as follows: articles concerning incidence, risk or conviction rates (the implicit message here being: 'we are talking to you'); articles concerning procedure, strategy, initiatives, reviews, inquiries and policy (the implicit message here being: 'we care about you'); and miscellaneous articles, including opinion pieces (the implicit message here being: 'we are angry on your behalf'). Suffice to say that in my review of these articles the overwhelming message implicitly conveyed in the omission of males is male victims are not real victims; ergo, male-on-male rape is not 'real' rape.

This is not just unfortunate, it is unforgivable. These articles not only could have included the male, but in addressing issues of policy, risk and justice they were obliged to be inclusive. Male rape is 'real' rape: it is *really* enshrined in law, it is *really* a risk for men in the community and it is *really* a lived experience for many men. It does not just deserve recognition, it factually demands it. At the simplest level, I would argue that in allowing this exclusion we enable the preservation of the hierarchies of and exclusions from victimhood that these authors ostensibly seek to destroy.

Unfortunately, such practices of omission, obfuscation and marginalization are not confined to newspapers. Examples can also be noted in television news bulletins, magazine shows and documentaries. For example in a BBC (2009) *News* broadcast, which discussed the impending change to rape investigations, protocol and interagency cooperation, with a focus on improving the currently low report and conviction rates, female pronouns were used throughout in reference to victims, whilst the male pronoun was exclusively used for reference to offenders. This was even the case in the contribution to the broadcast by the then Women and Equalities Minister, Harriet Harman. In the broadcast the only examples were female, and the only illustrations of victims were female. There was no room here for any male victims to validate their experience. In an episode of *The Wright Stuff* (2009) a discussion of rape (entitled 'Raped Stars: Police before Papers') was wholly gendered from the outset and was sustained throughout, even in follow-up the next day. The discussion began in reference to a single female celebrity,[29] but quickly became about 'all women'.

In a documentary, *Dispatches: Rape in the City* (2009), there was an entirely gendered presentation of the phenomenon of gang rape. Both the experts gendered their analyses, and the key researcher, Carlene Firmin, not only gendered her analysis and stated in her account of her research a very gendered research method (only females were interviewed), but also she was clearly wearing a T-shirt that with the caption 'Women's Resource Centre' on the back and 'Female Voice in Violence' on the front. The viewer is left in no doubt that this discussion is about female-oriented victimization. Any male viewers seeking validation of their own experiences are left with no room whatsoever.

In all, it would be fair to say that I was surprised at just how occluded male rape is in current UK reportage. All too often such pieces are quickly and pervasively framed as 'women's interest' and informed by spokespersons from feminist activist groups, thus inevitably facilitating the elision of the male. Yet simple measures could easily be adopted to foster inclusivity and/or neutrality – for example, to include gender-neutral terms throughout with no gendered pronouns or pictures, or to ensure a balance of gendered examples and illustration.

Feminizing rape is apparently not only ingrained, but entirely acceptable. This must stop. All rape is real rape – irrespective of the gender of the victim. We cannot possibly hope to positively impact on attrition whilst we continue to preserve the exclusion and privileging of victimhood for some rape victims only. The information media, in revalidating hierarchies of harm, techniques of minimization and responsibilization are necessarily culpable in resurrecting, legitimizing and sustaining rape's ideal victim – to the detriment of all.

Entertainment

Existing analyses of filmic depictions of male rape are few in number and in depth. For example, Projansky (2001) dedicates only three pages to this in her text on rape and the media, Lehman (2001) gives just one chapter to this issue in his text for the American Film Institute, whilst Demirkan-Martin (2009) gives just one chapter. These analyses all draw examples from drama/thriller genres, are beholden to the legislative construct that precludes women as rapists, and situate male-on-male rape as squarely oriented towards homophobia. None consider the wider ramifications of this as operating itself as myth-making – potentially writing-back to the 'totem' of female rape – nor do they consider its potential to undermine the tenability of feminism.

My research for this section involved identification and analysis of depictions of male rape and sexualized aggression towards males in film, television and popular music. These depictions will be used to illustrate the salience and significance of the ideal victim construct – ostensibly reconfigured as the male, but fundamentally attached to the explication of rape and sexual aggression in general.

Initially it was intended that film and television examples could be identified through the Internet Movie Database (IMDB),[30] but I did not find this to be particularly productive. Certainly, using the term 'male rape' revealed very few examples as those that were highlighted had already become standard in this area, whilst others that I was already aware of myself were not highlighted at all. Trying to identify incidents of male rape subsumed within the category 'rape' proper – without prior assumption of gendering in my own search criteria – was quickly revealed as unmanageable due to the quantity of hits that were in fact gendered as female.

I specifically wanted to move away from those examples that have become a staple of (albeit limited) discussion[31] in this area – for example, *The Shawshank Redemption, Deliverance, The Rape of Richard Beck* and *Pulp Fiction*, not least because these locate male rape as within the genre of drama or thriller, and thus the use of rape within these films is often part of a more fully developed story arc and character development, in some instances being central to the story itself. Therefore, each is inevitably aimed at a distinct audience and at the generation of a particular response, for example, pathos. This is not my interest. I was keen to seek examples from the genres of horror and comedy – not only because thus far this area has been somewhat neglected, but also because these genres can be contrasted with both drama and thriller, and are, as Wells (2000) asserts, 'allied' to one another, not least in their affective impact – laughter and fear – which Xu, Chia and Jin (2005, p. 2) note are both extreme and 'special' emotional responses that these genres elicit.

It was necessary for me to generate my own samples. The only way to do this was to watch and analyse films and television shows from the horror and comedy genres over a period of more than 18 months. Where film was concerned, I did not confine myself to samples obtained via the broadcast media, but also looked at that available via cinema and the rental market. Nor did I restrict my interest to Western or English-language forms. My only criteria were that they should be 'popular' (as determined variously by chart and box office rankings), produced in the last decade or so and easily obtainable. As far as possible I tried to challenge my own preconceptions about what might prove useful, deliberately sampling subcategories that I would otherwise dismiss. This was a tactic that proved surprisingly – and lamentably – productive, with references to male rape found even in Western and Chinese 'family' comedies.[32]

Films deliberately sourced for this project exceeded 100. But, in total, this produced just 21[33] relevant examples. In respect of material that was broadcast, rather than sample a specific channel over a period of time or many channels at the same time, I opted to keep a viewing diary over a period in excess of one year, during which time I challenged myself to view a range of material from within the comedy and horror genres – this involved prime time and off peak, premieres and repeats, terrestrial and satellite channels.[34] Because of the quantity involved here, I only noted relevant examples. This resulted in just 16[35] relevant sources.

What will be presented below are my findings in respect of the framing of male rape in the aforementioned sources. The examples presented are not intended to be representative of all depictions of male rape or sexualized violence, but rather are indicative. They are useful for highlighting themes and issues and speculating as to their interrelation with other forms of representation and other aspects of the triangulation.

I found male rape and sexualized aggression towards males to appear in disparate genres, but drawing on the same tropes and narratives (be they supported or subverted), in this sense contributing to the overall discursive construct of the male rape victim. As with the previous section, I examine selected sources with a view to ascertaining how the framing in each might be regarded as both drawing from and reinforcing the previously discredited notion of the ideal victim. Examples from horror and comedy will be discussed in detail.

At the most simplistic, one might say that horror establishes the 'fears' whilst comedy parodies them. Horror forms and exaggerates our 'monsters' whilst comedy perverts and trivializes them. Superficially then, given that horror and comedy appear to be posited as oppositional discourses, they might appear to be mutually invalidating – however, this would overlook Foucault's caution about discontinuity. It is arguably more plausible to seek to examine them as part of a mutually reinforcing symbiosis. It is their complex interrelationship that is of interest. In particular, my interest is in respect of how the various strands noted in each genre might together co-constitute the ideal victim.

In each of the examples, from horror and comedy, that follow one can again see that the previously discredited notion of victim precipitation is being subtly resurrected, even in supposedly pro-feminist depictions, with the male victim as the vehicle.

Horror

In each of the films under consideration here – *Ginger Snaps* (2000), *Battle Royale* (2001) and *Audition* (1999) – sexualized violence towards the male is seemingly valorized in a pro-feminist context, similar to that presented in *Thelma and Louise*.[36] Celebrated as role reversal, violent sexual assaults of men by women have significant support – for example Brownmiller (1975) states that she 'heartily agrees' with the following statement that she terms 'pro-woman commentary': 'I want to see films about men getting raped by women ... I want to see the camera linger on the look of terror in his eyes when he suddenly realizes the woman is bigger, stronger and far more brutal than he' (Sullivan, n.d., cited in Brownmiller, 1975, p. 303). Wish granted, but at what cost?

On closer inspection I would argue such depictions to operate as post- or anti-feminism.[37] A post-feminist depiction in this sense is one involving a female aggressor that at the same time valorizes the violence whilst demonizing the female actor and presents the male as enfeebled. Furthermore I note that in so doing such depictions undermine feminism in popular consciousness, as well as surreptitiously relegitimizing conventional rape myths.

We should remember the central tenet of Clover's (1987) work: that gender is not embodied on screen as male or female by virtue of the actor, instead it can be more fluid than that – depicted along a 'register' of indicative behaviours, with the genders 'collapsed into one and the same character' (ibid., p. 220). Thus male may become feminine and female may become masculine. Clover focuses on the trope of the Final Girl in this vein, noting that such characters have their gender 'compromised' by the exhibition and performance of more masculine traits; therefore she is in effect 'a male surrogate'. It surely follows that this premise holds for male characters also. As she herself goes on to state, 'angry displays of force ... belong to the male ... [whilst] crying, cowering, screaming, fainting, trembling, begging for mercy belong to the female. Abject terror is gendered feminine' (ibid., p. 212) – this being the case, it is the behaviour that signifies gender, not the body.

Clover (1987, p. 218, italics added) asserts in passing that – of the Final Girl – 'the same body does for both and that body is female ... it is gendered feminine *even when played by a male*'. I would argue that it is this much-neglected observation that should underpin analysis of fictionalized accounts of male victims of sexual/ized violence on screen and in literature, particularly as for our purposes we might conceive of the Final Girl as exemplifying a gendered morality that tallies in no small part with the ideal victim construct. This latter notion will be revisited in Chapter 5, but for now this observation about a body being gendered by behaviour (which corresponds with what Butler, in 1990, termed 'performativity') will underlie my analysis of fictional screen sexual violence towards men.

In *Ginger Snaps*, we have Ginger's sexual assault[38] of Jason; in *Battle Royale* we have Chigusa's vicious knifing of Niida; and in *Audition*, Asami's torture of Aoyama. The common element in each depiction – and each has a female protagonist – is the seemingly plausible rationale of vengeance/retaliation, or more accurately the rape-revenge trope. But in the cases considered here, this trope is only given the slightest of references and is not satisfied in full – in no instance is the female actually victimized or truly threatened, her 'retaliation' then is neither justified nor proportionate. As Clover (1992, p. 144) states 'for revenge fantasies to work, there must be something worth avenging', but the males depicted here do not conform with Clover's (ibid., p. 144) 'heinous crime – sweet revenge' logic. In addition, the 'punishment' meted out is frequently sexualized in itself. Thus, whilst we are invited to regard these as rape-revenge stories, they are more akin to rape *as* revenge, with the female as the aggressor. This could superficially be regarded as an inversion of standard depictions – subversive of gender norms – but this is not a reading I support, not least because in *Ginger Snaps* the sexual assault is driven by unbridled sexual aggression; whilst in *Battle Royale* and *Audition* the sexualized violence (which function as metaphorical rapes) is underscored by sadism[39] – both capacities that are very much of the male. In addition, in all instances the victim is effectively feminized through various behavioural tendencies and narrative motifs – culminating of course in the rapes themselves that Clover (ibid., p. 158) asserts are equated with 'quintessential femininity'. Thus the gendered subject positions are actually very much intact, with a 'masculinized' female aggressor and a 'feminized' male victim.

When coupled with sexualized violence, such narratives serve to lend credence to the rape/revenge model, an element of victim precipitation and counterpoint therefore to the ideal victim. One must also note that each film also draws on various other rape tropes that resurrect the spectre of myths thought long dead, for example, rape/sex, rape/seduction and rape/psychopathology. Thus such depictions are, in many ways, conformist and orthodox at their core. At the very least, simply reversing the gender roles in each instance can expose the problems.

Ginger Snaps is examined first. This film intertwines an adolescent girl's onset of puberty with her transformation into a werewolf – conflating the menstrual 'curse' with the curse of the werewolf. It is a horror with a darkly comic underbelly, a somewhat perverse 'coming of age' movie that explores themes of (amongst others) womanhood and sexuality. It has been widely received as a (pro-)feminist film and analysed as such (for example, Barker et al., 2006), but this is not a reading I support. It should be noted that the 'rape' scene that I regard as so pivotal has thus far been neglected, referred to only somewhat obliquely and problematically as 'a violent erotic encounter' in Barker et al.'s, (2006, p. 4) paper that is dedicated to this film franchise. Regarding this scene as 'violent eroticism' is to either ignore the aggressive coercion and vocalized resistance that occurs and/or to simply draw from a most definitely non-feminist understanding of the conflation of rape/sex.

Ginger's first love and loss of virginity involves the aggressive 'rape' of her boyfriend Jason in the backseat of his car – which is tagged rather tellingly as 'aggressive desire' in the DVD scene selection.[40] The way this scene starts clearly implies date rape. The scene opens with Ginger and her boyfriend in the back of the car; they are viewed from outside and are seen in a passionate clinch. This scene immediately sets up the vulnerability inherent in this situation – it is very dark and clearly isolated. The view quickly shifts to inside the car in a poorly lit and claustrophobic shot reminiscent of what Demirkan-Martin (2009) regards as a trope of (conventional)[41] male rape scenes. The audience is implicitly aware that rape is portended, but as yet is not aware as to who the aggressor is. Ginger removes her jacket, her stomach growls, she laughs – embarrassed. She smiles and tries to push Jason down onto his back. His response is probably not what the audience expects – he is reluctant to cooperate and, very quickly as this scene progresses, he communicates fear and clearly articulates non-consent. Given that other analyses have overlooked this, I feel it worth analysing in detail at this point. We should bear in mind that, were the genders reversed here, this would not so readily be dismissed as either 'erotic' or 'desire'.

On being pushed by Ginger, Jason responds 'hey, hey, take it easy' and pushes her upright, his hands, placed on her shoulders at the top of her arms, holding her off – the palms open and towards her – which reinforces his lack of consent; it is quite clearly 'blocking' body language. He regains composure to smile at Ginger, but is obviously uncomfortable and attempts to stall her: 'we've got all night'. Ginger responds, 'sorry. You just ... taste really good,' and proceeds to push him down again whilst kissing him aggressively. Ginger is evidently ignoring his discomfort and his lack of approval. Jason pushes her off again and in an attempt to gain some control over the situation instructs her, in a faltering manner to 'just, j … just lie back and relax'. The next exchange is what many interpret as part of a pro-feminist narrative, as Ginger responds to this request with clear affront. She is obviously offended and sharply retorts 'you lie back and relax', to which Jason exclaims 'hey, who's the guy here?'

Other analyses have overlooked the sudden transformation at this point of Ginger as (supposedly) a potential victim into an aggressor. Her demeanour quickly becomes menacing and she pushes Jason over, onto his back, and can be clearly seen pinning him down. The camera moves back to view the car from the deserted street so that we are reminded of the isolation and vulnerability of this exchange. The car rocks in response to Ginger's very aggressive physicality. When returned to the interior view, the camera focuses on Jason, in a claustrophobic close-up of his shocked expression – he is clearly scared. Ginger shouts in his face 'who's the guy here? Huh? Who's the fucking guy here?' a line and a role reversal that other authors have lauded, but what follows is indefensible and certainly should not be valorized.

Ginger pins his arms, shakes and pushes him down into the car seat. Jason again tries to stall her by articulating concern about their lack of contraception in an effort to disengage. He is clearly fearful – audibly stuttering and visibly cowering as he speaks; his last words in this sentence trail off to become a moan of pain, which rapidly becomes a scream as Ginger fiercely pushes his face into the car seat, disfiguring it with visible pressure. His face becomes contorted, he continues screaming and pleads with her to 'stop it', after which he screams again, much louder this time, whilst Ginger rips his shirt open. The camera shifts to give a shot from above; Ginger is clearly writhing on him. Again, Jason begs for her to desist, articulating 'no' and 'wait', his panicked breathing audible. Ginger looks impassive and mockingly dismisses his rejection: 'You're fucking hilarious.' She lunges at him, aggressively kissing and biting his neck whilst he continues to cry out in pain. We see Ginger move to cover his mouth – her overpowering of him is complete. This scene ends with his cries merging over the next shot of Ginger's sister asleep in bed.

This scene should arouse concern, and I am perplexed as to why it has not attracted opprobrium. Regarding the scene as pro-feminist is to wilfully ignore the deeper complex relating to sexual violence. This scene clearly inverts rape tropes about the vulnerability and innocence of women, but it does so by re-inscribing these on to the male. At the same time, this scene draws from and legitimizes old myths, not least of which is conflating rape/sex/desire, lending credence to the notion that arousal cannot be contained, that rapists cannot control themselves. This is indicated earlier by Ginger's physical hunger and is reinforced in the next scene when Ginger, in explaining herself to her sister, cries mournfully that 'I get this ache, and I thought it was for sex ...'; thus her 'rape' of the boyfriend is explained as uncontrollable desire/unbridled lust. This is reiterated later in the same scene, when Ginger explains her killing of the neighbour's dog – an act already intertwined in the minds of the viewer with the 'rape' of Jason due to a previous misdirection to the audience[42] – by sobbing that 'he, he, he barked, and he barked and he kept fucking barking and I, I, I just, I just, *I couldn't stop myself*' (italics added).

First 'rape' and first kill – Ginger just could not help herself. Such rationalizations serve to responsibilize the victim, making it their fault for 'triggering' or 'unleashing' sexual desire. This supports the notion of the ideal victim by placing victim behaviour (demeanour, personality, etc.) at the heart of explanations for rape, implying that some rape victims are 'asking for it'. As if this isn't problematic enough, later in the film we see Jason join his friends to watch the girls play hockey. He is visibly beaten, bearing contusions and lesions to face and neck. When his peers remark on this, he happily relays his victimization as conquest – 'Ginger Fitzgerald rocked my world' – a troubling reinterpretation of sexual violence as sexual congress.

Ginger Snaps draws on many previously discredited myths around the rape/sex conflation, such as rape is motivated by desire, and therefore the victim's behaviour can precipitate it; that it can become enjoyable for the victim, therefore no means yes; as well as serving to reinforce gender-specific male rape myths such as men always want sex/it is not really possible to 'rape' a man, and therefore successful coerced sexual congress of a male is by definition not rape. All of these myths serve to exculpate the offender and responsibilize the victim. Of particular concern is the notion of victim precipitation as this is a particularly pernicious barrier to justice for rape victims. I find it surprising that the reading of this film as subversive to patriarchal norms and therefore supposedly self-evidently pro-feminist persists.

The second film for consideration, *Battle Royale* (2001), is an apocalyptic vision of the future. The premise of this film is that Japanese teenagers have become dangerously disaffected, a conceit used as the core pretext in the film for the creation of legislation that empowers the state to randomly target secondary school cohorts via a nationwide lottery. These groups of teenage classmates are forcibly removed and dispatched to a remote island to compete in a televised survival game where there can be only one winner – hence the tag line 'could you kill your best friend?'. The film is graphically violent, but as a whole has been interpreted as condemnatory of violence, given that the public who sanction the legislation are culpable for the children's suffering, and the 'viewers' in the film and the audience of the film are also adjudged complicit. It can also be said to be optimistic of the human condition as many of the characters work together and sacrifice themselves to help others survive (Antoniou, 2004). Nevertheless, to my mind, a particular scene of female-on-male sexualized violence steadfastly detracts from these redeeming features.

The scene in question is between a female character, Chigusa, and a male, Niida. In this scene the sexualized violence towards the male is again seemingly valorized in a pro-feminist context that in reality operates according to the derogatory principle. Simply reversing the roles of these two characters in the violent attack reveals the supposedly pre-emptive 'retaliation' to be aggression that would simply not be acceptable if this were the traditional binary of corporeal female victim and male aggressor.

It is worth looking at this scene in its entirety. Taking one's analysis from the point at which Niida makes a threat to Chigusa, or from where Chigusa is injured, would inevitably lead to a stunted reading. It is important to note the character development within this scene as a whole, particularly the setting up of Chigusa as clearly dominant and Niida as weak, as this provides a context that reveals Niida's 'threat' to be empty and Chigusa's 'self-defence' to be aggression. This scene can only be read as pro-feminist in as much as one subscribes to a notion of this male as dangerous and this female as threatened. It is only this that could lead one to regard Chigusa's violent attack to be justified as some type of pre-emptive reprisal. This is not a reading that the scene as whole supports.

The audience begins this scene well aware of the female character's isolation. This is communicated by a flashback: she is shown training in the woods with the boy she wished were her boyfriend (Hiroki), who states he will always be there to protect her – whereupon the camera pulls back to illustrate that she is utterly alone. She is made bereft and communicates this in an anxious glance that is emphasized by foreboding music. When the male arrives we should be fearful for her and, certainly, taking the subsequent dialogue at face value – given that threats are made to the female – could evoke this, but the behaviour of these characters is in stark contrast.

The male is from the outset emotional, anxious and weak; the female is controlled, cool and hostile. The end result is to rapidly establish the male as vulnerable and the female as dangerous. The dramatic irony in this scene is that the audience is well aware of this long before he is and, most significantly, whilst the traditional rape trope still appears to be playing out.

When Niida arrives he is breathless, shaken, softly spoken and happy to see Chigusa. He is visibly armed, but his weapon (a crossbow) is held as a dead weight and is not aimed. Chigusa is nonplussed by his arrival, does not acknowledge him and immediately moves to leave. Niida continues to try to engage her attention, recalling that they were the topic of school gossip – presumably about a romantic relationship. This certainly attracts Chigusa's attention, but not in the way that Niida would like. She is cold, scornful and disdainful, dismissing that he was the source of the rumour. She turns away and stalks off.

Niida is shown plainly struggling to keep up, scurrying along clumsily and trying to catch her attention. He is wheedling: 'but you liked it. C'mon Chigusa, wait. Stay with me.' He reaches for her and catches her shoulder. Chigusa transforms from merely hostile to openly aggressive. She utters the rhetorical trope of sexual violence: 'Don't touch me', but displays none of the fear normally associated with it. At this point she pushes Niida, who stumbles. She is assertive, fierce and in control. He is a pathetic figure. She does not even stop to see if he collects himself, she just continues on.

This wheedling from Niida and mocking rejection from Chigusa continues. Time and again we see Chigusa as the dominant character and Niida as subordinate. When Niida tries to gain the upper hand by threatening her with his crossbow, Chigusa is not bothered at all by this seemingly open threat of violence. Niida then plaintively declares that he loves her. Once again he is rejected. Finally, Niida retaliates with a jibe about her virginity. This visibly enrages Chigusa who stops dead in her tracks and forcefully throws down her bags, her face contorted with rage. Niida propositions her, pleading 'we're gonna die anyway. Don't you wanna do it once, before you die?' She rejects and demeans him: 'Shouldn't you be worried about your life instead of that useless "pee pee" of yours.'

Now Niida is placed for the first time in the foreground of the shot, and revealed as clearly blocking her way whilst once more he threatens her with his crossbow – an act of superficial aggression that is belied by the fact that he is visibly shaking. At this point Chigusa, despite being unarmed, becomes the aggressor: 'drop that right now and let me go, or I'll assume you're deadly and kick your ass'. The camera cuts to Niida in close up. He is obviously afraid. As Chigusa walks towards him, he backs away. Niida is red, gestures wildly and spits as he speaks. He is aggressive, and clearly out of control. He gestures the crossbow towards her, and is still shaking whilst he issues his threat to rape: 'I've already killed. I could force you to do it now!' The audience knows that he has indeed killed, but we also know that this was only by accident and that this character is frightened and cowardly. His target of course is not privy to this, but his terrified body language in this shot plainly undermines the spoken threat. Indeed, Chigusa is not intimidated at all. She advances on him, is infuriated and defiant, retaliating: 'try it!'.

As she moves into his space, challenging him with her squared body-language, Niida again goes to move away; unfortunately he stumbles and falls. In doing so, he accidentally releases the trigger. At this point all posturing from Niida is over; he is immediately concerned for her welfare – but there is no corresponding change to Chigusa, instead her aggression is amplified. As the camera cuts to her, Chigusa looks up slowly through her trailing hair, a trademark Japanese horror motif that is used to communicate Chigusa as deadly.

To emphasize this, she is suddenly and vehemently angry. Her eyes are wild. As she slowly turns to face the camera, she is shown to have been grazed by the arrow and holds her fingertips to the cut. When she conveys her injury to Niida her voice by contrast is startlingly calm and devoid of emotion. Niida meanwhile is terrified and tries to make excuses – his manner is back to how we first saw him – wheedling, pleading, pitiful and desperate. He can barely hold the crossbow and makes no move to reload or aim it.

Chigusa calmly reaches into her bag and removes a flick knife. It is flicked open, skilfully, in close up, with her face in the background, her eyes focused on Niida. He gasps. He visibly begins to shift around, trying to flee. She makes an improbable challenge to the terrified boy: 'Come at me. Every inch of me will resist you!' He screams in terror and runs away; any threat he could possibly be construed as posing is now over.

The camera pulls back to show Chigusa in pursuit and gaining on him. We are again reminded of the isolation, but this time the vulnerability is plainly not Chigusa's. The music conveys panic and expectation. Chigusa wildly hacks at Niida's back and brings him down. She is determined to overpower him. There is a brief struggle on the floor and they roll – all the while the only sound is Niida screaming. There is seepage of blood shown against his white shirt. Only when he struggles free and tries to escape do we hear Chigusa, who screams what sounds like a battle cry. She overpowers him again, hacks at him in the back and throws him face down. He is prostrate, unarmed and wholly defeated. The viewer can be in no doubt as to his vulnerability.

Whilst Chigusa is screaming in anger, Niida is crying out in pain and fear. As he tries to escape, Chigusa can be seen in full frame trying to slit his throat. When he falls, onto his back with his legs splayed, she kneels over his prone body, faced towards his feet. He tries to push himself up onto his elbows and importantly, he does not reach out to touch her – he is concerned only to try to scramble away. She calmly raises the knife in both hands, over her head, and proceeds to hack at his groin, twice. At this point he instigates physical contact by trying to push her off, still struggling away from her and now clutching at his blood-stained crotch, all the while screaming in agony and fear, and still on his back. Chigusa calmly rights herself, turns and – kneeling beside him – stabs him in the heart. She finally stops her attack and flees herself only when interrupted by another female student who we also know to be deadly.

This scene clearly draws on established rape tropes to seek to establish a threat that can go some way to legitimizing the lethal response. We are supposed to interpret Niida as an ineffectual rapist, with this encounter an attempted rape. Chigusa can then be viewed as 'fighting back' to save herself, with her success in this regard celebrated. Certainly it is the case that in the film Chigusa remains a sympathetic character for the audience – hence we are later treated to her being reunited with her unrequited love, she is accorded closure and forgiveness before she dies, and her death is peaceful in contrast to other largely graphically sadistic demises. It is also the case that this character is a favourite of many authors who have analysed this film (Harper, 2009); and she has a dedicated fan-following online, and certainly garnered new fans when I screened this to my own students – indeed this particular scene was one that elicited laughter from the largely female audience and was later remembered fondly for the enjoyment it elicited.

But this is problematic. Chigusa's violent, sexualized attack on Niida is not proportionate to the threat – if indeed there ever really was one. Seeking to celebrate this as role reversal and empowerment is to overlook that here the male is clearly enfeebled and made to bear markers of behaviour more consistent with female gender stereotyping. The sexualized assault therefore is on the weaker, more vulnerable party. Not only that, but as the assault is seemingly provoked by the victim, the attacker therefore is seen to be justified as engaging in retaliation of sorts. This is enormously problematic as it clearly draws on aspects of the ideal victim construct in making Niida responsible for his own fate and exonerating Chigusa. But we should remember in doing so that

Niida has been made feminine whilst Chigusa has been stripped of her femininity – consequently this is not the role reversal it is commonly lauded to be, as we still have a feminized character bearing the sexualized assault and made culpable for it.

In the final horror film for analysis, *Audition* (1999), the audience is well aware that the female protagonist Asami is a sexually aggressive psychopath, so the victim precipitation facet of the ideal victim construct, or more specifically what I call 'redemption by provocation' that has been played out in respect of the female aggressors (in some form or another) in *Ginger Snaps* and *Battle Royale*, should not be relevant here. Yet bizarrely it is.

The plot centres around a widower, Aoyama, who decides he wants to get remarried after seven years alone raising his now teenaged son. He confides to a colleague and friend about his reservations and the difficulty he anticipates in trying to find a wife, at which point the friend – a film producer – suggests that he set up an audition that will have the purpose of finding both his film and Aoyama a 'leading lady'. Whilst the film funding never materializes, the auditions still go ahead. At one level this is intended to reveal the 'casting couch' at work in the service of immoral men, but in actuality, Aoyama never fully satisfies this conceit – though his friend most definitely does. Instead, Aoyama's intentions are honourable and not only does he treat Asami well, but he also falls in love with her. Asami meanwhile is revealed to be a sadistic psychopath who makes a sport of killing the men with whom she becomes either physically or emotionally intimate.

Various authors demonstrate a subscription to the victim precipitation model in their analyses of this film. How else can Asami be regarded as an 'avenging angel' (Balmain, 2008, p. 98), a 'female avenger' (McRoy, 2005, p. 58), meting out 'punishment' (Choi, 2008, p. 8). These authors predicate their analysis on an implicit acceptance of rape/revenge – for example, Balmain locates a discussion of Asami within a chapter entitled 'The Rape-Revenge Film: From Violation to Vengeance' – and frame their analysis as pro-feminist. However, to do so requires a very selective analysis. As Bowyer (2004) notes, the director Miike Takashi plainly denies any feminist intention, and indeed one may argue that elements within the film concerning Asami's characterization and behaviour should steadfastly detract from such a reading. What underlies such interpretations is a privileging of Asami's revealed childhood abuse that posits the violence against Aoyama as a substitute for, or extension of, retribution against these men. But to do this necessitates that the audience see one man as all men. This is not sustainable, not least because Miike Takashi goes to some lengths to sympathetically depict Aoyama as romantic, sensitive and sentimental, with Aoyama's intentions towards Asami as noble. Consequently, I would argue that he cannot be construed as deserving his fate through this model, though it is certainly significant that this reading persists.

However, whilst the rape/revenge model does not bear here, victim precipitation of sorts can still be seen. Miike Takashi depicts Aoyama in a positive fashion, to Western eyes, but to a Japanese audience many traits he displays are profoundly feminine and as a consequence whilst Western audiences might perceive him as a 'good' man, he is not a good 'man'. His masculinity is impinged upon and it is this that can be argued to conform to a notion of victim precipitation, as the viewer is led to understand Aoyama as weak and vulnerable. To my mind this element of victim precipitation is of far more significance than any notion of 'retribution'.

Aoyama is a widower and single parent who is still very much in mourning, despite seven years passing since the death of his wife. There are extended scenes that illustrate him as having primary responsibility for parental and domestic duties – such as counselling his son, helping with his homework, cooking and doing the washing up. Aoyama is clearly the carer. When he agrees to 'audition' in an effort to find a suitable candidate to be his wife, it is significant that Aoyama does not take the lead or the initiative. It must also be noted that this search is for a wife and not a conquest, that the deceit involved in setting up the audition is at the behest of his friend and is mitigated by the reassurance that the TV project will go ahead, so it is not fake per se, but merely dishonest. The overall aim – for Aoyama to find a wife – is with the express encouragement of his son. Aoyama does not take the lead in any aspect; his primary motivation is simply to please others. His sense of conflict at betraying his dead wife results in palpable reluctance and guilt. Only when he sees Asami's picture on her CV does Aoyama fully commit to the process: for him, it is love at first sight.

The attack from Asami is very much a symbolic rape – not simple retribution. Her assault takes the form of sexualized sadomasochistic torture, and should the viewer be in any doubt – despite insertion of needles that presumably symbolizes penetration, accompanied by Asami softly crooning 'deeper, deeper' – we can also note that during the removal of Aoyama's foot, the aggression is clearly and explicitly encoded as sexual, as we are provided with a cut scene showing one of Asami's childhood abusers masturbating whilst she is simultaneously shown to openly relish the pain of her victim's dismemberment.

Asami sees all men as one – 'You're all the same. Every single one of you' – but the audience should not. Aoyama is vulnerable precisely because he does not conform to the patriarchal ideal of hypermasculinity. It is his feminine traits that render him vulnerable to Asami, not any machismo. Thus we are presented with a male character who is introverted, nervous and reserved. As his feelings grow he becomes reckless – ignoring his friend's caution and the evidence he himself has amassed that indicates Asami is not to be trusted. He is ruled by his heart and not his head, or his libido. These feminine traits are reinforced in specific scenes: when he and Asami first sleep together it is she who takes the lead, undressing, lying down and instructing him to 'come here', whilst he clearly requires persuasion; when Asami abandons him in the middle of the night, he is distraught and becomes increasingly emotional because of their separation; when confronted by his friend he is defensive and protective of his romantic notion of Asami. Indeed, even during the attack, Aoyama escapes in his unconscious mind to revisit romantic dreams and treasured memories of his brief time with this woman, seemingly turning her from assailant to partner. At the finale, when both lie incapacitated on the floor – Asami with her neck broken, Aoyama with his body paralyzed and foot dismembered – he clearly sustains eye contact with her and 'hears' her previous dialogue from their dates. He is still wistfully reminiscing.

It is such feminized traits that render the assault on this male character possible and that invalidates the pro-feminist rationale. Aoyama is as vulnerable, naive and trusting, as presumably Asami was in the past. At the point at which he is attacked and tortured he is made feminine. An attack on Aoyama cannot represent an attack on predatory, sexist or immoral men and, consequently, when Asami attacks him ostensibly for the purpose of retribution, she transgresses the limits of the rape/vengeance scenario and instead becomes the 'rapist'.

Thus we have two myths of note here: the feminized Aoyama who does not abide by a precautionary principle and thus is seen to render himself vulnerable to attack, whilst Asami's motivation for rape seems to be explained through reference to her childhood trauma and is therefore psychopathological. Both are dangerous tropes to fall back on when explicating sexual violence. The first implies that 'weakness' invites rape and thus responsibilizes the victim, whilst the latter posits that rapists are abnormal and different, not responsible for their actions. These directly undermine core contributions from feminist theory that compel us to regard rape as indiscriminate and normalized.

It is particularly important to note that Aoyama's friend, who conceived of and orchestrated the audition that discovered Asami, routinely abuses his position as a casting director to exploit women. He is depicted as clearly misogynistic, encouraging the women to talk about their sexual histories and to audition nude – yet no 'vengeance' is visited on him. Perhaps we are to understand that it is precisely his sexism and machismo that protects him; if so, this is a troubling message.

In contrast to many existing analyses, I argue that the examples discussed above do not challenge rape myths – they revalidate them. The notion that real men cannot be raped whilst feminized men can; that victim behaviour precipitates sexual aggression; that rape is sex; that rapists are compelled and not responsible for their actions – all of these myths are alive and kicking, revealing supposedly pro-feminist depictions as surprisingly orthodox at their core, and the superficially subversive as insidiously normative.

Comedy

I found many more examples of comedic depictions of male sexual victimization than horror examples, which should be a concern in itself given the function of this genre. Key examples to be discussed in depth here include episodes from the television series *Supernatural* (2007b) and *My Name Is Earl* (2007 and 2008), the films *Me, Myself and Irene* (2000), and *Bruce Almighty* (2003). First I will look at the episode 'Tall Tales' from *Supernatural*. It must be noted that this series is not usually comedic in the main, but this particular episode is a departure from the usual style of the series and is mostly concerned with comedy – particularly in its presentation of the material of interest to this project, hence its inclusion here.

Overall, this episode minimizes the impact and significance of rape in that it renders it comic fodder. The narrative pivots on notions of rape as a deserved act of retribution. This draws on and reinforces notions of victim precipitation, 'asking for it', responsibilizing the victim in this scenario. We should also note and be troubled by the comparison throughout, with tropes established regarding 'date rape' scenarios – blacking out, confusion, shame, etc. The most striking thing for me when analysing this film was how much of the comedy throughout the episode pivoted on this single incident. It was referenced numerous times despite being only one of three varied scenarios throughout the hour-long show. Also, most disturbing for me, was just how central the victim's very clear trauma was to the comedy. Watching this with the sound off, and then in freeze-frame, the trauma and anxiety of this character is clear.

The relevant segment begins with a very frightened young male being supposedly abducted by aliens; he is 'beamed up' in a manner reminiscent of science fiction shows such as the *X-Files*. The scene is shot to communicate isolation – it is dark and quiet, the campus is obviously deserted. The victim is heard screaming in terror. Later we see this young male, who is introduced as Curtis, in a bar, lining up a row of alcoholic drinks – shots, possibly whisky – and knocking them back in quick succession. The camera is tight on him, framing his upper torso with his shoulders clearly hunched over the bar; he is cradling a drink. He looks dishevelled and pensive. The entire scene, whenever the camera is on Curtis, is conducted with him in close-up, or with him clearly visible in the foreground. The viewer is left in no doubt that Curtis is traumatized. He is brooding, his body language is closed off and protective and at first he is uncommunicative. Because *Supernatural* is usually a 'straight' series, the tone that is established is very serious.

Curtis is asked to relay what happened, to which he replies that nobody would believe him. He is persuaded to trust his questioners, Sam and Dean – the two lead characters in the show – and he haltingly begins to tell his story: 'I, uh. I blacked out. I lost time. And when I woke up, I didn't know where I was.' At this point the viewer is party to a flashback – presented with a close-up of Curtis, unnaturally close – deliberately invading any sense of personal space. This is a technique common in films about rape and sexual violence as it communicates violation. Curtis is shot as if he is on his back. When the camera pans slightly it is to show an 'alien' figure encroaching on the scene, leaning over and towards the prone figure of Curtis. His confusion, fear and vulnerability are clearly communicated. Sam asks him to elaborate. Curtis concedes, but he is visibly emotional, stumbling over words and speaking through clenched jaw to state: 'They did ... "tests" on me.' His voice audibly choked with emotion. At this point there is another flashback, re-emphasizing the previous prone and powerless Curtis. The camera returns to Curtis in the present as he tries to continue: 'And, erm ...' He knocks back another shot of alcohol, looks very uneasy and is obviously reluctant to go on. His reply is painfully drawn out. He coughs, 'They, erm ... they "probed" me', at which point the camera turns to Sam for a reaction shot. So far the scene has been emotionally linked to Curtis, but at this point Sam sets the tone – in stark contrast to the emotion of Curtis, Sam is visibly trying not to laugh. This is the point at which the viewer is repositioned. The empathy that had arisen when tied to

Curtis's painful and emotional story is now dissipated and replaced with a mocking tone.

Whilst this is significant in itself, given that it potentially condones rape-scepticism in general, as this scene progresses it becomes even more significant – not least because the straight delivery by Curtis does not change. The configuring of the 'probing' as rape is completed when Dean asserts 'Some alien made you his bitch!' The audience is made complicit with finding Curtis's assault, and his evident pain, funny. At the risk of pointing out the obvious, this would not be appropriate had Curtis been cast as female – it is solely his status as a male victim that enables this. It is even more pertinent that the scene clearly draws on the 'confessional' scenes in rape films, with Curtis relaying his attack in a style reminiscent of the post-rape 'interview' or exposition in mainstream drama, complete with visible shame and barely contained emotion.

In this episode, not only is rape mocked and trivialized, but also the particularly pernicious rape myth of victim precipitation is given credence. Curtis's selection as a victim is explained in line with 'just world' theory – in essence, that he deserved it. The focus in explaining the rape is entirely on Curtis, who is solely responsibilized. This is explicitly articulated by Curtis's friend who states 'Whatever happened to Curtis, he had it coming', and by Dean who states that he knows the connection between the victims – that they are all 'dicks', with the implication therefore that they, including Curtis, were 'asking' for it. An authority figure in the show, a character called Bobby, explains that the modus operandi of the perpetrator in this case is to 'target the high and mighty. Knock 'em down a peg. Usually with a sense of humour.' For the purpose of this episode, the rape of a male is rationalized as clearly instigated, 'deserved', and trivialized as 'humorous'.

In the TV series *My Name Is Earl*, there are two episodes of note: 'Bad Earl' (2008) and 'Early Release' (2007). In the first, the episode revolves around Earl' trying to adjust to life outside prison. He meets an escaped ex-con and friend, Ralph, who in flashback reveals how he managed to evade capture. Ralph is seen running down a largely empty highway in only his underwear, socks and shoes. He is then seen trying to hitch a lift and is eventually offered one from a male resident of the county, who the audience knows from previous episodes is a middle-aged gay man struggling with his homosexuality. This eventuality is accompanied by the narration from Earl that Ralph 'was so desperate to get away from that prison, he got in the first car that would pick up a man with no pants' – despite the intended humour, this is a line that simultaneously conveys Ralph as at risk and the driver as a risk.

The sexual assault in this episode is not made explicit; it is only ever implied. The driver is shown to be clearly and inappropriately excited by Ralph's appearance. This man then offers to take off his shirt too and begins to unbutton it, at which point he quickly drives off. The next scene is Ralph demanding that the rapidly speeding and erratically driven car be brought to a stop. After he exits the vehicle, a visibly shaken Ralph proclaims, 'You're lucky I can't drive stick or I'd kick your ass and take your car, pervert.' As the car drives away, Ralph shouts after it, 'And if you ever tell anybody what we did I'll kill you.' He then walks towards the camera for a close-up framing of his now grief-stricken face. The viewer is invited to assume that a sexual act has occurred between the two men, whilst Ralph's emotional reaction leads us to assume this was without his consent. The comedic tone deliberately robs the victim of any audience sympathy, and instead invites ridicule for what the narrator has implied are the inevitable consequences of Ralph's reckless behaviour – a swift and succinct exercise in victim blaming.

This incident is revisited again later in that episode, and its nature is clarified somewhat. During an intervention to persuade Earl to reform his character, Ralph's assailant declares that without Earl's assistance 'I never would have experienced the love of another man.' Ralph, in the background of this scene and clearly in shot, interrupts his assailant's speech by aggressively shouting 'next' whilst the man looks dismayed and hurt. This clarifies the incident as sexual in nature, but simultaneously seeks to negate Ralph's previous trauma. At this point the incident is seemingly reinterpreted as consensual and the assailant is depicted as akin to a jilted lover.

This episode conflates rape with sex and in doing so rationalizes rape as driven by sexual desire and according with sexual orientation. We are also given to understand that Ralph invited this attention by being 'provocatively' dressed and that he therefore put himself 'at risk'. Moreover in the close of that last scene, the viewer is positioned to empathize with the assailant, because he is depicted as the more sympathetic and vulnerable character.

In the second relevant episode from *My Name Is Earl*, 'Early Release', we see Earl trying, unsuccessfully, to escape from prison. There are several instances of sexual assault and violence towards men used as comedic devices in this episode. The implied off-screen anal gang rape of Earl's friend Frank is the first – this is implied to be a consequence of his attempt to escape from prison whilst disguised as an overly attractive female nurse. This character is shown sashaying down a corridor and attracting lecherous attention from other inmates who are fooled by his disguise. In defiance of the precautionary principle, Frank is openly enjoying this. When Frank is attacked, there is no dialogue – but there again it simply is not necessary. The camera positioning accords with the rape trope by having a claustrophobic focus on the victim's face. Thus there is a close-up of Frank, his fear and pain are clearly emoted, and he is heard crying out in anguish. Multiple men's hands then invade the foreground of the shot to pin him down, with a rhythmic movement thereafter to indicate penetrative sex. Frank is regarded as inviting this attention by being effeminate, attractive and provocative, and thus is responsibilized for his fate. The humour is derived from the fact that the audience sees this as an inevitability given his choice of disguise, whereas Frank is oblivious to the 'risk' he is taking.

The next film worthy of close examination is *Me, Myself and Irene* (2000). The basic plot of this film centres around Charlie who is presented as mild-mannered, kindly and meek, a low-ranking, largely ineffectual police officer, and a cuckolded single parent raising children who are not genetically his own. Charlie is well liked, but he is pitied – he has little respect from co-workers or neighbours and he is depicted as repeatedly being taken advantage of and demeaned.

The comedy stems from Charlie's mental health problem – he has a multiple personality disorder, wherein lies his polar-opposite personality, Hank. It is Charlie's struggle and failure to contain Hank that contrives the situations from which humour is derived. The audience is intended to see Hank as the 'repressed' elements of Charlie's personality, and it is certainly the case that Hank's exploits are largely 'wish-fulfilment' and retribution of which Charlie is not consciously capable.

When Charlie is given responsibility for escorting a female prisoner, Irene, back to New York, he quickly develops a romantic interest in her that he is not capable of pursuing. As with other 'problems' in his life, it is his alter ego Hank who emerges to resolve this. About two-thirds of the way through the film, Charlie confronts Irene about sleeping with Hank. The joke here being that Hank successfully masqueraded as Charlie to achieve this conquest, something that Charlie who is genuinely in love with Irene would not be able to do. This scene has connotations of 'date rape' as Charlie has been overpowered by his alter ego and thus has been unwilling or unable to give consent to the various sexual acts that his body has received, whilst Irene was able to consent, but is mislead into having sex with Hank, whom she despises, whilst actually being in love with Charlie. The comedy however is focused not on the deception Irene has suffered, but on Charlie and the horror he experiences in having to face up to what happened to his body.

On discovering that Hank hijacked his body to seduce Irene, Charlie is clearly indignant and hurt. He sits down hard on the bed and visibly fidgets in discomfort, and in seeking the source of this he finds and removes a sex toy from under the blankets: a large comedy rubber dildo. He holds this in plain view and moves it around to mock Irene whilst stating: 'Well look who joined the party! [talking to the dildo in full frame] did you have fun? [Jiggling the toy, he replies in a mocking cartoon voice] Ooh, yes I did, yes I did. [Turns to Irene, dildo in foreground, larger than life.] So I guess old Hank-y-panky wasn't enough for you?' To which Irene states, reluctantly and clearly ashamed, 'it wasn't for me'.

Charlie is evidently repulsed by the implication and throws the offending object away, into the far corner of the room and off-camera. He physically crumples to sit with his head in his hands, shoulders visibly convulsing, audibly weeping and moaning in revulsion. In the next scene the date rape reference is made plain when Charlie is presented in a parody of the post-rape shower scene trope – he is sitting, trousers around his ankles, underwear visible, whilst balancing precariously on the sink, desperately trying to rinse his anus.

Later in the film, Charlie and Irene are discussing the incident. In case the viewer is in any doubt that it is Charlie who bore the sexual acts and who regards them as assault, he accosts Irene with a vehement: 'I turn my back for one minute and you stick it up my ass, literally', to which Irene shouts in response: 'You stuck it in your own ass!' This could be construed as ameliorating the assault by recasting it as self-harm, but it must be remembered that Charlie was not in control of his own body – this was an act performed on him, done to him against his wishes and without his consent. Unsurprisingly, his repugnance and trauma are not erased at this revelation. This segment resolves with a kissing scene between Charlie and Irene, during which he laughingly complains about his 'sore' rear. Consequently, the trajectory here appears to be a parody of the rape/rescue/romance trope.

Charlie can be said to bear markers of more feminine traits, whilst Hank is an archetypal macho chauvinist. Like the example from *Supernatural*, this film includes and mocks many orthodox rape tropes. Unlike *Supernatural*, but in accordance with the examples from the horror genre, this film also appears to be pro-hypermasculinity – it is significant that the sexualized aggression and degradation in general only happens to Charlie and not to his macho alter ego Hank. Other characters who experience sexual assault and degradation, in particular, are also presented as 'weak' in some way. This message is clarified in that redemption for Charlie is in embracing his more masculine traits and thus effectively subsuming Hank into a single personality. Masculinity therefore affords invulnerability. Where vulnerability is incurred it is because of failure to conform to masculine ideals – thus supporting the myth that real men cannot be raped, and that victim behaviour precipitates or at least facilitates assault.

In the film *Bruce Almighty* (2003) there is a clear example of supposed victim precipitation through the use and sanction of retributive 'rape'. The central character Bruce has been imbued with God-like powers and throughout the film uses these for wish-fulfilment, including supposedly just retribution. The key example I discuss is where Bruce as 'God' confronts a gang that had previously beaten him up. He sets about achieving vengeance, in this instance, through sexual assault and degradation of the lead gang member.

This scene begins with Bruce skipping past the entrance to an alley – he is deliriously happy and drunk with power. To emphasize this, the music in the background is an upbeat pop song by Snap entitled 'I've Got the Power'. Bruce stops skipping when he recognizes the gang; he is obviously pleased to have spotted them and says his catchphrase to emphasize this. At which point he inflates his chest and adopts a macho stance, advancing brazenly towards the gang.

The gang members remember Bruce as the victim of their attack. They proceed to laugh uproariously at him and to openly mock him. Bruce in a roundabout fashion demands an apology from them – the audience knows this is unlikely, and because of Bruce's previous behaviour we anticipate a punitive consequence, though we do not know what. The lead gang member retorts with an unlikely scenario, stating that he'll apologize 'the day a monkey comes out of my butt'. This suffices as provocation, and Bruce gleefully informs him 'That's today.' The film then cuts to the gang leader in full frame and bearing a shocked expression. He looks visibly in pain, is shaking and sweating. He audibly moans. The sound effects at this point include gurgling and wet noises. There is a close-up of his rear – full screen. Something is seen to emerge (presumably from his anus), and it moves under his trousers. The camera returns to his face, to show he is still in shock and pain. The punch line is delivered when we return to his rear to see a monkey jump free of his trousers. In case the audience is in any doubt as to what has just happened, another gang member queries, 'Did that monkey just come out of your crack man?' At which point the gang leader collapses and all the other gang members flee the scene.

In a clear inversion of Bruce's own vulnerability and physical assault earlier in the film, the gang leader is now alone in the alley with his assailant – prostrate and vulnerable – defeated. He is utterly vulnerable in comparison with the now all-powerful Bruce. As this man is seen slowly and carefully picking himself up off the ground, clutching at his rear and groaning, Bruce initiates another assault by addressing what he terms the 'anal dwelling' creature, to tell it that 'It's time to go home.' The monkey cries out and pelts towards the leader who runs screaming to the end of the alley, desperately trying to get away. He screams the rhetorical rape trope 'No, NO!' and is shown wildly trying to scale a wire fence in a desperate but utterly hopeless bid to escape. The monkey gains on him. The visual rape trope of a claustrophobic close-up of the leader's face is accompanied by an auditory 'pop'. He screams at first, then is very still and quiet, shown to be in shock, wide eyed and open mouthed. He collapses again, falling off the fence to lie still on the concrete ground. The assault is complete.

The comedy in this is supposed to derive from the inversion of the roles between the gang members who are made vulnerable whilst Bruce – who the audience identifies with as 'everyman' – is made omnipotent. The violence is intended to be seen as righteous and deserved – some type of 'divine' justice for the degradation Bruce felt in being beaten up by the gang members earlier in the film. This is Bruce taking his manhood back, and the audience should root for him. Unfortunately though, the victim precipitation element of the ideal victim construct can be noted here in the form of provocation, albeit most certainly not sexual, as can the notion that rape is made possible by weakness, or at least by being weaker. Neither of these are cause for celebration.

Other examples from comedy I noted that use the same repertoire of myths in explicating male rape and sexual assault include those that draw on 'weakness' as the rationale – films such as the Chinese family comedy *Dummy Mommy Without a Baby* (2001), the Korean *The Spirit of Jeet Kune Do: Once Upon a Time in High School* (2004), and TV series such as *Supernatural* 'Folsom Prison Blues' (2007a), those that draw on notions of 'provocation', be it sexual or retributive include films such as the American family comedy *The Hot Chick* (2002), *Scary Movie 1* (2000), *Scary Movie 2* (2001), *Scary Movie 4* (2006) and prime-time TV series such as *The Kevin Bishop Show* (2009), *Two Pints of Lager and a Packet of Crisps* (2005), *Commercial Breakdown with Jimmy Carr* (2008), *Never Mind the Buzzcocks* (2005), *Mock the Week* (2007, 2009) and *Supernatural* 'Pilot' (2005). Certainly from my sample, these myths, or subscription to the same, appear pervasive.

The central myths that can be seen as operating in the above examples all draw from and reinforce notions of victim precipitation. Principally these can be distilled as: 'weakness' invites rape and rape is provoked (as either sexual desire or retribution). These myths are underscored by, and in themselves support, problematic conflations in our 'understanding' of sexual assault – namely the following conflations: rape/sex/ sexuality that convey the implicit message that rape is in some way deserved and that 'real' men cannot be raped. We should also note that in rationalizing the motivation of the rapist the enduring message is that they lack self-control – be this understood as regarding sexual desire, mental illness or violence. These tendencies necessarily implicate the victim as their behaviour is understood to in some way 'unleash' the assault – thus drawing on the precautionary principle that operates in respect of female rape to render the victim culpable.

Music

Homophobic themes are common in certain music genres; their salience in certain types of rap, for example, are well documented. This is not my interest. I am more concerned to identify themes relating to same-sex sexual aggression, particularly where such rhetorical acts might be interpreted as threats to perform acts otherwise construed as serious sexual assault or rape. Whilst these can and do intersect with homophobic discourse, this is not my prime interest. I am solely concerned to identify rhetorical threats of sexual aggression, by men to men, or rhetorical claims to experiencing the same. More generalized threats that use sexual references, for example, 'fuck you' or 'fuck you up', are not included, nor are passages that might be interpreted as implying male rape, but are ambiguous. I have focused solely on the explicit and overt here.

In the genre nu-metal, lyrics pertaining to same-sex sexual degradation and aggression can be discerned. For example, in my examination of Korn's back catalogue, out of eight albums released between their launch and the time of writing, six albums in total contain songs with such lyrics. Twelve tracks – to be discussed below – include lyrics that either explicitly relate to rape or to sexualized violence between men or towards men. Suffice to say that examples of victim precipitation such as rape/revenge, rape/sex are particularly notable here.

Korn is an American band with worldwide distribution and chart success. Since their debut in 1994 they have held successive top-ten positions in singles and album charts around the world, earned platinum, multi-platinum and gold discs for individual albums, achieved numerous awards, made frequent appearances on prime-time music television shows in various countries, featured on soundtracks for high-grossing

Hollywood films, such as *I Know What You Did Last Summer* (1997) and *Tomb Raider: the Cradle of Life* (2003), whilst their back catalogue of music videos is frequently looped on popular music channels such as Scuzz and Kerrang. At the very least, we can see that their material is popular and high profile, with wide dissemination and longevity.

Korn's track 'All in the Family' (1998) parodies an MC duel with 'rival' lead singers from Korn (Jon Davis) and Limp Bizkit (Fred Durst) hurling progressively more distasteful insults and sexually explicit threats at one another – clearly using male sexual victimization as an extension of aggression. Throughout the track, lyrics that are intended to communicate the weakness of those to whom the threats are made can also be noted and include terms of endearment used in a sarcastic fashion to belittle and demean when placed in context (such as 'You pumpkin pie/I'll jack-off in your eye'), and reference to physical development or lack thereof intended to infantilize (such as 'nappy hairy chest'), as well as those intended to feminize ('Raggedy-Anne'). There are also references to supposed previous sexual assaults – the implication being therefore that they are pre-established as violable, or perhaps innately so, thus drawing on the notion that weakness is precipitative. The final line of this song communicates sexual violence as conquest in an effort to establish a victor – it is noteworthy that these are conflated.

The track 'Ball Tongue' (1994) is about exploitation and betrayal. In this song, lyrics around incapacitation, powerlessness and sexual degradation intertwine to produce a notion of defeat and conquest that draws from an understanding of sexual aggression as invited by weakness. The sentiment of this track is revisited in many others, but is expressly coupled with reference to rape in 'Freak on a Leash' (1998) and 'Wish You Could be Me' (1999).

The track 'Faget' (1994) draws on the rape/revenge arc. It is easy to be distracted by the supposed homophobic[43] themes in this song, but it must be noted that Korn frequently use such terms in self-reference, almost akin to self-flagellation, rather than as terms by which to derogate others – due in no small part to the bullying the lead singer and lyricist Jon Davis has reputedly experienced himself (Walters, 1999). In this track the lyrics describe a subject who over the course of the song is transformed from being a powerless victim of an implied rape to an aggressor. Speaking in the first person, the lyricist initially uses self-deprecating and feminizing terms such as 'pretty boy' to communicate shame and self-loathing. He describes feeling disempowered and violated by a more powerful male assailant, with rape intimated through reference to this man having a firearm and 'having' the singer's body – presumably the mention of a gun here is intended to function as both a literal weapon and a metaphorical penis. When the lyrics shift to convey the victim's transformation to aggressor (such as, 'Y'all can suck my dick/and fucking like it'), it is posited as positive – intended to communicate his empowerment and salvation; this role-reversal culminates in his dismissal of his tormentors as 'queers' at the close of the track. He has gone from being threatened to making threats, from demeaning himself to demeaning others. This is to be seen as righteous and redemptive. This song draws initially on a notion of vulnerability as making rape possible, and thereafter follows a rape/revenge arc. This narrative or rape script is echoed in 'Reclaim my Place' (1998), 'Bottled Up' (2002) and 'Thoughtless' (2002) which will be discussed in detail below.

Reference to (innate) vulnerability as predisposing one to sexual victimization is revisited in the track 'Daddy' (1994), which is about child sexual abuse. The lyrics also draw on rape/sex in setting up the victim as desirable, and are written in the first instance from the point of view of the assailant; the intended victim is described as 'pretty' and 'sweet', with the desire to rape made explicit in specific use of that term, rather than implied. The rape scenario is clarified as moving from intent to actuality in the chorus, when the point of view shifts to being that of the victim recalling the rape. At this point the lyricist communicates shame, pain and betrayal. There is no resolution or redemption provided in this song, only the story of the assault. The track closes with the vocalist audibly in tears. The notion of desire as driving rape, and thus of desirability as precipitating it, draws from established myths. Thus the weakness of the victim enables the assault, which is itself supposedly instigated by the attractiveness of the victim. Although clearly about child abuse this still reverberates in line with the ideal victim construct to configure rape as precipitated, and configures this as female in accordance with the emphasis on the powerless child – as Clover (1987, p. 211) states, 'the helpless child is gendered feminine'.

The track 'No Place to Hide' (1996) can be argued to draw on the rape/romance arc. The lyricist intimates a violation that he describes as akin to rape, and communicates that the victim of this cannot escape or evade his assailant, but – crucially – has that victim state that they enjoy this. This draws on the notion that rape can become pleasurable, that therefore rape is invited and welcomed as sex, a theme and sentiment revisited in the track 'Break Some Off' (2003).

The track 'Thoughtless' (2002) includes both implied and explicit reference to male rape that takes the form of a revenge fantasy. The lyrics are emphasized in the accompanying music video, directed by the Hughes Brothers, and both are relevant. The video is set in a high school and, in line with the lyrics, quickly establishes its topic as bullying. The narrative arc of each is around empowerment, with revenge and redemption clearly using male rape as a contingent of hegemonic masculinity. This will be examined in depth.

The visuals follow the routine victimization of a young male by his peers. The video opens on an external shot of a high school. The start of the day is signified by the bell sounding and by the hurry of a mass of students to get inside. In contrast with the album track, female laughter is audible. As the camera closes in on the school entrance, a sign on the wall is visible in the foreground of the screen, declaring ominously that a safe school is 'everyone's responsibility' and impotently urging students to 'report any weapons on campus'.

The protagonist is first presented through close-ups of his feet and lower torso; he is abstracted and objectified. As the camera pulls back, he is shown walking through the school corridor; he is alone, pensive and holds his head down. The pace seems unnaturally slow and is almost dream-like. At this point the subject breaks the 'fourth wall', acknowledging the audience by raising his eyes to look directly into the camera, staring, unblinking directly at the viewer. There can be no question as to with whom the audience should identify. The viewer is then repositioned to see what he sees – that he (and by extension the viewer) is the subject of unwanted attention. This is first by a group of males – 'jocks' – who exude hostility, and then by a group of young women who stand clustered together and appear to be mocking him. Both the music and visuals are foreboding. This changes only when he is suddenly and inexplicably jumped by the group of males who drag him forcibly into the lockers, which run either side of the corridor, and proceed to beat him viciously. In contrast to what has gone before this is suddenly in real time with each swing fast and each impact jolting. They leave him sitting on the floor, a pathetic figure alone and hurt. As if to emphasize this, the banner declaring 'senior prom' peels away from the wall immediately above his head – his rejection, humiliation and defeat is absolute.

When the song begins, the lyricist communicates in the first person, maintaining the audience's identification with the victim: he describes himself revisiting daydreams and simultaneously striving to divest himself of any compassion. The latter is significant, as this can be understood as a feminine trait and therefore underscores his weakness. That he is wrestling with this particular aspect of his character is revisited later in the track and the video.

The visuals show the youth drawing in a journal – from context it can be deduced that he is plotting revenge scenarios concerning his attackers. The writing visible includes titles from other Korn songs, whilst the images sketched are dark and tormented. The viewer is reminded again of his vulnerability and isolation when in a hectic and boisterous classroom he is the only one sitting alone and engrossed. To emphasize this, the lighting is suddenly modified to pick out only him in the middle of a blanket of darkness. In the security of his journal, our victim's imagination is emboldened – the lyric communicates bravado and vengeance, and explicitly articulates retaliation as reciprocation: 'take a swing at me/.../gonna put you on the ground'. At this point in the video the youth's body starts to blister; this is the physical beginning of a transformation that will enable him to visit retribution on his bullies and redemption for himself. The form this revenge might take is intimated as rape by the lyricist, who describes a desire to see his enemy weeping whilst revenge is exacted on his 'dirty ass'.

This is clarified a short time later when the youth is shown being attacked in the school pool by the jocks. Whilst he is held under, punched and kicked, the visuals cut to show Korn – visually indicated to be playing inside the young man's brain – and the lead singer once again describes a desire to retaliate in kind, but the form that will take is now explicitly articulated by the lyricist as rape and justified as vengeance: 'I wanna kill and rape you/the way you raped me'. When the video cuts back to the pool it is to show the youth floating face down with visible contusions to his face and chest; the accompanying lyric declares a statement of bold intent, 'it's on', a colloquialism that indicates acceptance of a challenge or intention to compete. This then is the pivotal moment, his breaking point, where the youth's physical transformation and his attitude will empower him to take revenge in the real world. It is surely no accident that the lyric includes oblique reference to a gun – a weapon understood as a phallic symbol.

The next scene has the youth alone in the locker room, crying; but it is not through despair, it is anger, and the blisters on his back further communicate this as the lead singer's face is shown pushing up through the boy's skin whilst repeating a line that indicates that our victim will no longer be victimized. His full transformation from victim to aggressor is communicated when he later throws a TV out of his bedroom window – an overt display of anger and force that newly configures him as demonstrably masculine.

The climax of this music video is the youth's triumphant entrance to the school prom. He throws the door open and stands at the top of the stairs demanding the attention of his peers on the dance floor below. Accompanied by a beautiful female escort, he is presented in dramatic contrast to how the viewer first saw him – now he is confident and commanding with an image designed to match this new machismo: he is dressed as a 'pimp', an image that simultaneously communicates heterosexuality and male chauvinism. He throws his hat into the crowd and leers down at them; he rips his shirt open to reveal his bare chest and the band members of Korn are revealed, pulsating under his skin. He then projectile vomits over all of his tormentors who are shown at length being soaked by this putrescence, whilst his beautiful companion points at them and laughs uproariously. The inversion of roles is complete, his revenge enacted. The final lyric reinforces the notion of aggressor as empowered: he will leave them 'screaming' – it is a celebratory promise of merciless retribution.

The overriding message in both the song and the video is that victimization (which in the lyrics expressly includes rape, although in the video is limited to physical aggression) can be explained by weakness, and that retribution for past victimization (which in the lyrics again includes rape and is communicated in the video as degradation) is just – thus subscribing to notions of rape/revenge and victim precipitation, as well as communicating that machismo is empowerment and invulnerability. The narrative arc and myths here share commonalities with the film *Me, Myself and Irene*, not least in the fact that redemption and salvation for both lead characters lies in their embracing hypermasculinity – thus reinforcing the notion that 'real' men cannot be raped.

All of the above examples pivot on logics around victim precipitation and thus victim blame. In Korn's back catalogue we can see subscription to rape/revenge, rape/sex and rape/weakness. To make the male rape-able, he is made violable by being constructed as weak, demeaned and feminized. This includes examples where attractiveness explains rape, where revenge justifies rape and where romance reconfigures rape as sex. Significantly, where redemption is contained in the narratives it is achieved in all instances through reference to hypermasculinity, and in some instances through transformation from victim of rape to rapist. In this sense it shares some markers with the pro-feminist vengeance scenarios and I would argue that in doing so it casts a far harsher light. This trend – for rape/revenge to be understood as redemptive – should be a concern. Valorizing rape in any context is exceptionally dangerous.

4.4 Conclusion

The media is a key site for the co-constitution and dissemination of 'truths' around victimhood. For male victims of sexual violence this truth pivots on difference – both in terms of rape of the male being conceptualized as differing from the normative female and as bearing what Sivakumaran (2005) termed the 'taint' of homosexuality. The particularization of the construct of male rape is overwhelmingly concerned to explicate and rationalize what is otherwise assumed to be the inviolability and invulnerability of the male. Hence it simultaneously marks those so affected as aberrations from the masculine norm, and – in drawing on the precipitative element of the ideal victim construct – it marks them as intrinsically culpable. Thus, paradoxically, it is the case that to be recognized as a male victim of rape is to be simultaneously designated as undeserving of victim status.

Thus in both information and entertainment media, male victims of rape and sexual assault are not considered to be real victims. The former largely overlooks them, whilst the entertainment media responsibilizes, trivializes and even vilifies them – in some instances daring to valorize their aggressors. Either way, male victims are clearly not considered worthy of the victim mantle.

In many ways male rape appears to have arisen to take the place of female sexual victimization – where once this was omitted from reportage, so now is male rape; where once this was gratuitously depicted in the entertainment media, so now is male rape. We should be sensitive to the fact that male victims often bear feminized traits to mark them as rape-able. Consequently media depictions of male rape can be regarded as functioning as effective substitutes for the female, and as such they support a patriarchal normativity despite appearing to invert it. The implications of such tropes around male rape go beyond mere 'depictions' of rape of the male, and indeed beyond rape of the male per se. In lending credence to previously discredited myths about rape, such as the conflation of rape/sex/sexuality and the tropes of rape-revenge and rape-romance, we can see the enduring and intersecting myths of rape is sex (it is therefore low harm and explained through sexuality and desire), rape can be incited or invited (through weakness or other provocation), rapists cannot help themselves (they are governed by passion or paraphilia), only certain types of people get raped (reckless, feckless or promiscuous), all of which clearly place responsibility for the assault with the victim and invite the inevitable supposition – if rape is something one can be readily protected from, why did the victim fail to do so? Hence this supports the pernicious myths that victims 'ask' to be assaulted, and/or 'cry' rape. Thus the construct of the male victim impacts on our understanding of all acts, and victims, of sexual violence and rape. Therefore it does not just deserve our attention, it demands it.

This chapter has discussed the accepted 'truth/s' of the male rape victim discernable in certain sections of the media. Media frames are significant for their privileged dissemination to worldwide audiences, and hence can be taken to indicate consensus and normalization. In Chapter 5 I will shift the focus from the media to the audience, specifically the single unit of an 'active' audience: the fan. Constructs are significant if ubiquitous and pervasive, for sure, but thereafter they must be internalized and credibilized to become normative – as this is what gives them the potential to become guiding rationalities. With this in mind I will be moving from an analysis of 'knowing victimhood' to the 'imaginings of victimhood', specifically looking at how fan fiction conceptualizes male rape and how this interrelates with academic and media discourse.

5
Biopolitics – Imagining Victimhood

5.1   A focus on the 'horizon' of male rape: the imagining, thinking, reasoning subject

In a criminological analysis, one might expect at this juncture a shift on to state institutions and statistical data in order to ascertain the 'truth' of victimhood – perhaps looking at recording practices and conviction rates, hospital admissions and counselling referrals, etc. Thus, if one were to examine 'the individual' it would most likely be in their interaction with those institutions, reporting practices and support services indicated above, or otherwise as delineated groups whose 'truth' might be established through interviews and surveys. My interest, however, is guided by Foucault's caution that power is constituted 'from below' and 'transactionally', not top-down, and that people often act without understanding the consequences of their actions. Consequently, one may argue that the usual criminological focus on the state here would be effectively a misdirection; as Nadeson (2008, p. 5) cautions – governmentality scholarship must 'look beyond the disciplines and surveillance technologies of enclosed institutional spaces'.

Instead of looking at what is assumed to be an aggregation of subject behaviours telling us about this population, we should attempt to look more closely at the population as a construct, and moreover at the individual as self-constructing, to discern subjectivity. As Dean (2010, p. 19) asserts, 'government encompasses not only how we exercise authority over others, or how we govern abstract entities such as states and populations, but also how we govern ourselves'. Instead of following the established path from the media to the state, I will now examine the audience. Or rather, the contemporary artifacts[1] of the active audience: fan fiction. In so doing, I am using 'the fan' as an example of the imagining, thinking and reasoning subject – one who conceptualizes victimhood for themselves and for others, and who, therefore, illustrates the 'horizon' indicative of biopolitics and the 'success', therefore, of governmentality.

Once again, my aim is to identify that 'violence', by noting traces of discursive regularity and concordance in respect of the understanding of male rape and the male rape victim. I am particularly interested to see to what extent the ideal victim construct and its counterpoint of victim precipitation are given credence, along with the salient myths of rape in general and male rape in particular. My specific interest in the fan and fan fiction is threefold, to critically examine the following inter-related, and indeed mutually supportive, suppositions that I find wholly problematic: fan fiction as 'active' (Abercrombie and Longhurst, 1998, pp. 32–33); male-rape as desexualized (Wlodarz, 2001); and slash fiction as supposedly pro-feminist (Suzuki, 1998) or 'cyberfeminist' (Kibby, 2001). Keeping in mind Foucault's caution that 'Individuals are vehicles of power, not its point of application' (Foucault, 1997, cited in Hay, 2003, p. 167), underlying this will be consideration of the second aspect of the triangulation and of Foucault's notion of governmentality: 'biopower'.

5.2 A focus on fans and fandoms: the audience and governmentality

This chapter will draw on the marginal area of fan studies,[2] and in doing so will seek to credibilize the fan and fan (slash) fiction as valid areas of criminological and victimological concern – both in general terms as sites within governmentality, and specifically in relation to the discourse of male victims of sexualized violence.

Given that the purpose of governmentality is to 'constitute populations' and impact on the 'conduct of potential conduct', the purpose of this section is to examine audience frames. In particular, it aims to engage with audiences as communities and foreground their roles within the new media as active audience and contributors – specifically dealing with fans and fandom. It can be argued that the notion of the fan and fandom are of particular importance to a Foucauldian analysis, as they provide the 'antidote' to the hypodermic notion of media power by providing an opportunity to investigate the more transactional relationship so key to Foucault's notion of power. Although we must do so with Jenkins' (1992, p. 293) caveat in mind: 'fandom does not prove that all audiences are active; it does, however, prove that not all audiences are passive'.[3]

My interest is to ascertain whether 'regularity' is notable in this arena. I am also interested to see how such frames might have been re-imagined and/or ostensibly subverted and thus how they become 'reconstituted' through the active audience – exemplified in the fan and collectives organized around fandom. In particular, online fan-authored fiction provides a readily accessible source which is not only produced within an online community, but in its fluid and reflexive nature is actually more often what Youssef (2004, p. 64) terms 'communal writing'. Furthermore, its authors often attract fans themselves.

I am not so concerned with investigating 'the fan' as a homogenous, distinct or pathologized entity. I do not wish to carve them out as 'Other', but instead I am interested in them as visible and attainable representatives of the audience. In this sense, I am drawing on 'third wave' fan studies that situate fandom as part of taken-for granted knowledge and everyday life (Gray, et al., 2007). I am interested in their artifacts as constituting an indication of the 'horizon of experience' (ibid., p. 10) and their 'horizon of activity' (Mendieta, 2002, p. 6), not them per se.

Whereas much work in the current vein of cultural criminology is drawing on what Gray et al. (2007, p. 3) call the 'Fandom is beautiful phase'[4], from media and cultural studies, given the multilayered, contingent, performative, fantastical and contradictory nature of ascribed and adopted identities; I do not regard this as worthwhile – except of course in what such works can reveal about the nature of the researcher and their bias in those instances. As McKee (2007, p. 92) states: 'The fact that fans are "active" ... does not mean that their practices are subversive or progressive'. I would suggest that fan-fiction that deals with male rape is a case in point here.

The fan fiction I will be focusing on is 'slash',[5] which is solely concerned with placing characters in a male homosexual relationship[6] regardless of their copyrighted author's source material (Youssef, 2004) or 'canon'.[7] Where this becomes of more obvious concern to this project is the salience of male-on-male and female-on-male sexual violence and rape (known as either 'rapefic', or 'non-con' to denote non-consensual sex) in fan-authored endeavours. It is important to note here that such 'events' often take part outside of and as a prequel to a character's development as homosexual.[8] Unfortunately, because of this, the analysis that has taken place so far has only been imagined in terms of 'queering' and resistance to patriarchal gender norms,[9] rather than in respect of the discourse of sexual violence or hegemonic masculinity. For researchers engaging with this niche topic, the main draw of attention is decidedly related to the predominantly heterosexual[10] female authors' imaginings of male homosexuality,[11] rather than the depictions of sexual victimization. Yet, I would argue that this is clearly a fertile site for their re-imagining and re-inscribing, and as such should demand our attention. The very fact that slash involves male victims and is frequently written by women is regarded by many authors as redeeming it.[12]

Suzuki (1998, p. 258) states that the authors of such works 'describe homosexual sex – including apparent rape – in order to register this resistance as a self-assertion against the social image of the female gender. They portray male protagonists, loved by the very partners who apparently rape them, as imbued with innocence.' She asserts that this demonstrates resistance of gender norms.[13] I disagree – clearly this simply re-inscribes female attributes of femininity, passivity, etc. onto the dominated male. It is not subversive then, but instead subtly conformist and normative. This is in stark contrast to what Chin (2007, p. 214) asserts as the overwhelming conclusions of most Western research that 'stresses the active participation of fans ... suggesting there is resistance of sorts to the official culture', and is contrary to the findings of a great many feminist interpretations of slash; for example Bacon-Smith (1992, p. 203) supposes 'the women of the fan community construct a safe discourse with which to explore the dangerous subject of their own lives' – in essence postulating that it is about 'self', going on to assert slash as fundamentally about confronting male sexual violence, and thus concerned with what she terms 'the conservation of risk' (p. 204). Ostensibly, for sure, but we shouldn't overlook the end result here regarding the preservation of patriarchal norms.

It is striking to me that in slash fiction it is the weaker and/or (often supposedly latent) homosexual male who is forcibly penetrated – failure to be a 'real man', and moreover to be made an effeminized man, is what conspires to make these characters rape-able. It is what enables this supposed aberration to make sense. Significantly, this conforms to hegemonic masculinity, it doesn't challenge it. It also reveals the female audience[14] as having internalized dominant rape myths by re-inscribing them onto a caricatured and ostensibly heterosexually gendered 'homosexual' relationship.

Here then, there is the clear conflation of rape/sex/sexuality. Returning to Suzuki's (1998) statement above, the tentative strands of another myth can be noted that should be of concern: the conflation of rape/sex/ desire, as intimated in her use of 'love'. In analysing such fiction, what should be notable is the presence of previously discredited myths around female rape resuscitated and revalidated in respect of the male – not least of which are those narratives that accord with legitimate victim status and victim precipitation (for example: rape/romance; rape/retribution; rape/revenge). This illustrates the pervasive and potent nature of such frames, as well as the conformist nature of supposed instances and expressions of resistance.

There are many difficulties faced when attempting to research 'fans' and their 'fandoms', let alone when this is done wholly via the medium of the Internet. Suffice to say that, as Gray (2007, p. 81) said, the material garnered as sources for this piece are the result of a 'brief peek', an exploratory snapshot which makes no claim to being either 'scientific' or 'accurate'.

Initially, when I decided to identify audience engagement, I had intended to prioritize discussion boards and blogs in response to various news articles and television episodes that were analysed in Chapter 4. However, this was quickly dropped as it became clear that the level of engagement is often quite superficial and/or exclusionary (through the frequent use of jargon and references to previous posts, or long-standing disputes from invested participants). I instead decided to prioritize fan-authored fiction on the basis that such works, where they featured male rape, would be capable of analysis in a similar vein to that already completed and, frankly, I fully expected this to be a rather niche topic for fan-authored story arcs and hence to be quite straightforward – thus effectively expediting this chapter. Then I discovered slash, and my preconceived notion of what this chapter might look like changed irrevocably.

The initial literature review I performed in respect of the audience, the fan and fan fiction failed spectacularly to prepare me for the material I found myself reading. Many of the authors dealing with fan fiction may deal with slash, but they deal predominantly with a certain type of 'sanitized' slash – most often simply homosexual love stories and erotica – known colloquially as 'fluff'. What they frequently overlook, or briefly acknowledge but steadfastly minimize,[15] is the area I found myself focusing on – the genres of hurt/comfort, domestic discipline and the rather less euphemistically entitled bondage, dominance and sadomasochism (BDSM). These are the genres frequently highlighted in searches for 'rape' and its obfuscated forms 'non-con' (indicating non-consensual sex) and 'dub-con' (a contraction of 'dubious consent' – supposedly indicating a grey area between persuasion and consent).

In the interests of clarity – which would have certainly helped me – slash, as a whole, can be regarded as pornography. Rather than the soft-core porn which many authors have elucidated and celebrated as pro-feminist self-expression and subversive social-commentary, the material

I encountered was hard-core[16] porn, with the rape/s not part of a story arc per se, but rather the focus in and of itself. This, then, is how male rape is predominantly 'known' in slash – as eroticized sexual violence.[17]

I was initially interested solely in identifying popular slash archives, and anticipated using these to identify popular stories for analysis. Unfortunately this was not particularly workable, as the genres I sought were often either not presented as a distinct category and/or the ability to search these archives for what I required was limited. Difficulties were also experienced due to my status as an outsider – searches were hampered by my having only a rudimentary grasp of relevant jargon, and by exclusion from fandom[18] and canon-specific[19] language. For example, after realizing I could overcome some of the difficulties I was experiencing by limiting my focus to a fandom relating to a series I was myself familiar with – specifically *Supernatural* (analysed in the previous chapter) – I identified an archive that appeared to be generic slash, and included non-con, but could not find anything other than fan fiction dedicated to *Harry Potter* on there. Had I been even remotely associated with this fandom I might have realized that a site called 'the silver snitch' might prove to be somewhat preoccupied with what I now know to be the 'Potterverse' (Harry Potter fandom).

As a consequence, my next tactic was simply to search for 'supernatural slash', initially on Google, which produced several relevant hits by popularity;[20] then within LiveJournal,[21] which resulted in lists of recommended pieces of individual work and lists of relevant interest groups. At this point the amount of possible slash fiction revealed, even with specifying this single fandom and non-con/rape, was simply far too prolific to be manageable for this study.[22] This is not what the academic works I had read led me to expect. What is marginal in the literature is certainly not minimal or neglected on the Internet. Fortunately, through preliminary research on LiveJournal, I noticed several recommendations and hits for 'The Supernatural Slash Oscars'[23] – this appeared first within a LiveJournal search for 'SPN slash', second for 'Supernatural slash'; whilst on Google it was listed within the top three of a search for 'Supernatural slash' and the top four for 'SPN slash'. At the very least an argument could be made that this site was 'popular', as indicated by Google, and endorsed within the slash community and *Supernatural* fandom as indicated by users of LiveJournal.

There is a convention of sorts in present analyses of slash: an inevitable temptation to regard slash, especially that dealing with non-con, as being in some way deviant. This neatly segues into analysing this fandom and its participants as a subculture of sorts – being transgressive perhaps, or even in some way acting out of 'abnormality'. This school of thought effectively castigates and demeans. There is also the response to this, those who write in defence of slash, pre-empting such criticism by asserting rebellion and empowerment that arises from the inversion of the gaze and of the gender-roles. I do not subscribe to either of these stances. On the one hand, I think it dangerous to effectively marginalize and psychopathologize this expression of the 'active' fan; on the other, I also regard it as inherently naive to romanticize or even idealize this as subversion or resistance.

Instead, I am interested to see how 'normal' this is. Or rather, to note instances where this realm and its members draw from and replicate and/or reconstitute and transform the tropes, stereotypes and myths evident in other aspects of the triangulation. It is my contention that this realm does not serve to disrupt the discursive regularity evident in male rape, rather it compounds and consolidates it. I regard this as an activity and expression that is very much part of normative culture, not separate from it, and most definitely, therefore, not at odds with it or symptomatic of paraphilia.[24] I am interested in how orthodox rape myths are re-inscribed onto the male, thus gaining a new credibility. In this way I argue that such works do not challenge hegemonic masculinity, they reinforce it; they are also, therefore, not deviant: instead, they are decidedly conformist.

Traditional analyses are preoccupied by the apparent 'gender-bending' that seemingly inverts the orthodox female victim rape scenarios and tropes by virtue of assigning victim status to the male, but this overlooks that this male is effectively 'feminized' in order to create a narrative logic to justify him as rape-able. The techniques most readily discerned to enable this can be delineated along the logics of the ideal victim binary as those that seek to exonerate the male victim versus those that blame him. In the former a high level of violence and/or coercion can be discerned. In the latter the victim is constructed as complicit or culpable. In each instance the male is feminized in order to make him rape-able/penetrate-able. This is precisely why these logics contribute to, rather than challenge, hegemonic masculinity, and why they undermine feminism rather than act as pro-feminism.

Using LiveJournal SPN Slash Oscars and other techniques mentioned above, I identified four pieces of fan fiction[25] by two authors.[26] When aggregated, this gave me 789 pages of text – in excess of 260,000 words to analyse.[27] Each was read in full and annotated in turn, with salient themes and issues noted. Each was then read as a 'rape-story' in context, with the depiction and framing of the rape and associated plot and character development deemed a priority. This was very time consuming, but very rewarding. Reading these as 'rape-stories' enabled me to discern the 'rape-script', including myths, tropes and stereotypes. Reading them alongside each other allowed me to note commonalities and established formulae, as well as supposed departures from these.

Within this selection of material, a particular piece of fan fiction has been singled out for more detailed analysis here. *Deadly Temptation*, was written over a three year period[28] (November 2005–April 2008), and comprises 52 separate chapters, 699 pages and a total of 226,982 words. This work is also listed as the winner of best work in progress (in the category of 'Supernatural Fictional Person Slash, other pairings') at the 2008 LiveJournal SPN Slash Oscars. Most significantly, it is something of a 'communal' project – the author not only sought and received frequent feedback, as is fairly standard in this medium, but she also invited her audience to contribute to plot and characterization by posting surveys and dedicated discussion points with which her followers were invited to participate. As such, the resultant material is not just a product of, or reflection of, this author but something far more than that. It could be argued that this piece doesn't just meet with the approval of this fandom, it seeks to represent it – as such the depictions of rapes therein are of particular interest and importance.

There is a tendency to regard the audience as either utterly passive or absolutely active. The former attracts criticism as it maximizes the impact and role of 'the media', the latter because it minimizes it. In respect of the former, such critique – taken at face value – has served to stifle 'effects' research and indeed devalue a great deal of that which has been implemented. But just because direct cause–effect cannot be clearly established, does not mean we should cease attempting to establish co-contingency between audience and media frames, nor that we cannot seek consensus over those forms. We might not be able to claim that '*X* caused *Y*', but that is not the concern of a Foucauldian analysis. It is the very presence of discursive regularity that is important, and the impact this may have in the social realm, not who is to blame per se. Indeed, a transactional notion of power defies such attributions, although Foucault does recognize that transactions might not be equal but rather asymmetrical.

As Boyle (2005, p. 192) states 'the intertextual nexus in which [a] program and its characters are situated reminds us of the difficulty of studying television in isolation ... The activity of the viewers – as consumers and producers of their own texts – also challenges the conceptualization of the viewer as being passively exposed'. But this is not to say that the viewer is completely free. We must be mindful that 'the continuation of hegemonic gender relations in web-based discourses illustrates cyber-spaces *entrapment* in wider social and cultural relations' (Scodari, 2007, p. 12, italics added). The activity of the audience, whilst not as 'unfree' as the maximizers might assume, is neither wholly free, as the minimizers assume. Limits on freedom, or rather the limits inherent in freedom, are, after all, the crux of governmentality.

For Foucault, governmentality – understood as the conduct of potential conduct[29] – pivots on self-regulation, which Dean (2010, p. 20) expounds as 'the action of the self on self'. He clarifies that 'to define government as the "conduct of conduct" is to open up the examination of self-government or cases in which *governor and governed are two aspects of the one actor*' (p. 19, italics added). Dean quickly moves away from any detailed examination of this,[30] preferring a more orthodox state/government focus, but his observation is astute. Self-regulation, after all, might be most easily understood as the point at which we become complicit in our own 'subjugation'. The construction of self and identity in the achievement of subjecthood is key, and is greatly neglected in much Foucauldian scholarship,[31] despite its express articulation in Foucault's concept: 'ethics'. I will argue that, for the purpose of this piece, slash might be regarded as illustrating the ethics of the fan; and furthermore, where concordance is noted in respect of rape myths and 'truths', that this reveals governmentality.

Foucault's concept of 'ethics' can be understood as both the technologies of self-constitution and the practice of freedom. Examining ethics for the purpose of governmentality necessitates 'thinking about the linkages between questions of government, authority and politics, and questions of identity, self and person' (Dean, 2010, p. 20). This is feasible if we understand biopower as disciplinary – it then invokes the individual as a necessary vehicle, and the self as a key site, given that disciplinary power is atomized and diffused within governmentality to multiple sites within the social rather than state body. Biopolitics can, therefore, be understood, as Dean (2010, p. 36) endorses, to operate 'at the level of ... individuals and populations'. I suggest that the significance of this is far clearer if expressed thus: if we are to accept biopower as operating in the constitution of populations for the purpose of governance, then the individuals that comprise those aggregations should not be elided but foregrounded. After all, what is a population – be it also expressed as community or group – but a collection of individuals?

The significance of the fan to political economy is becoming well established in media studies. Van Zoonen (2005, p. 64) conceives of fans and fan culture as bearing the traits of 'ideal citizenship', noting emotion and imagination as foundations of fandom 'that are relevant to political involvement'. Building on this, Gray et al. (2007, p. 10) identify fans and fan-like engagement as intersecting with the civic role and duty, and thus go on to elevate the significance of the fan above issues of popular culture: 'studies of fan audiences help us to understand and meet challenges far beyond the realm of popular culture because they tell us something about the way in which we relate to those around us, as well as the way we read mediated texts that constitute an ever larger part of our horizon of experience'.

Suffice to say that if we recognize the value of culture, pop-culture and otherwise, and of community and the social, we must recognize the importance of the fan. Citing Rose (1999), Hay (2003, p. 182) asserts the importance of community in forming political actor-subjects, enabling states and citizens to 'govern through community'. His interest is primarily community as geography or spatial areas, however, I would argue that much of his work might be extrapolated to populations not delimited by space but by identity as 'communities' – especially online communities, as surely by virtue of the Internet these are not just physical spaces anymore but virtual spaces; as Kirby-Diaz (2009, p. 27) clarifies: 'last century's *public* is today's *virtcom*' (virtual community).

Identity is key here regarding self and community, where elected and/ or ascribed, as this contrives both individuation and massification. Or, as Foucault might conceive of it: 'individualization' and 'totalization'. This is relevant in two ways regarding discursive regularities (that enact regulation) in fan fiction: the knowing self as author and the knowing self as reader. This must be understood in the delimited context that one's 'grounds for self-assessment and self-knowledge'[32] (Nadeson, 2008, p. 153) are intrinsically situated. As Simons (2004, p. 193) states, 'technologies of power/knowledge have constructed what we know as psyche, subjectivity, personality, consciousness'; the 'self' so understood is always relational and contingent – not outside of biopower as an essence, but intrinsically a part of it. After all, 'the relation between government and the governed passes, to a perhaps ever increasing extent, through the manner in which governed individuals are *willing* to exist as subjects' (Gordon, 1991, p. 48, italics added).

Thus, pastoral power and technologies of the self are interlinked/ interdependent with self-policing one of the 'practices of subjectification' (Nadeson, 2008, p. 213). Burchell et al. (1991, p. 5) note that Foucault was fascinated by the power over and within freedom 'the "soul of the citizen", the life and life conduct of the ethically free subject, as in some sense the object of its own suasive capacity'. As Lazzarato (2002, p. 8) clarifies, 'the "government of souls" is always at stake in political struggle'. Hence, Foucault came to view his own work as not so much about power, but about the subject. This, then, is where identity and identification become important. As Bratich et al. (2003, p. 9) assert, 'self-governance is secured through a deployment[33] of a series of ethical techniques of self-fashioning, ones that can have a strong cultural component'. Fans, their fandoms and 'fannish' creations will be argued to exemplify this.

Bratich (2003, p. 68) alleges that 'thought has been governmentalized', going on to state that 'thought infuses practices as an ethos of self-reflection, a task that in its performance requires a provisional yet persistent dislodging, which is the condition for (and enactment of) freedom and alterity' (p. 70). To my mind, this supports a focus on fan fiction as the product of the imaginings, fantasy, self-reflection, insight and wish-fulfilment of the fan. Hence, I use fan fiction as a 'way in' to the active audience's 'thought' and to the internalization and acceptance of myths and tropes therein. Fan fiction – and indeed the discussion boards around this – is a site in which to examine this 'governmentalization of thought' in action.

Indeed, only popular fan fictions are recommended, linked and promoted and the examples I have seen all conform to existing myths. Rather than conforming *despite* the substitution of slash over heterosexual encounters, perhaps – it might be argued – it is *because* of it.[34] The focus for resistance is corporeal gender only, not behaviours or subject positions, which is enormously problematic as these become in themselves signifiers of gender. Certainly, the victimized males I encountered in slash were very much in keeping with Clover's (1987) precept – acting simply as female surrogates or substitutes, with their corporeal gender being effectively 'overwritten' by behaviours that explicitly gender them as feminine. As a consequence, such works simply cannot be regarded as subversive, as it is the 'feminization' that renders the characters rape-able. Furthermore, as in the examples from music, it is interesting to note that the salvation and/or redemption of male victims in slash comes from their overt (re-)masculinization – embracing their machismo and rejecting homosexuality is precisely what enables them, ultimately, to save themselves and wreak vengeance on others. After all, being the 'hero' is the preserve of the (hegemonic) male.

Thus, I would argue that slash is very much in the service of hegemonic masculinity and patriarchy. Both 'just world' and the ideal victim binary can be readily noted, indicating that these persist in respect of meaning-making around rape. Considering that the vast majority of such authors are women,[35] some of whom are very young women,[36] the persistence of these in their writings should be a cause for considerable concern. After all, these women are conceptualizing victimhood – for others and also for themselves.

5.3 Pretty when he's broken:[37] slash and the eroticization of male sexual victimization

In this section I will provide a critical reading and analysis of the fan-authored fiction *Deadly Temptation* (by the author writing under the username and pseudonym 'Darkestangel'). In this fan fiction, an obvious effort is made to explain the supposed anomaly of the heterosexual male rape victim. In essence, a narrative is constructed – albeit often contradictory and confounding – that seeks to make the male rape-able. In doing so, he is set apart from other men and marked as different, distinct and Other. A recurrent issue for the author seems to be the imperative to overcome the male's inherent invulnerability derived from norms around masculinity/strength/power – the difficulty in overcoming the notion that men cannot be victims of sexual violence.

There is a constant need to explain why the male either cannot or does not fight back. The former seeks to exonerate him, the latter seeks to responsibilize him, thus creating an ideal victim binary that I would argue acts to recuperate masculinity and resurrect rape myths. Thus, in this fiction, for the 'innocent' victim there is the use of extreme violence, multiple assailants, weapons and other forms of coercion, including threats of harm to family members and finally brain washing, mind control and nervous breakdown. For the 'culpable' victim there is reference to latent homosexuality and subconscious desire, sexual promiscuity and sexual deviance, self-indulgence and reckless self-endangerment.

In analysing this fiction, it is interesting that not only are these narratives all applied to a single victim over the course of the story to explain successive instances of repeat victimization, but several antagonistic and contradictory narratives can be found in the explication and exposition of *single* instances of his victimization. Utilizing the binary as a whole to explain the victimization seems to be of far more importance to the author than satisfying the logics of any particular aspect of it.

To be blunt, making the victimization plausible (in the incredulous face of the totem of heterosexual masculinity) – through reference to any and all logics – is far more important than making the explanation itself consistent or internally coherent.

As previously described, *Deadly Temptation* is an explicit pornographic story within the genre of slash, and more specifically hurt/comfort and BDSM. Whilst the author draws on elements of established canon regarding *Supernatural* in her first few chapters,[38] she does not regard these as intransigent – she deviates from this and regards her later chapters as Alternate Universe.[39] The author is a regular, prolific and experienced slasher, with a significant investment within this genre and a significant presence on the Internet and in fan forums – her work is widely recommended and is hosted on several separate fan sites as well as on her LiveJournal site and her own website. This was her first *Supernatural* slash and was commenced whilst season one was airing in the US.

Before looking at examples drawn from the rapes themselves, I want to look at the prequel to the first rape, to consider how the author first introduces her readers to the various characters, specifically the lead characters from the show (Sam and Dean) and an original protagonist (Christian) – noting the innate and salient characteristics that the author has chosen to foreground for us and questioning what significance this might have in terms of rendering one male, Dean, rape-able.

The plotline as a whole essentially revolves around the older brother Dean and his selection, abduction and – lengthy and varied – sexualized torture at the hands of numerous sexual sadists. As is faithful to the canon, the key protagonist in question is a vampire – a potentiality that would not strike this fandom as unbelievable. Arcs within this overall plotline concern Dean's 'awakening' to a supposedly latent homosexuality and of a repressed incestual desire – which are initially triggered and then sustained by a series of vicious and degrading sexual assaults at the hands of both his original abductor and his brother, both of whom eventually become Dean's 'lovers'. This culminates in a 'love' triangle, the negotiation of which sets up the means for Dean's redemption, which is communicated not least through an express rejection of homosexuality *and* a denial of his rapes – which is to say that Dean eventually comes to recognize his rapes as consensual acts, attributed to his underlying homosexuality, whilst explicitly disavowing homosexuality as a valid identity or practice for himself.

A recurrent technique used by the author is to contradict and radically reinterpret Dean's experiences through flashback, asides and internal monologue. She frequently presents a brutal, explicit and degrading rape scene, only to then reinterpret it as in some way consensual. Likewise, the author presents apparently consensual homosexual intercourse which is later reinterpreted as in some way coerced. There seems a recurrent tension in her narrative to explain away the rape as homosexuality, and then to reject the homosexuality through rape. Various aspects of these intertwine throughout chapters and story arcs to become mutually supportive, in terms of making the male rape-able through reference to homosexuality and latent desire which then serves to negate the rape as he becomes complicit. The overriding message, despite the ambivalent and seemingly contradictory rationalizations herein, is that male rape is not possible.

I would argue that this is due to the narrative's orientation to the rape/sex/sexuality conflation and the assumed inviolability of heterosexual masculinity. Both scenarios serve to protect hegemonic masculinity – in the denial of rape (by reinterpreting it as consensual homosexual sex) and then in the rejection of homosexuality (by reinterpreting consensual homosexual sex as coerced, and, therefore, as rape). The fact that these positions are mutually negating and contradictory seems to pose little problem for the author or her readers, of the utmost importance instead is to preserve the internal logics of the rape myths and of hegemonic masculinity. This is decidedly problematic, as not only is male rape here expressly eroticized, but it is presented in ways that legitimize the notion of victim precipitation in general and ultimately cast doubt on the possibility of male sexual victimization full stop.

Prequel to the first rape

Readers are first introduced to Sam and Dean in a context and manner that fans of the official show would be comfortable with. The author is not only setting up her own arc here she is also demonstrating credibility within this fandom by drawing her respective characters and the context for this story as faithful to the original source text.

The story starts with a scene featuring a squabble between Dean and his brother. Sam is frustrated, aggrieved and indignant that Dean was content to idly stand by and leave him to eradicate a nest of six vampires by himself. It becomes apparent that Dean watched Sam from the safe vantage point of 'leaning up against his car', whilst Sam proceeded to 'get his ass kicked by bloodsuckers'. The situation is made more dangerous as the author clarifies that Sam has only recently returned to 'hunting' after five years absence, during which he was studying at College. When Sam confronts Dean about this wilful neglect, the response is one of dismissive sarcasm, which culminates in Dean clearly demonstrating somewhat skewed priorities for his possessions over his family when he chides his brother for countenancing the possibility of getting into his 'precious' car with ash on his clothing.

Sam is quickly established as the responsible, knowledgeable and sincere sibling; Dean – in stark contrast – is established as his polar opposite. He is presented in this scene as superficial, lazy, unreasonable, careless and selfish. In doing so, the author has chosen to foreground only certain aspects of temperament and personality that are presented in the official show. In essence she has chosen to present Dean at his worst and Sam at his best. This obviously resonates with just world theory, making Dean rape-able so that his victimization is understood by the reader as in some way deserved.

The primary factor that is presented to explain Dean's forthcoming victimhood is his level of desirability. Dean is quickly established by the author as universally physically attractive and sexually irresistible – knowing no boundaries. In the first eight pages Dean's 'beauty' is explicitly translated as inciting sexual desire in others and is noted as influencing: his own brother, the supernatural in general, teenage girls, victims, clients, delivery men and 'half the people we meet' (p. 1).[40] This is significant, as in providing the context for the forthcoming rape the author firmly establishes it as within logics around a rape/sex/desire conflation and thus rationalizes rape as provoked/incited/precipitated by qualities and factors intrinsic to the victim themselves. Perhaps most importantly, the focus at this point is almost entirely on explaining Dean as a sexualized and eroticized being. This is the background given to facilitate understanding of Dean's selection as the victim. The drive here is to rationalize Dean's victimhood as plausible within an expressly sexualized and personalized frame of reference.

Contrast this with Christian, the offender, who is first introduced three pages into the story but escapes a similar amount of attention and explication. His motivations are expressly oriented around Dean himself – the offender in this instance is understood only through his victim. Put simply, it's all Dean's fault: he is irresistible. The author states that Dean's attractiveness influences Christian, plausibly sufficing therefore as provocation: it 'captivates' Christian, makes him 'lustful', and compels him: 'he *had* to taste the beauty' (p. 4, italics added). This is corroborated by other characters, such as: the 'pizza delivery guy', who openly leers at Dean and rebuts criticism from Sam by stating 'sorry Dude but I'm not blind' (p. 7); the two teenaged victims of a poltergeist, who incredibly manage to recover enough from their immediate ordeal to make inappropriate advances toward Dean; and indeed his sibling, Sam, who confronts and justifies his own sexual attraction to Dean as inevitable and inescapable given that 'even the supernatural had the hots for his brother' (p. 7).

The focus is on constructing Dean as explicitly eroticized and objectified. The author makes reference to his 'pretty mouth', 'angelic face', 'well defined body', 'succulent flesh' and 'smooth wet skin'. These all seek to essentialize qualities in Dean himself as provoking or inciting attraction from others. The inherent or innate nature of such attributes is bolstered by the author when she states his would-be attacker is not only 'captivated' by such appearances but also by Dean's smell and the anticipation of his taste. We must also note there the choice of phraseology – there is no use of the more traditional gender specific descriptors such as handsome, rugged, athletic or muscular, instead the author uses terms that are imbued with femininity: 'pretty', 'angelic' and 'beautiful'. These draw on and appropriate established myths around the responsibilization of women and exculpation of men for rape – that beauty unleashes desire, she can be 'irresistible', men cannot control themselves, etc. The extended logic of this being that women need to guard against provoking attack through adherence to appropriate manner and dress. This is significant, as the author goes on to establish Dean as clearly in violation of this precautionary principle and thus as deserving of victimhood but not victim status.

These first steps towards feminizing Dean are plausibly in order to render his fate 'knowable' and understandable. These interlink with other significant aspects of characterization relating to his behaviour and personality. In addition to noting Dean as eroticized, he can also be discerned as infantilized. This is communicated mostly through Dean's interaction with his brother Sam. Dean is established as intellectually inferior to Sam, he is rendered childlike through descriptions of his immature behaviour and attitude and through Sam's opprobrium and his evident frustration with this behaviour.

We might think that through infantalization Dean is absolved of responsibility, but this is not the case – he is imbued not with the innocence of childhood but with the failings of immaturity and youth. Dean is openly described as insincere and duplicitous: 'Dean faked a hurt expression' (p. 2). Other descriptions draw him as selfish, short-sighted, sarcastic, superficial, lazy, temperamental, reckless, devious, manipulative and cunning. He willfully antagonizes those around him for his own amusement, '[Dean] loved getting Sam riled up' (p. 7); is careless of his own safety and that of others; is conceited about his appearance;

and is arrogant. Importantly, the reader is to see him as being self-aware and having insight – he is presented as fully knowledgeable of the impact and influence he has on others and he clearly enjoys it, much to the exasperation of his brother. This is in obvious defiance of the precautionary measures that the logics around rape precipitation would dictate.

This combination of feminized beauty coupled with infantilized reck-lessness serve to responsibilize Dean for his fate. Both his physical self and his moral self are culpable. This is emphasized further in the notion of Dean having a 'sixth sense'.[41] This intuition is used by the author to introduce doubt as to the level of Dean's complicity with his own victimization and thus with whether he ever really is raped – a constant ambivalence that runs throughout the text.

The first rape

The first rape is established by the author through what the reader is led to believe is a dream. It is presented in italics, which has been encoded by the author as specifically denoting dream sequences, and follows Dean clearly falling asleep in bed. However, it later transpires that the assault is not only dreamt. Christian is able to manipulate Dean's dream-world to leave him vulnerable to assault in the real world – the dream is a cover for and facsimile of a very real sexual assault that happens to Dean whilst he is incapacitated. This provides two levels to assess: the assault contained within the dream and the assault in the real world.

I would suggest that the author presents us with two levels in order to introduce doubt for the reader around whether Dean consents. We can note that this 'doubt' is reinforced through contradictory and confused physical responses and articulations from Dean throughout this section. Irrespective of this, it is important to point out here that for my pur-poses any sexual activity that is performed whilst someone is incapable of consent – as in the case of Dean being unconscious or sleeping – would satisfy the criteria for rape. Any dreamt will or want is simply not relevant beyond its use here as a literary device, by the author, to communicate a supposed subconscious desire, which is used to render Dean complicit, and hence negate the rape. Consequently, I regard this section as clearly the first rape and deserving of analysis as such.

Dean's first rape occurs in his motel room, with his brother in the next bed. The assailant, Christian, has incapacitated Sam by putting him in a deep sleep. Dean is likewise incapacitated by sleep but is made to appear lucid in his dream state. It transpires that Dean has encountered this dream before, that Christian has been tormenting and 'grooming' him for two nights in preparation for this physical attack. Interestingly, this familiarity is one of the factors used to suggest that Dean consents on some level – this resonates with the stereotypes and myths around repeat victimization in general and sexual and/or domestic violence regarding women in particular.

In the dream, Dean is driving alone on an isolated stretch of road at night when he engages in what is to be regarded by the reader as 'risky' behaviour: he stops for a hitchhiker, Christian. Dean is then made to participate in various sexual acts accompanied by degradation, threat of and actual violence, culminating in digital penetration.[42]

Christian is depicted as an intimidating figure: physically larger, stronger and more aggressive than Dean. The reader is given to understand that in this scenario Dean is unable to physically fight back and that Christian is more than capable of overpowering him. This clearly draws from the myth that only weaker males are raped.

This physical enfeeblement is reinforced through infantilizing language – Christian repeatedly refers to Dean as 'boy' or 'little one'. There is also use of endearments to imply a pre-existing relationship, and to indicate Dean's status within it, for example 'my sweet'. This establishes Dean's inferior and subordinate role whilst appearing to mitigate the otherwise vile and degrading nature of the assault. It also subtly reinforces more explicit feminization by casting Dean as a 'helpless child' along the lines argued by Clover (1987).

In this scene, Dean is presented as conflicted, and this is used to responsibilize him. Although described unambiguously by Christian's internal monologue as his 'unsuspecting prey' (p. 8) there is an attempt throughout this section to render Dean complicit and cast his victimization in doubt. The key way the author achieves this is in repeatedly having Dean draw on his intuition to indicate his awareness of what is going on, and then having him consciously ignore it. For example, when Dean first stops to pick up the hitchhiker the author clarifies that it is 'against his better judgment' (p. 9), going on to narrate that 'something at the back of Dean's mind warned him that this man was potentially deadly, but he couldn't stop himself' (p. 9), and then having him consciously master his own 'sense of panic' (p. 12) by actively repressing it. Dean is revealed as feeling out of control and fearful, yet he is made to explicitly articulate consent: 'every fiber in Dean's being wanted to defy the strange being's command. "Yes" he [Dean] reluctantly answered' (p. 11). But of course, for the purpose of this analysis it is important to assert that consent that is coerced or compelled cannot be consent, thus the rape is not negated.

The rape/romance trope is particularly important for this scene. Christian articulates that he can sense Dean's distress and apprehension but that this 'would soon turn to passion' (p. 10). When Dean refuses Christian's advances, however, Christian states 'it really doesn't matter what you want' (p. 11), which should serve to clarify the act as rape, but the author soon attempts to cast doubt here as she implies that Christian is insightful and knows Dean's true will better than Dean himself, that he can sense Dean's desire. She also attempts to rescue Christian from the role of 'villain' by revealing Christian's feelings for Dean as in some way noble – using terms such as 'loving' and 'tender'. These are techniques that attempt to reconstruct this scenario as consensual and seductive, rather than coercive violation, and furthermore cast this as rape/romance – which in itself should be perturbing.

Post-rape

Although the author goes to great lengths to cast the assault in the previous scene as in some way consensual, in the scene that follows various post-rape tropes used to communicate stereotypical trauma are notable. These include indicators of physical revulsion, such as extensive showering (asserted as lasting from 6 a.m. to 1 p.m.), repeated vomiting and dry-heaving and uncharacteristic loss of appetite; and behavioural and personality changes, such as over-sleeping, being withdrawn, agitated and crying. Dean's childlike vulnerability is also referenced again, with his brother finding him sat in the foetal position in the shower, a way of self-comforting. From these it is clear that the author intends to communicate that the encounter with Christian was rape. This is emphasized for the reader in the fact that it is the stronger, more dominant brother (as the author depicts him), Sam, who finally draws this prolonged episode to a close and 'rescues' Dean, temporarily, from Christian's influence and his own tortuous thoughts by going to his aid in the bathroom and 'pulling his brother up off the shower floor' (p. 18). The 'rescue' is important at this point in subtly communicating and reinforcing the non-corporeal gender, as Clover (1987) notes – females are rescued, whilst males rescue themselves. We can also note Dean as a 'vulnerable child' (Clover, 1987), emphasized here by Sam's paternalistic actions: wrapping him in a towel, checking his forehead for a fever, chiding him and putting him to bed.

However, at the close of this section, and just prior to the next rape, the author yet again introduces an element of doubt. The scene is closed with Dean reflecting consciously on his experience and expressing confusion over whether he wants to repeat it: 'Part of him was terrified to go to sleep while another part of him wanted to be with the mysterious stranger. Part of him wanted Sam to keep driving away from the shit town while another part of him never wanted to leave' (p. 22). This notion of conflict and ambivalence about his rape is continually interwoven throughout this story.

The author frequently seeks to wrong-foot the reader in reinterpreting Dean's feelings towards the assaults and his role in them – but, although the author and her readers are distracted by this, academic inquiry should not be. It must be remembered that Dean could not give consent to the acts that were engaged in as he was asleep; notions of latent desire, subsequent arousal or confusion do not nullify the crime that has occurred – it is of great concern to me that this author and her readers apparently believe otherwise.

In this first rape and its context many rape myths can be noted, not least of which are rape/romance, latent or subconscious desire and provocation. These are all key elements of victim precipitation and thus form part of the negative aspect of the ideal victim. Dean is cast as both deserving of victim status (in that he is coerced, overpowered, incapacitated and suffers physical violence – he is therefore innocent of any blame: the archetypal deserving victim) and undeserving (in that he flirts, supposedly consents, doesn't fight back, gets aroused and ejaculates – he is therefore deemed complicit in his fate and is undeserving of victim status).

Feedback posted on one of the author's discussion boards in respect of this instalment indicates subscription to the rape myths evidenced here, thus a user called 'Cheryl' states in one post that 'I'm a sucker for slut! Dean'[43], whilst in another post she goes on to praise this chapter as 'so hot'[44] – the rapes for this reader have been effectively minimized as consensual, hence Dean is a 'slut', with the assaults consequently able to be reconfigured as homoerotic and, therefore, 'hot'. The trends, tropes and motifs established by the author in the first section are repeatedly referenced throughout *Deadly Temptation*. For this author and her readers, the myths congruent to these clearly have power as explanatory devices for her male victim and his assailants.

In addition to this first rape, and contingent on the rationales therein, there are two narrative arcs within the text as a whole that deserve analysis: the first involves the refiguring of Dean's relationship with Christian as what slashers would recognize as 'domestic discipline', but what would be more accurately conceived of as domestic violence;[45] and the second pivots on the introduction of 'Wincest' (a contraction of Winchester – the brothers' surname – and incest) to eventually comprise a 'love' triangle between the brothers and Christian. These are a concern not only because of the issues they raise in themselves, but because of the continued emphasis on Dean's non-con that underscores them. These arcs are used by the author and her readers to import superficial 'relationships' that supposedly mitigate the offence of rape and thus enable the incidents to be perceived as erotic. In doing so, they draw on what should be problematic notions of spousal rape, date rape, fraternal rape, etc. The context of 'family' or 'marriage' does not negate the offence of rape and yet here we can see evidence that, for this writer and her readers, it plainly does. For me, what is so problematic here is not the BDSM themes, but the emphasis on non-con as supposedly erased through the relationships that contextualize it. This has obvious resonance with the ideal victim and various rape myths – not least of which is that rape can become 'romance' (therefore it's an effective tool in courtship and a mere extension of seduction) and that a pre-existing relationship confers implied consent; both of which are significant and very real barriers to justice for victims where 'domestic' or 'date' scenarios are involved or can be misconstrued.

The 'domestic discipline' arc is introduced very early on. It is first referenced through Dean's initial ambivalence towards Christian, where the reader is invited to infer the tentative beginnings of a relationship through Dean's expressed 'love' and 'desire' for his assailant – sentiments expressed in reflections on, and even during, attacks of the most violent and gratuitous kind. It is quickly clarified by the author in the use of the term 'boyfriend' to refer to Christian, even whilst the unfolding narrative reveals this character stalking the brothers with the intent of capturing, abducting and 'breaking' Dean. The first penile-penetrative rape of Dean by Christian is used by the author to 'consummate' Dean and Christian's dynamic as a relationship, and to verify Dean as homosexual.

Christian sets the agenda and motivation behind the rapes as one of conquest and ownership: 'He wanted to be inside Dean's body and mind, and he wanted to own Dean's body and soul' (p. 16). This is a theme revisited by the author numerous times within each arc and given credence by her victim. Thus, Dean, reflecting on his first assault and about to experience another, states: 'He could feel the stranger's hands caressing his thighs and his crotch. He could feel the seductive voice that promised nothing but pleasure, and he could feel the excitement of being totally out of control' (p. 23). Bearing in mind that this is a reflection on a penetrative assault that results in this character suffering from various physical and emotional indicators of trauma, to see this reconfigured in such positive terms – 'caressing', 'seductive', 'pleasure' and 'excitement' – is more than a little troubling. Having rape expressly configured as all of this precisely because it is 'totally out of control' is simply abhorrent.

The author shows Dean to be the weaker, subordinate 'partner' in this 'relationship', being uncharacteristically (out of canon) quick to apologize, meek and deferential. The first penile-penetrative rape to be precipitated by Dean is presented as retributive – provoked by Dean's defiance of Christian and enabled by his weakness. Interestingly, Christian is also presented as regretful that the first intercourse would be forced, with the onus placed clearly on Dean as having 'made this necessary' (p. 25). Thus, Christian is posited as having to resort to rape at Dean's instigation, for Dean's own good and for the sake of their 'relationship'. Christian is depicted as a reluctant and pragmatic rapist, with rape merely 'a necessary evil' (p. 26).

The rape/romance theme is cemented with Christian 'kiss[ing] and lick[ing] at Dean's neck tenderly even as he tore at his body with no remorse. "It will be sweeter next time, I promise"' (p. 26). Though Dean experiences this as rape, and articulates it as such – 'he had been raped in his own fucking bed' (p. 32) – the author has Sam identify this as an erotic encounter with the assailant, termed as Dean's 'mystery lover', and Dean as conferring retrospective consent of sorts by admitting to himself that he wanted to be 'raped' again. The author eventually confirms this as a consensual homosexual relationship when, on the fourth occasion of rape, she states 'Dean looked up into Christian's eyes and saw nothing but love and tenderness as he was claimed by the vampire. "yes" ... he whispered' (p. 46). This is consolidated with Christian stating: 'I made love to you' (p. 47), to which Dean responds in the affirmative whilst coyly admitting reciprocation. Finally, the author has Dean refer to Christian as his 'blood-sucking boyfriend' (p. 50) prior to establishing and interweaving her second arc.

Rape is thus established as the means by which Christian 'wins' Dean, and subsequently as the means by which he keeps him – the author utilizes violent rape as discipline for transgressions, referring to such acts as 'punishment' and an 'act of contrition', with the assailant frequently apologetic and regretful; whilst Dean is depicted as appreciative and needy, for example petulantly asking 'don't I at least get a kiss' (p. 61). Furthermore, it is cast as flattering, as Dean reveals: 'I hate you but at least you want me' (p. 82).

In setting up the 'domestic discipline' arc, the author characterizes Dean as initially ambivalent about his rapes and his sexuality, and uses the rapes as a means by which to develop Dean's character as homosexual. This is disturbing as it draws on the myths that a male victim can be 'made' homosexual by the experience of rape and/or that only homosexual men are raped. It is certainly the case that many victims of rape experience confusion around their sexuality, but this is precisely because of such myths – it does not and should not lend credence to them. Having Christian depicted as knowing Dean's sexuality before Dean himself does, and supposedly unleashing Dean's desire through coerced sexual intercourse, is profoundly dangerous. For this author and her readers 'no' certainly seems to mean 'yes', with latent desire waiting to be 'unlocked' by the noble (insightful, altruistic and didactic) rapist. Rape is hereby cast as an extension of courtship, the epitome of true love and unbridled desire, which can precipitate the same, demonstrating a clear resonance with classic rape myths.

The 'domestic discipline' arc intersects with the 'Wincest' arc, to quickly establish a rather perverse 'love' triangle, with Christian and Sam first working together, then in competition to 'own' Dean through successive and ever more graphic and sadistic rapes. Many of the myths and tropes noted above are recast here.

As previously indicated, Sam is established early on by the author as the younger but dominant brother, who wrestles with an attraction for his sibling. Sam is protective of Dean, which is in canon, but is also revealed as proprietorial and sexually territorial, which is not. Sam sets about 'rescuing' Dean from the abusive relationship he has with Christian by drugging and abducting him, but is quickly seduced himself when he is made to watch Dean get 'punished' in a lengthy episode that culminates in a degrading and explicit anal rape. This turning point is revealed in a narrative retrospective and was forewarned by the author's use of behavioural and rhetorical echoes between Sam and Christian. Thus, just as Christian is described as physically the larger man, so is Sam; just as Christian assaults Dean with slaps, grabs and physical restraints, so does Sam; Christian pets and protects Dean with gestures such as carrying him, wrapping him, touching him 'tenderly' and putting him to bed, as does Sam; and Christian uses diminutive pet names for Dean, likewise Sam.

The author is again drawing on the rape myth of 'the weaker man' here as a rationale for and portent of rape, and the conflation of rape/sex/desire as motivation. In combination these 'explanations' serve as indictments of the victim and present a particular barrier for heterosexual male victims of rape as they struggle to understand their experience through this prism. It is especially troubling as in reality neither 'sex' nor 'weakness' are necessarily in evidence in male on male rape – the assailant does not need to be homosexual to rape other men (Groth and Burgess, 1980; Struckman-Johnson and Struckman–Johnson, 1992; Scarce, 1997); nor does he have to be physically more intimidating to overpower or incapacitate his victim, as – in common with women – many men have reported 'freezing' during the assault, being effectively paralyzed with shock or fear (see vignette R v. Armstrong in Rumney and Morgan-Taylor, 2004). Unfortunately, the persistence of these myths comprises an effective barrier to justice for male victims of rape who either do not report the assault for fear of condemnation (Kaufman et al., 1980; Calderwood, 1987; Canter and Hodge, 1998), or, on reporting it, find that they do not satisfy the Crown Prosecution Service requirements for a 'strong' case to take forward for prosecution,[46] or, if taken forward, find that juries are unconvinced by their account of the assault and do not convict. These myths have been found to be prevalent amongst juries,[47] who subscribe to the resultant 'precautionary principle', which – if the victim is found wanting in this regard – effectively implicates them in a manner similar to contributory negligence, as such, the notion of 'asking for it' persists as a significant barrier to justice for all victims of sexual assault.

An extension of the 'weakness' rationale is the preference for the use of excessive force, weaponry and/or multiple assailants as more adequately providing the vulnerability deemed as necessary for male rape – the author does not have scenarios involving completed rape where one or more of these factors is not in evidence. This should be a concern, as none of these elements is in fact necessary, but it is becoming the case that more reports of male rape contain them.[48] Rather than assuming that this reflects a real rise in sadistic assault, 'tooled-up' rapists or gang rape as a phenomenon, we must consider whether this myth is becoming prescriptive to the extent that victims are more inclined to report an assault if it meets this criteria, whilst those whose assault does not may plausibly choose to exclude themselves from the pursuit of formal justice.

The author has her 'love' triangle commence in earnest during a torture scene in which Sam is physically incapacitated by being bound to a chair, cut and mutilated; after which Dean is forced to fellate Sam whilst simultaneously being anally raped by Christian. In line with the 'noble rapist' theme established earlier, this assault is cast as didactic – Christian wants Sam to admit his incestuous attraction to Dean, going on to state 'you have nothing to be ashamed of ... I mean, look at him; he's fucking beautiful' (p. 102). Once again, Dean is responsibilized, whilst those around him are absolved of all responsibility.

During the assault, Sam, who was initially unwilling, is transformed into a willing participant who 'hisses' and 'moans' in pleasure, and clearly articulates encouragement for his brother to continue. He later begs God for forgiveness for his 'inappropriate desire', whilst the author clarifies the dynamic here in narrating through Dean that 'Christian's game in the basement had caused Sam to face some realities and one of those was that he found his own brother sexually attractive' (p. 117). Thus Sam's supposedly repressed and controlled desires for his brother have been effectively unleashed. Once again, the author draws on the notion that rape and sexual assault can become pleasurable, that those assaulted are latent homosexuals who have invited the attack in some way and, furthermore, that the rapist knows his victim's desires better than they know themselves. Moreover, as it draws on myths that rape is a consequence of natural sexual appetite and that rapists cannot control themselves, we can see the reinforcement of the victim as precipitator.

From this point on, the author continues to furnish each arc with successive abductions and escapes, with Dean made perpetually vulnerable to those who profess to 'love' him, 'protect' him and 'rescue' him. Sam is depicted as wrestling constantly to control his desire to rape Dean, something the author then has him do freely – in dream sequences at first, then later as part of a group retribution when goaded by Dean. Christian and an assortment of other villains are likewise unable to control themselves around Dean, who is 'too pretty for his own good' (p. 173), even betraying one another for him; whilst Dean is explicitly held culpable for this influence, for example, Sam states: 'but it is your fault Dean ... all you did was spread your legs like some fucking whore' (p. 181), a condemnatory sentiment echoed by one of Christian's group who tells Sam 'your brother is nothing but a little bitch who can't keep his legs closed' (p. 151).

Dean's assailants are frequently described as penitent or conflicted about being unable to prevent themselves from raping Dean, for example, Sam is challenged by his father who asks if he can control himself around Dean, Sam confesses that he is unsure and is frightened of what he might do, whilst one of the vampires confides: 'Dean ... you've made me do things I knew are wrong ... you've made me lose control' (p. 416). The implicit message here is that we should pity the poor rapists who are so clearly remorseful and unable to control themselves – it is not their fault.

Dean, meanwhile, maintains ambivalence about his rapes and rapists, often moving from fear and hatred to pleasure and affection, even during the most violent assaults and in reflection upon them. The author frequently undermines any articulated confusion or non-consent by positing Dean's achieving orgasm as equivalent to, and indicative of, pleasure and desire; but in actuality male victims can be made to physically respond, through stimulation of either their penis or prostate, or even just in response to fear itself (King and Woollett, 1997; Davies, 2002; Rumney and Morgan-Taylor, 2004), and consequently this in no way mitigates the assault or the lack of consent. This of course is strikingly similar to classic rape cases cited by early feminist researchers where police, barristers and judiciary regarded the 'truth' of a case to pivot on evidence relating to physical indicators of the woman's supposed desire – such as vaginal lubrication or erect nipples – something we regard as utterly abhorrent now and yet continue to validate in respect of male victims. Indeed, the notion that ejaculation belies the 'cry' of rape is so widely held that rapists reputedly utilize this to ensure their victim does not report his assault (Groth and Burgess, 1980), or if he does, that he is not believed.

In line with this, Dean is depicted as a liar who in effect 'cries' rape, and is even noted to be deceiving himself by suppressing a deeper or repressed truth. The vampires, speaking of Dean, state that 'He likes to be on the edge and out of control ... he won't admit it but he likes being dominated and used' (p. 274). Sam interprets Christian's successful relationship with Dean to be a consequence of Christian's understanding of Dean's 'need' to be raped: 'Dean needed more than that [a loving tender relationship]. Obviously the vampire had figured this out early on, why else would Christian use this method [rape] to entice Dean?' (p. 287). This is enormously perturbing given that the notion of the 'victim as liar' has been revealed as so resilient, irrespective of gender.[49]

Time and again, Dean's love and lust is regarded as attainable through rape, with the rapes described in the most graphic manner, involving ever more debasement and violence, and an increasing numbers of assailants. The author depicts rape as a tool of seduction and confirms its veracity with Dean's internal post-rape monologue. For example: whilst Dean is beaten and raped by Christian, he fantasizes about his brother's first anal rape of him and reveals that he wishes that this time it was Sam once more; when Dean is raped by Christian again, receiving penile-oral penetration from his assailant, he is surprised and ashamed to hear himself moaning with pleasure, whilst the author then clarifies that 'there was something primal and erotic with the way Christian forced submission upon him, and *even though he feared for his life and safety*, Dean couldn't control the shudders of desire' (p. 222, italics added). This is perturbing, as the notion of 'wanting to be raped' persists as a rationale that denies victimhood for some people, especially those in 'date' or 'domestic' scenarios;[50] whilst coercing compliance on the basis of this misapprehension – effectively perceiving rape as a valid component of seduction – continues to be revealed as a widely held belief.[51]

Correspondingly, rape is frequently cast by the author as motivated by 'love', whilst in retrospect various rapes are then consequently rendered consistent with this by being recast as 'lovemaking', with Dean eventually coming to reciprocate that sentiment for his rapists, including his brother: 'I love you, I hate you ... I want you' (p. 437). This is extremely dangerous on several levels, not least because of the notion of consistency and reciprocity, but also because, once again, the idea of the 'noble' rapist is given credence, as well as the notion that rape can become consensual. All of which, of course, give tacit approval to interpret no as yes – that the victim's denial is neither final nor reliable given that they might be persuaded to change their mind.

Interlinking with this, the author frequently has Dean commence a consensual act then withdraw his consent, articulating this clearly through the usual verbalization, but has both the assailant and Dean render this withdrawal of consent invalid. Thus, the assailant is invariably aroused by pleas to 'stop' or 'don't' and are made to articulate rejection or disbelief of the denial, either as it is made, or in reflection. The victim, meanwhile, is made to reveal that the withdrawal of consent is without integrity by eventually responding positively to the assault, either in the moment or in reflection afterwards. This not only compounds the above regarding the insightful rapist and desirous victim, which functions to render consent irrelevant, but it superficially lends weight to the myth that consent cannot be withdrawn once given – an enduring myth that is widely held, despite legislation clearly deeming otherwise (Lyon, 2004). Either way, consent for male victims is considered to be inconsequential.

In addition to the rape myths and tropes noted above, certain rape-tropes are inverted or contravened by Dean to imply tacit consent. For example, when Dean is rescued by his family, after being held hostage and brutalized by the vampire clan for several weeks, he is asked by his father if he wants a shower, but Dean declines. This is presented as a significant breach of genuine victim behaviour and elicits the following comment from the author: 'Surely a person who had been as violated as Dean had would want to get his attacker's smell off of him' (p. 376). This reluctance to comply with what is evidently regarded as a valid display of rape-trauma is referenced three times in this short scene. This element of doubt is quickly validated when the author recounts a graphic dream sequence featuring three assailants, including Sam, that Dean interprets positively as 'subconscious needs and wants' (p. 386), even going on to declare that he loved Christian. Here, failure to conform to appropriate victim behaviour reveals the falsity of claims to victimhood – in this sense these myths have become prescriptive and normative.

In the finale of this piece, the author has Dean embark on a quest for vengeance against the vampire clan. In doing so she is drawing on the rape/revenge trope and is, therefore, providing some clarity as to how the reader should interpret Dean's previous experiences. It is significant that Dean does not seek revenge in respect of Sam, meaning that Dean's experiences at the hands of his brother are implicitly lent credibility as a consensual relationship. Indeed, her final motif here is to cast Sam and Dean's relationship as one of 'forbidden love', with Sam made to gain control over his aggressive sexual impulses and Dean made to openly reject homosexuality.

Dean is re-masculinized by the author by becoming the aggressor. Dean hunts, traps and kills his rapists using cunning and deceit – the author posits that the same 'charms' that made Dean vulnerable to his assailants makes them vulnerable to him. In essence, their sexual desire for Dean is used against them. His first vengeance kill is cast as cold and calculated, with the victim dispatched by three bullets to the head at close quarters. Dean does not display any extremes of emotion here and remains clearly in control. His second kill involves far more in the way of sadistic torture, but with Dean presented as reluctant, or at least repentant.

Together, this refiguring of Dean as more pro-active, aggressive and – at times – merciless, with a clear rejection of homosexuality, serves to recoup his masculinity. Although we must note that even in the final chapter, Dean still does not 'save' himself. That action is reserved for his father, who wreaks vengeance on behalf of his son with an enthusiasm and determination reminiscent of the film *Last House on the Left* and then saves Dean from himself when he and Sam reverse Dean's transformation from vampire to human. Indeed, the author closes this piece with Dean reflecting on his loss of masculinity because of his rapes, confiding in Sam that 'it's going to take some time for me to forgive you … and for me to feel like a man again' (p. 684), before finally breaking down in acknowledgement of his ordeal.

In closing, the author has Dean explicitly 'looking to reclaim his masculinity' (p. 687) by becoming more aggressive and sexually promiscuous with members of the opposite sex. She then explicitly equates the two by stating that 'Dean had finally rediscovered his manhood and his sexual appetite' (p. 687), emphasizing this with an internal monologue where Dean confesses that 'he loved the power he felt when he was inside a woman and when his fist was crashing into another man's face' (p. 689), an equivocation that of course precisely echoes that displayed by Dean's aggressors. For the author, closure is achieved when corporeal-gender equilibrium is restored.

5.4   Conclusion

In the above examples, drawn from a single article of BDSM, non-con slash, we can see recurrent reference to various rape myths for what is assumed to be their explanatory power. This might not indicate advocacy of such myths, but it certainly indicates subscription to them. That such works have been interpreted as subversive or as pro-feminist is more than a little perplexing. To my mind this should provoke consternation rather than commendation.

I would argue that the significance of such work goes beyond the fandom of which it is a part and pervades the very notion of self as an individual and as a citizen. Discursive regularities here go towards providing the guiding rationalities that enable the 'regulation of life' (Mendieta, 2002, p. 6). Celebrating aspects and instances of these regularities as supposedly liberationist or subversive is to be deflected by their nominal target, but we should remember that, as Clover (1987) so astutely observed, a body can be made feminine or masculine by virtue of the gender traits assigned to it. In the example discussed here, Dean has been made feminine – not just, as Clover (1987) would note, by the rapes themselves, as that would be something of a tautological argument, but by the traits and behaviours that he is made to perform. Lest there should be any doubt as to this, we must note that the slasher in question never allows Dean to 'rescue' himself, nor does she allow Dean to actively penetrate others.[52] There are a few instances where Dean receives fellatio, but he is always in some way subdued or restrained and it is made clear by the author that this is something done *to* Dean; whereas when other characters have Dean perform fellatio on them, it is also depicted as an aggressive act done to Dean – referred to numerous times as 'face fucking'.

Irrespective of the myriad of other ways that Dean is feminized, his requiring rescue and being penetrated are what Clover (1987) has called pivotal markers of the 'feminine' gender. As a consequence, there is no subversion here; the character 'Dean' must be read on two levels – superficially this depiction is about male rape, but fundamentally I would argue it reconfigures itself as about female rape. Dean is an effective female substitute, to ignore this and celebrate the recycling and resuscitation of rape myths as resistance is something of a pyrrhic victory. The 'ethics' of the fan here are revealed as remarkably patriarchal at their core.

6
Individuation – Acting on Victimhood

6.1 Normativity in the 'practices' around male rape: the acting and acted upon subject

This chapter will ostensibly address the issue of access to justice, but rather than do so through reference to data indicating need versus official incidence, or reporting versus attrition, I will be seeking to place this discussion steadfastly outside of any appeals to justice or demand per se – knowing only too well how these issues can be the effective undoing of a Foucauldian analysis. Access to justice as a topic has been covered before – comprehensively and passionately – by many of the authors whose work was addressed in Part I. I will be looking instead at concrete and irrefutable examples of discursive regularity, those 'practices of violence' in what Foucault termed 'dispositifs'.[1] For my analysis, this is the dimension in which the male rape victim as a subject acts and is acted upon.

Of particular concern for my analysis is that, despite formal recognition of male rape in law, we continue to see the male rape victim redacted[2] from official research, policy, funding, provision and activism. This illustrates the regime of truth linked to objectifying and subjectifying practices in the realm of sexual violence and victimization that continues to declare that male rape is not real rape, and in doing so contributes to the preservation of the ideal victim construct that 'writes back' for all victims of sexual violence.

Unfortunately, such is the routinization of the 'legislated into existence'[3] approach to the issue of male rape that – as indicated in the introduction – it has achieved the status of a convention. It has become, simply, what we do. Indeed, in work with my own students, be it essays, presentations or dissertations, they – without fail – do the same, and when challenged they tend to speak of 'logic' and 'necessity'; both of which highlight the importance of this area to a Foucauldian. In essence, this approach has become not only what we do, but what we should do. Of course it is precisely for this reason that I decided to adopt a different approach within my triangulation. Thus far I have taken great pains to detach, or at least temporarily derail, this problem from the usual administrative focus. And I have to say, it is with some trepidation and reluctance that I finally address this aspect.

In so doing, however, I am mindful of the following: normativity in practices and technologies, be they conceived of as transactions at the level of individuals or groups, as private citizens or through the authority of official agencies, comprises those behaviours that constitute what Bratich et al. (2003, p. 4) call the 'materiality of discourse' and resonates with the observation by early sociologists Thomas and Thomas (1928, cited in Merton, 1948, p. 193) that situations we define as real become 'real in their consequences'. This is the site of the acting and acted-upon subject, where technologies of the self simultaneously and reciprocally co-constitute the Other. This is the final act of 'deployment'; moreover, it is the very visible and tangible site of deployment – and as such is a core aspect of governmentality.

At this point it is important to note that a focus on individuation and dispositifs is not in itself equivalent to governmentality per se. This is an important distinction, as many governmentality studies limit themselves to just this aspect of the triangulation, precisely because it is so very concrete and therefore 'graspable'. But to do so is to be deflected from the myriad of other circulations of power throughout the social body that I have raised in previous chapters. The visible, the substantive – dare I say – the obvious, is not all there is. Hence, I have addressed this latterly, in order to foreground the more neglected aspects of the triangulation.

So, here we have a chapter – the final aspect of the triangulation – that might be received as the supposed end to this 'process', which contrariwise thus far reads like a beginning. But in reality, of course, it is neither. The triangulation, after all, is determinedly non-linear – despite limitations in its form as presented here. Thus, this chapter, which may otherwise read as the final flourish that demonstrates that what has been examined over the course of this monograph really does have concrete significance in the social realm, must instead be approached with rather more caution than that plea to 'justice' might appeal. However tempting this might be, to read it as such invariably invites oppositional polemics between those who accept the data, and the 'reality' implied from this, versus those who do not. It posits this debate once more as within the administrative realm and invites simplistic 'quick-fix' solutions. This is not my aim. Rather, I am concerned simply to continue tracking those constancies and inconstancies, the regularities and contradictions, looking for consensus and concordance. My interest in the construction of the subject in this sense is to use his conditions of materialization to critique the 'victim industries'[4] that contribute to his creation – as knowing and known – and thus invite a circular reading[5] of the triangulation chapters, with clear imbrications expected from the reader, and simple delineations confounded. This is a direct attempt to prevent a simplistic cause–effect conclusion being drawn.

6.2 A focus on policy and provision: redaction and governmentality

In this section I will examine the technologies around male rape, from the specific intellectual or 'expert' invested and trapped within the 'victim industry', to the normalized 'self', whose experience is detached and understood through the myopia of the 'normal'. Two specific aspects will be addressed: that legislative recognition of male-on-male rape has yet to make a significant difference to the 'experts'; and that the 'experts' continue to produce the data that justifies precisely that lack of change. Of most concern for me is that almost two decades since male rape was formally included in statute, it is still largely omitted from policy and provision. Moreover, even where tacit recognition is ostensibly made, the male rape victim is often quickly redacted in subsequent policy, pronouncement, discussion and provision. It is this effective sleight of hand that underscores the continued resistance to take male rape seriously.

Not a simple matter of omission or exclusion then, rather it is a process of gradual redaction, indicative of the subjugation of knowledge. This results in the formal recognition and protection accorded to male rape victims, as enshrined in law, being subsequently marginalized in policy and provision. Although I recognize problems in the current legal definition of rape, in this instance my interest is not in how to create a better law; quite frankly, I think that rather futile, given that in this instance it is how the law is enacted that is problematic.

It is my contention that this process of redaction might be better understood as representing a shift towards discursive equilibrium in line with the regularity in constructions of male rape across the various levels and aspects of the triangulation. A focus on formal rights, justice and due process, therefore, is doomed to fail whilst the predominant construct of male rape remains configured within the ideal victim binary. Consequently, rather than perceiving poor access to justice as being indicative of the failure to achieve equality for male rape victims, we should instead seek to understand this as indicative of the success of governmentality in this instance.

This chapter will include case studies of three concrete examples to illustrate this phenomenon – the erasure of the male – at work: in the first instance, I will examine the development of the legislative construct of 'rape', this will include the 1994 Criminal Justice and Public Order Act and the 2003 Sexual Offences Act; secondly, I will look at resultant policy arising from this – the most significant of which in the current landscape is the 2010 Stern Review – subsequent interpretations and responses to this will also be examined. Finally, the resultant provision will be scrutinized, with an explicit focus on voluntary, as opposed to statutory, agencies and Rape Crisis provision will be highlighted.[6]

In the first section, the inclusion of male rape in law will be critically considered. I will conclude that the legal construct of rape has yet to become fully gender neutral, but that recognition of sorts has been achieved. In the second section the impact of the legislative construct on policy will be considered – the Stern Review (2010) will be taken as a case in point. It will be noted that this review did include the male rape victim, asserting the need to make efforts to include the male within policy, research and provision precisely because of current elision, but that he was nevertheless marginalized in the review as a whole. What is most interesting is that agencies that were compelled to note the review's findings failed to do so – in official government responses to Stern (2010) and the subsequent voluntary sector reports, the comments originally made about male rape were omitted. It follows that provision for the male in the voluntary sector (as directed and funded by government) is slim. Despite receiving public funding from the Ministry of Justice to provide support services to victims of sexual violence, Rape Crisis – the largest such agency in the UK (and indeed with a significant international presence), provides no routine provision for men. The provision of services to men by this organization will be considered in depth. Ireland will be noted as an exemplar of good practice and contrasted with provision in mainland Britain (England, Wales and Scotland), which is patchy at best.

It will be concluded that, despite being enshrined in law and given specific rights within policy, victims of male rape are denied recognition and provision by agencies 'on the ground'. Thus, irrespective of statutory recognition and protections the male is still excluded from these 'gate-keeping' victimology/victimization industries.[7] This contributes to their continued invisibility, which is disingenuously reconfigured as evidence for a lack of demand and is then cited to support their continued exclusion. This is the folly of 'intelligence' and 'evidence', and is where managerialism becomes governmentality.

6.3 All victims are not equal: the phenomenon of the invisibilized man

In this chapter I will show that male rape is readily invisibilized: moving from being given absolute recognition, rights and protections in statute, to tacit inclusion and marginalization in government reports, which is further weakened by outright redaction in voluntary agencies' interpretations of the same and exclusion in their subsequent enactment of such in provision and practice.

Law – now you see them ...

Discussion of the legal forms relating to rape often begin with section 142 (2) of the 1994 Criminal Justice and Public Order Act[8] which amended section 1 of the 1956 Sexual Offences Act to effectively extend the definition of rape by recognizing anal rape, where previously this had been classified merely as non-consensual buggery (buggery being a lesser offence that carried a lower penalty than vaginal rape). The next significant change to the law is contained within section 1 of the 2003 Sexual Offences Act, which includes penile penetration of the mouth as rape and effectively gives express recognition to transgender populations by recognising gender re-assignment surgery (male–female). Often overlooked in the same discussions is that the 2003 Act also creates the new offence (in section 2) of Assault by Penetration, which covers penetration by objects/appendages other than a penis.[9]

These changes are indeed significant – the first amendment renders the victim gender neutral, the second de-privileges genitalia as the site of assault and recognizes gender rather than sex – but the new offence of Assault by Penetration, whilst indeed an improvement to the old offence of Indecent Assault, is by no means wholly satisfactory and, in fact, goes some way to illustrating the enduring problem with rape legislation – that the legislation is far from gender neutral (despite claims to the contrary) as the offender is still very much gendered. To satisfy the offence of rape the assault must be one of penile penetration – no other appendage or indeed object suffices to qualify as 'rape', as the use of such becomes merely assault by penetration. I would argue that privileging the penis (even where it is 'reconstructed' through surgery in female–male transgender populations) does a disservice to male and female survivors. Considering that the use of objects is a common component to sexual violence, why then demean it in legal recourse? I would suggest this is more about a refusal to accept females as assailants.

Interestingly, in her section on developments in rape law, Abdullah-Khan (2008) laudably recognizes the potential for women to be rapists,[10] but the manner in which she does so is rather odd. She cites a case that might be better regarded as 'incitement' to rape or 'aiding and abetting' rape, as there is no physical contact, let alone penetration, by the female assailant indicated in her example. I take her point, but can't help but wonder why she did not use more explicit examples of, for instance, women achieving intercourse without consent through coercion, duress and incapacitation of their male victim; or of women performing non-consensual penetrative acts on males. They do exist.[11] As a consequence, I regard this rather impoverished example as reflecting her internalizing of the feminist, gendered, model of rape.

Women as sexual predators encompass more than just child abuse or molestation. Unfortunately, much of our 'understanding' is restricted two-fold: not only in respect of penile penetration being necessary, but that it is something which is done to a victim. These aspects necessarily mean that we omit female sexual predators from the criteria necessary for rape; we also omit them from serious sexual assault unless they have used an object or an appendage. Thus, where a female successfully engages in full intercourse against the will of her male victim, this is not rape (because the penetration is received by the assailant, and we do not and cannot recognize that under either rape or the most serious form of sexual assault, as this is assault by penetration). Likewise, where a female engages in sexual penetration – using an object or an appendage – this is not rape (it is demoted to serious sexual assault).

As recognition of female perpetrators of domestic violence in heterosexual populations gains credence and recognition,[12] more examples of women as aggressors in sexual violence will doubtless be uncovered. Until then, I'm left wondering why we have yet to make the connection that coerced sexual congress – entailing penetration of the anus or vagina of either party with any body part or object – full stop, is a serious sexual assault, deserving of recognition as rape. Given that such sexual assaults are commonly regarded as a key component of abusive relationships – irrespective of the gender of the assailant or indeed the victim – it seems to me that it takes a concerted effort to continue with the omission of female assailants from the crime of rape.

I understand the arguments commonly invoked against extending the definition of rape to be fully gender-neutral,[13] but I find these unconvincing. Without fail, these draw on the self-same constructs of gender, history and systematizations derived from patriarchy that are already popularly problematized – ironically by the very groups who had strived to defend precisely the continued exclusion of men as victims of rape and continue to prevent recognition of women as rapists. Often the core argument seems to fall back onto the tautology that rape is a gendered crime, therefore we need to retain it as gendered. I do not dispute that women are targets of rape, but like Scarce (1997) and McMullen (1990) I do dispute that they are the only victims; furthermore, I also dispute that only men are the aggressors.[14]

Nevertheless, recognition for victims of male-on-male rape is now on statute and, as such, statutory agencies must enable access to justice. This much is indisputable. However, the landscape of the criminal justice system is not just one of the law and state agents,[15] such as the police, Crown Prosecution Service or courts. The voluntary sector also plays a significant role in constructing, interpreting and implementing policy. Furthermore, it plays a significant role in raising awareness, lobbying for change and delivering certain provision. In this latter role the sector becomes an adjunct to and gatekeeper for the criminal justice system;[16] this is particularly important. It is to a consideration of the male rape victim in policy, and thereafter within a key provider of post-rape support services, Rape Crisis, that I now turn.

Policy – smoke and mirrors ...

Policy and law-making do not occur in a socio-political vacuum. They are very much a product of perceived 'need' and 'public interest'; neither of which are unproblematic. Neither 'need' nor 'interest' can be regarded as self-evident, although – and this is precisely the problem – they often are. Thus, just as we can see moral panics leaving their institutionalized 'trace', a plethora of activity that produces substantive forms penetrating the fabric of civil society; we should also recognize that subjugated knowledges, their marker being incredulity rather than fear, instead result in grudging acknowledgement, tacit assimilation and stymieing. As Ivison (1998, p. 144) states, the 'law operates increasingly as a norm rather than a sword in liberal jurisprudence', thus, legislative reform is not and cannot be a magic bullet. Policy is intimately related to law, but need not be one and the same. Indeed, law, policy and provision together are what determine the criminal justice landscape.

Case study: the Stern Review

The Stern Review (2010) was commissioned by the Government Equalities Office and the Home Office. It is an independent review, led by Baroness Stern, charged with investigating the treatment of rape complaints by public authorities, specifically to look at the response of public authorities to those reporting rape. The key finding of this report is that 'the policies are not the problem. The failures are in the implementation' (p. 8). I concur: however, the report lays clear responsibility for what it terms 'patchy provision' solely at the door of state agencies, and of voluntary agencies notes only that 'whilst treatment of victims has improved considerably, we heard of areas where victims' organizations struggle to have their concerns heard' (p. 8), thus appearing to regard victims' organizations as above reproach – this is naive, and I would argue that this is an assessment that can only be made if one excludes provision for male victims from the review itself.

The report's assessment of voluntary agencies' provision (that is wholly without recourse to any research or review) is very revealing in this regard, being entirely and overwhelmingly positive. In particular, Rape Crisis is singled out for commendation – they are seen as central to the way forward for access to justice for rape victims in the future:

> We are fortunate in this country that since the 1970s we have had Rape Crisis Centres which have provided support and counselling. These were originally for women only, but *some* now also help men. Their dedicated work over many years to raise awareness of sexual violence *against women* has led to many of the improvements that we have described in this report. They provide a safe place where victims can go to be supported, listened to and get counselling. (p. 102, italics added)

Men are included here almost as an afterthought, and it is recognized that provision for men is not the norm. Surely this begs the question: if it is recognized that only some Rape Crisis Centres help male victims of rape, how can they be celebrated as acting for or serving all victims? Some is clearly not all. Exclusion by gender is a barrier to accessing justice and should be inexcusable – predicated as it is on prejudice and discrimination; essentially reinforcing, legitimating and reifying those myths that the Stern Review has supposedly set out to problematize. Why then does this not attract any opprobrium? I would argue that this reveals the implicit gendering of rape as female and the male victim as anomalous – which is utterly indefensible.

This review posits voluntary agencies as key to an effective multi-agency approach, and I would agree. However, I find it enormously problematic that a greater role for them is asserted without any scrutiny of their present adequacy to deliver on equality. So far as Stern (2010) is concerned, the way forward merely involves assimilating more of these organizations into the mainstream criminal justice system and giving them a greater role in service provision. Apparently there is no need for these organizations' current practice to change. This is wholly problematic and in actuality would function counter to her express aim of achieving justice for all and, even more damning, appears to give tacit approval for such discriminatory exclusions to continue.

In my review of policy statements, interpretations and provision by the voluntary sector, with the male rape victim at the forefront of my mind, I have found core voluntary agencies to be key to exclusion along gendered lines. This is not to say that statutory agencies are above reproach, but as problems with them are well documented, my concern is to shift the focus. Resolving problems within statutory agencies is important, but unless we embed recognition and provision for male victims within the voluntary sector we have little hope of affecting change that will benefit all victims. We must stop idealizing the voluntary sector, as in its present form it is a site of exclusion and discrimination for male victims of rape and sexual assault.

Stern (2010) investigates current provision as gender blind, however, this 'blindness' does not operate in the interests of neutrality or inclusivity, precisely the opposite in fact. This is plausibly because the review falls back onto the construct of rape as gendered. A close reading of the text in the document will be performed to illustrate this.

From the start the document makes a concerted effort to be inclusive – 'This report should make clear what anyone who has decided to report a rape, whether a man or a woman, can expect from a public authority' (p. 4) – unfortunately, prior to this clear expression of inclusivity the foreword has already cited only cases regarding female victims, research that highlights solely females and government initiatives that likewise focus on the female. Thus, a feminized bias is already perceptible.

In the Executive Summary, it is stated that 'Women, men, children, and people of all ages and all social groups can become rape victims' (p. 7). Consequently, the term 'victim' appears gender neutral, however, this is not actually the case given that asides are later made to men as victims and to the male experience, the necessity of which reveals that supposed neutrality as intrinsically gendered female. For example, after a lengthy passage detailing 'what we have learnt about rape' in which gender is not mentioned, it is then stated that:

> around eight per cent of recorded rape cases are rape of a man. Men find it very difficult to talk about what has happened to them because of the common view that a man should be able to fight off an attacker. Male victims 'find it less easy to identify as victims and ask for help'. (p. 12)[17]

This leads one to reconfigure that previous neutrality as inherently gendered.

This technique of elision, whereby apparent neutrality is in reality fundamentally gendered, is repeated throughout the document and is strikingly similar to techniques evident in the media. 'Gender not specified' is most certainly not the same as 'gender neutral', thus indicating subscription to rape as gendered female – despite the legislative neutrality that should guide and bind a formal review.

Even where the analysis appears neutral and should be neutral, it becomes gendered:

> a number of polls, conducted by various bodies, give a flavour of the range of views and the balance of public opinion. They tend to show that the majority of people have a view of who is to blame for rape that is in line with the definition of rape found in the law, and this is good news. However, the polls also show us that a substantial minority hold *women* partially responsible for the crime'. (p. 50, italics added)

This denotation of the female is compounded by 'box 5' which details facts and statistics in regard to blame that are solely female centric (two) and gender not specified (three) – where the latter, of course, has been previously established as implicitly gendered. Thus, male victims are excluded from this analysis.

This understanding of rape as feminized is persistent and stubborn. Under the sub-heading 'rape is controversial' it is stated that:

> Strong opinions are held and often voiced about rape ... This should be no surprise since rape is about sex, violence, power, intimate

relationships between men and women or between men and men, society's attitudes to what is acceptable behaviour and where blame and responsibility lie for non-consensual sex acts. Many people feel that the way rape is discussed and dealt with reflects unacceptable attitudes towards *women*. (p. 12, italics added)

This is an interesting passage – note the subtle shift here from inclusion to exclusion: male-on-male victimization is included, but the final note clearly genders the issue as female in asserting 'towards women'.

Other omissions can also be noted, for example, having stated non-consensual sex acts rather than rape per se, the scope could be broadened to include female-on-female and female-on-male (as per the offence of serious sexual assault), but it is not. This can be taken to indicate the prescriptive function of the feminist model of rape: those latter permutations of sexual victimization are simply inconceivable for many operating with this model in mind.

Frequently, this report has the rather unfortunate tendency to recycle rape myths, even whilst overtly disavowing them. This is achieved through a consistent trend to relate rape myths to women and female examples, with the exclusion of men; indicating either that these myths do not apply to them – which is simply erroneous – or that they are in some way less problematic when they are – which is indefensible. For example:

There is a view that women are in some way to blame for being raped if they go out wearing revealing clothes and have too much to drink. Some complain of the tendency to lecture women on what they should and should not do rather than making it clear to men that sex without consent is rape. (p. 12)

Rather than being the myth-busting assertion it is intended to be, by orienting this as a problem of men against women this paragraph is key to perpetuating the biggest myth of all – that this doesn't affect men as victims. Yet, the notion of precipitation that underlies this myth is a rationale applied equally to men – irrespective of sexuality – and arises in various forms, as may be readily discerned from the previous triangulation chapters.

This can be seen again in a section about raising awareness, where it is stated that campaigns to educate women on personal safety 'should be matched with an equal, if not greater, effort to educate men about rape myths and their responsibility to ensure consent' (p. 53). These are certainly valid points, but they would have more impact had male victims been included. As it stands, this once again configures the rape victim as female, configures the assailant as male and does not challenge the precautionary principle underlying the notion that women should 'keep themselves safe', nor that assailants are motivated by sexual desire and thus should 'ensure consent'. As a consequence, this passage actually re-validates myths around the feminization of rape, victim precipitation and rape as sex – all of which could have been disrupted through the simple inclusion of male victims.

The myth of the 'weak' victim is also revalidated. Time and again attention is drawn to 'vulnerable victims' – I have a particular problem with this comprising part of our conventional understanding of rape, as vulnerability often has little to do with this crime. The notion of vulnerability as femininity, or at least as antithetical to masculinity, is a pervasive and entrenched myth that is a significant barrier for the recognition of male rape, and indeed of female victims who do not readily meet the 'feminine' stereotype. As was demonstrated in the previous chapters, in this sense 'vulnerability' becomes a core component of the ideal victim construct and is, therefore, a pernicious barrier to justice for all. It is ironic then, that this is so readily included in this report in the supposed interests of facilitating access.

Another myth which is revitalized in its rejection is the victim as liar – in rebutting this, the authors gender their discussion around women, but there are no grounds to intimate that male victims are not likewise impacted by incredulity arising from the suspicion of false allegations. As illustrated in the previous chapter, myths relating to victims as liars are readily applied to males and, as a consequence, this pronouncement reflects a careless slip into rape as gendered. This fails to give due consideration to the male victim population and in doing so could be regarded as giving tacit approval to the application of this myth to men – at the very least it enables the rationale that to regard women as liars is unacceptable, whilst to regard men as liars is not.

Talking about vulnerable victims in more detail – and still not including men – explicit attention is drawn to gang culture, and yet the report configures this as associated solely with female victims. The omission of men is significant here in particular, given that gang culture is one of the few areas where academic study has most readily accepted male victims.[18] This particular instance of gendering reveals precisely how robust that underlying notion of female victimhood really is.

Male victims are eventually included, but as a separate issue, and once again in the rejection of a myth, it is actually legitimized – the only myth detailed for men is in reference to prison rape and homosexual communities. By including men in this manner the subtle message is that they are marginal to the real issue of female victimhood and that they are in some way an anomaly. The reader is surely led to ask why, if rape of men does not occur solely within these populations, are other example not included? Thus, by choosing to refer to men only in respect of these populations, the discussion of male rape is oriented to precisely that which is criticized.

Accordingly, an important omission for prison and same-sex relationships must also be noted: reference to sexual violence by women on women in those communities. This reveals a value based assumption, rather than the empirical approach claimed, as women within those populations are most certainly not free from sexual violence by other women.[19] Once again the choices here reveal the delimited field of enquiry and understanding.

The implicit gendering of this piece is most readily revealed in the section 'is the law understood', where it states: 'It is important that the 2003 law is understood. It says that one person having sex with another when that person has not agreed to it is rape' (p. 13) but in actuality this statement is simply not an accurate interpretation. The legislation is clear – penetration by a *penis* must be *done to* the victim – thus precluding the interpretation of female-on-female and female-on-male sexual assaults as rape. It is (unfortunately to my mind) not as inclusive as 'sex without consent'. That the authors assume so simply reveals the subtle yet rigid demarcation of this issue – not that they assume that it does include those populations, but rather that they cannot conceive of them as being included in the first place. Once again the feminist model is in effect here.

As well as subtly gendering statute, there is also gendering of case law evident in the report. Where citing from Court of Appeal rulings relating to cases with female victims, which as a consequence have female gender pronouns, these remain in their replication in the report. These pronouncements clearly should have been paraphrased in this report to make them unwaveringly gender neutral – this very simple action would have remedied any gender exclusion. I find it quite telling that this was not deemed necessary.

The various examples detailed above are not exceptions; there are numerous other instances of apparent neutrality that is then revealed as implicitly gendered either through asides regarding men (though these are infrequent) or examples – case studies, quotes, statistics, etc. – detailing only women. Despite pretensions to be inclusive, recognition of male rape in this report is infrequent, marginal and peripheral at best. Given that this document marks the way forward for the Ministry of Justice's implementation of rape policy from this point on, we can safely assume that male rape victims in England and Wales will continue to be sidelined.

Provision – now you don't ...

If the *Interim Government Response to the Stern Review*[20] (Home Office, 2010), published by the Government Equalities Office, is anything to go by, continued redaction of the male victim from the anti-rape agenda is assured. Their opening paragraph commences with the assertion that 'Violence against women and girls in all its forms, and whatever the circumstances, is unacceptable' (p. 1), citing statistics that solely relate to females 'Around 10,000 women are sexually assaulted and 2,000 women raped every week, and over a third of all rapes recorded by police are committed against children under the age of 16. Over three million women in England' (p. 2). Men are eventually mentioned, in passing: 'Men can also be victims of rape – the most recent Home Office statistics (for 08/09) show that around seven per cent of all recorded rape cases concern a rape of a man' (p. 10); males are mentioned only once more: 'While rape is overwhelmingly perpetrated against women and girls, Baroness Stern also draws out important messages about services and support for male victims' (p. 28). The remainder of this response is wholly gendered as female, and where apparently neutral, it is readily reconfigured as female via subsequent examples and pronouncements. In this instance, however, perhaps we should note that the task force in question is merely continuing with the precedent for acceptable priorities and elisions established by Stern (2010).

In terms of immediate policy, the IGR (Home Office, 2010, p. 15) states that they intend to undertake 'Publicity campaigns challenging drunken behaviour, warning people of the risks of excessive alcohol intake and supporting responsible choices also have a role to play in preventing sexual violence'. So far, so neutral – or so it seems; unfortunately they go on to state that the plethora of activity will be solely focussed around women as victims. Planned media campaigns, new guidance for journalists, resources through the National Health Service and materials for the National Curriculum are all, without fail, oriented towards female victimhood – awareness raising, therefore, expressly excludes male victims of rape. This continues in the realm of service provision, where they state that 'when *women and girls* suffer sexual violence it is essential they have access to help and support that meets their needs' (p. 17, italics added). Even in terms of attrition, risk management and protecting the public, the onus once again is on females:

> Government priorities in this important area are to: provide end-to-end support for all victims through the criminal justice system, from report to court; bring more offenders to justice by improving reporting and conviction rates; and rehabilitate offenders and manage the risk they present to *women and girls'* (p. 21, italics added)

Not only are male victims of sexual violence not considered a priority, in a manner similar to Stern (2010), here male victims fail to be considered at all.

Given the wholesale exclusion of male victims from this response, voluntary groups providing services for male victims of rape might well suspect that male victims are not included within government agendas or state funding. Unfortunately, as the Stern Review (2010) has been absorbed within the government's *Violence Against Women and Girls* strategy (for which there is no corresponding strategy concerning violence against men and/or boys), I imagine this eventuality to be rather inevitable. It can be readily noted that statutory recognition of male victims of rape and sexual assault does not readily translate into public sector priority.

One might hope that the voluntary sector is rather more egalitarian than this. Stern (2010) singles out Rape Crisis[21] as a paragon of support provision for victims of rape, and it is – so long as the victim is female. There is rather less provision for male victims. In England, Wales, Scotland and the European Union, exclusion of men is the norm. The exception to this is Ireland, which is exemplary in its gender neutrality. But for England and Wales – the regions where the impact of Stern's (2010) recommendations are felt – RC provision is marred by the active exclusion of male victims. This will have serious repercussions for this victim group should RC be given more power without any onus on them to achieve equality in provision. In the next section I will illustrate RC's discrimination and exclusion by gender in two forms: an analysis of their written response to Stern (2010) and a detailed examination of RC provision across the UK.

Rape crisis: response to Stern (2010)

As a specialist organization dedicated to raising awareness and fighting injustice for victims of rape, RC's response to Stern (2010) should remedy the partisan and exclusionary failings of Stern (2010) and the IGR (Home Office, 2010). After all, RC is not just the frontline in terms of delivery; it also plays a key role in the multi-agency approach and is at the forefront of policy development and intelligence gathering in this area. At the very least, RC should be able to include the male victim of sexual violence simply because their own experience of service provision reveals a need to do so. Unfortunately, this is not the case. RC's response, published as a press release on their website,[22] instead represents the epitome of redaction. Indeed, it is here that the male victim of sexual violence is eliminated entirely. Given their significant role in service provision to victims of rape and sexual violence, the enhanced role that Stern (2010) envisages for them in the future and their significant ongoing funding from the public purse, omission of a victim group on the basis of gender is utterly indefensible; yet despite it being glaringly evident, there is a wholesale reluctance to problematize this.[23]

In common with other pronouncements, their statement starts in a seemingly neutral fashion, which is not sustained, and the gendered construct of the rape victim as female is readily revealed: 'in order to respond holistically to the complex range of support and advocacy *women and girls* need after experiencing sexual violence' (p. 1, italics added). They go on to state that '*Women's* negative experiences of the criminal justice system are sadly a common reality' (p. 1, italics added) and that '*women* still face a postcode lottery when they try to access support' (p. 1, italics added). All of which may well be true, but these situations are not ones that are faced exclusively by female victims of sexual violence – a reality of which RC should be well aware.

As a consequence, their assertion that 'the recommendations within the Stern Review should be added to the overhaul required to address significant change needed to ensure uniformity of response nationwide for all victims' (p. 1) sounds incredibly hollow. Male victims are not mentioned at all in this initial response to the Stern review. So far as this statement is concerned, the agenda for RC centres is wholly female-centric. It is as if the legislative change never happened, and as if the asides from Baroness Stern and the tokenistic inclusion of the IGR simply passed them by. To say that provision for male victims is not a priority for RC is a considerable understatement. That RC in particular is invited to play an increasingly significant role in provision of services and policy development must be an excruciating prospect for anyone concerned with male victims of this crime.

I do not intend to undermine or belittle the role that RC has played in successfully putting rape on the criminal justice and public agenda.

I simply raise concern that they have failed to adapt their 'mission' to include male victims of rape and sexual violence.[24] As the single largest third sector provider of such support in the UK[25] their continued failure to assimilate male victims into their remit produces – intentionally or not – a significant barrier to justice. This is somewhat ironic considering that the core aim of RC is precisely to enable justice for 'all victims' of rape. Their assertion can only be considered to have any integrity at all if the construct of the victim is implicitly and fundamentally understood as gendered female.

Of course, it could be the case that service delivery is not compromised by gender – perhaps the response has no concrete impact and is a simple error that does not truly reflect RC as an organization. With this in mind, I duly sought to ascertain precisely what level of inclusion RC achieves. Unfortunately my findings in this regard do not exonerate RC from the charge of excluding male victims – quite the opposite in fact.

For RC agencies on the ground, not all victims are equal. Female victims are provided for by all RC centres, male victims by very few indeed. It is a damning indictment of this charity that male victims in some regions of the UK have zero access to support outside of statutory agencies. Given that statutory agencies depend on the voluntary sector to effectively 'prop up' and supplement their provision, it is perfectly feasible that some male victims will have only a modicum of support available to them – if any – in stark contrast with female victims in the same locale. This puts RC centre stage in creating the very 'postcode lottery' for male victims that they so vocally decry for females.

It is accepted that such voluntary organizations, like RC, will deal with far more victims than will ever make a formal report. The discrepancy here between official statistics and data gathered by the voluntary sector becomes part of the dark figure in relation to rape and sexual violence, and it is the case that organizations like RC have been instrumental in using this data as part of the overall picture of 'attrition' in rape, drawing attention to rape as a serious and common crime worthy of greater provision than official statistics would otherwise support. But, of course, this contribution only holds true where 'rape' is gendered female.

For my part, I am concerned that the continued exclusion of males by organizations such as RC has precisely the opposite effect – producing limited data, or rather inhibiting data collection, which thereby justifies male rape as of small significance and low priority. Rather than helping to shine light on the dark figure of male rape, RC instead exacerbates the darkness.

Rape crisis: addressing the postcode lottery?

RC has been instrumental in calling attention to what they call the 'postcode lottery' that victims of rape and sexual assault face when trying to access support services in the UK. They have taken a leading role in attempting to redress this, and have made great strides. However, to date their efforts have been largely focussed on widening access for women and girls, not for male victims. As a consequence, RC as a movement and a provider might now have the very same accusation levelled against them. In this section I will examine the regional disparity created by RC for male victims.[26]

Looking first at RC England and Wales, using the 'find a rape crisis centre near you' interactive map[27] I attempted to ascertain what provision was made for male victims of rape and sexual violence by region. It is important to note that this map is intended to be one of the first points of contact for prospective clients – i.e. victims. Failure to be accessible at this stage could mean victims progress no further in seeking support. This is of staggering significance once one takes into account that research has indicated many victims of rape and sexual assault contact agencies other than the police in the first instance. These agencies then play a pivotal role in intelligence gathering and, crucially, in helping to refer cases on to the police they are also performing a 'gate-keeping' function in respect of access to justice.

Of most concern to me is that one may readily note areas with zero provision for male victims of rape and sexual assault. Male victims attempting to locate support services via RC in the North East, South West or London, will find that there is no such support available to them.[28] To male victims in these regions, Stern's (2010) wholehearted commendation of this organization would be antithetical to their own experiences. Victims in the remaining regions: North West, Yorkshire and Humber, East Midlands, West Midlands, Wales, East of England and the South East, will find only limited availability of support, that provision made is different for males in comparison with females and, furthermore, that support is frequently far more restricted and impoverished than for females. In the North West, five providers are listed,[29] only two of which make provision for male victims;[30] in the Yorkshire and Humber region, six providers are listed,[31] but only two include men;[32] in the East Midlands five providers are listed[33], only two of which include men;[34] in the West Midlands three providers[35] are listed, only one of which includes men;[36] the East of England has the most providers listed – a total of seven,[37] but only two of these include men;[38] in the South East six providers are listed,[39] only one of which includes men.[40] The only region with 100 per cent provision is Wales, but this is rather less impressive than it sounds given that Wales is massively under-represented by RC – with only one centre in existence.[41]

Of those regions found to provide no support to male victims, one might expect to see at the very least that male victims are acknowledged by individual centres and some measure of referral is offered – be that in the form of contact details or links posted to specialist organizations such as Mankind[42] or to umbrella organizations such as the Survivors Trust[43], or by simply detailing the UK's national helpline number.[44] Unfortunately, in each of the regions with nil provision for men – the North East, London and the South West – even these simple measures are not undertaken. Male victims in these regions are not just neglected by RC, they are denied and abandoned.

Areas with limited provision have some interesting trends in their manner of inclusion. It is often the case that those centres that do cater for men make different provision for them, either in respect of segregating services or in limiting services. Some centres cater for males, but only young males up to the age of 19; some centres recognize male victims but provide referral services only; some centres provide support to males but then undermine this and marginalize men through mission statements or logos that depict only women; whilst some centres superficially appear to recognize males but in actuality only do so as supporters of survivors, not survivors themselves. Thus, even where 'recognized', support and services for male victims of rape and sexual violence is limited at best. These findings will be discussed in more depth below.

Different provision, in itself, may seem of little significance – and certainly if this merely resulted in gender specific appointment times or sites that would be the case. However, it can be seen that RC does not just make different provision, but less provision. Given that the vast majority of centres do not deal with males at all, to have those that do accord less priority to men sends a clear, if unintended, message to that victim group. For example, RASASC[45] state that 'Male clients have specific time slots in our main building and we use a women only centre for counselling and ISVA support in Halton'. At first glance this might appear of little impact, but in actuality this is significant as clearly drop-in is precluded for men in this instance; the NRICC[46] states that 'appointment times are staggered to provide women only space', which is perfectly reasonable but the priority implied here is inexcusable. Savana[47] reiterates this implied priority with its statement that they make 'Women only provision in separate unit'. Contrast these with the KRASACC[48] which clearly states that 'There are separate space and times for men and women', thereby achieving what the others intend, but without the overt gender priority and with no explicit limitations to support services – a far more equitable pronouncement that cannot be interpreted as indicating barriers to inclusivity.

Some centres expressly exclude adult male victims, despite including young males and children. For example, CARA[49] states that they provide 'support, information and counselling for children, young people of both genders and adult women who have experienced sexual violence, either directly or indirectly, in the recent past or historically'. They then go on to clarify 'Service also for young men *up to the age of 19.* Young men seen at different times', so we can discern from this that adult males are excluded. This differentiation is a little perturbing – why should it be the case that, for example, a woman recalling a historic case of sexual abuse or a recent experience of the same is free to seek counselling without restriction, but a male can only do so up to the age of 19? Whether intentional or not, this appears to support several problematic notions such as the gendered hierarchy of victimhood, that adult males are not worthy victims whilst concomitantly reinforcing the notion that weakness – indicated in the focus on male children – does. This centre redeems itself somewhat by providing a referral service (see below), but once again the gendered priority communicated here is clear.

Several centres that recognize male victims do so only through the provision of referral to other agencies. CARA states: 'At present we do not work with male survivors but their calls will be treated sympathetically and we can provide details of other agencies that can help'; SERICC[50] do the same. Unfortunately, even those centres that provide this modicum of support succeed in actively excluding through their profiles, for example, AVRC[51] genders their blurb as female in its entirety, despite going on to state that 'Men can be given initial support by phone and email.' The WRC states clearly in their profile that they deal solely with women and girls, compounding this by stating 'Confidential support to women who have suffered sexual abuse or rape at any time in their life', but they do then state that they provide telephone counselling to men – 'We will also listen to male survivors' – but unfortunately this appears almost as an afterthought. These techniques of inclusion seem begrudging at best, and certainly lack clarity – in itself this is significant as a lack of clarity in these centres' profiles could well preclude males from utilizing these valuable services.

Where services are provided, males are also excluded or marginalized through a similar lack of clarity in the textual profiles, for example,

CRASAC[52] state that they deal with women and girls only, but then go on to say: 'We provide a telephone support line and ISVA service for Women and girls, Men and boys'. This is also the case in the use of logos and slogans that gender rape as a female experience, for example, Savana includes male victims but readily undermine this by their corporate slogan that states 'women growing stronger'. A lack of clarity at this stage could lead men to overlook the services these centres provide, which leads one to wonder just how committed to providing them these groups are.

Unfortunately, some centres do not provide even a modicum of recognition for male victims, instead according males legitimacy solely as supporters of female survivors. Oxford[53] states: 'we provide help and support for those supporting a survivor (the caller can be male or female)', but they do not cater – at all, not even in referral – for male survivors. For them, the only legitimacy a male can have in the dynamic of rape is as offender or partner to a female victim. I initially misread this; having focused solely on 'the caller can be male or female' I assumed that the provision of telephone counselling was inclusive. Were a male survivor to make the same error I imagine this would be nothing short of devastating.

Others state that they recognize male victims but then go on to relegate males to support roles; for example, MRC[54] does recognize male victims, but in its main blurb excludes them as victims by stating that their telephone helpline is for women survivors only, going on to clarify that 'we also provide information for those supporting survivors including male relatives and friends'. Evidently their provision is not truly equitable, and males are only recognized in supporting roles in this instance.

From this examination, it seems that exclusion of male victims from RC centres in England and Wales is the norm rather than the exception. Where support is offered it is often less than that to which a female victim is entitled. Furthermore, there is frequently a lack of clarity for males that might lead them to exclude themselves when support can be accessed, or to attempt to access support when it is not provided. The present state of affairs satisfies and measure of 'patchy'.

It might be hoped that RC are working to remedy this, after all as a charitable organization with limited – indeed declining – funding, they cannot be expected to make adaptations to existing centres across the board, as to do so could result in limiting provision for all because of budgetary constraints. However, whilst that might be a reasonable supposition by which to attempt to defend existing centres, new centres are a different matter entirely. In this vein, SARSVL[55] is interesting to examine: 'SARSVL is a brand new Rape Crisis centre offering services in LS1 – LS29; WF3; WF10; BD3; BD11 areas. From 7th April 2010'. Indeed, it is the only new centre flagged on the website. As such they carry a particular responsibility to overcome present limitations within existing service providers; to fail to do so would unequivocally reveal that RC has no commitment to male inclusion – after all it is easier and cheaper to include males from the outset rather than adapt provision at a later stage.

It is disappointing then that SARSVL is actually one of the worst offenders at this time – with neither provision nor recognition for male victims; only female victims are recognized and included. Whilst it might be reasoned that making changes to existing centres to enable the inclusion of male victims would be precluded by organizations largely dependent on public and charitable funding, such an excuse certainly does not hold for a new centre, where male victims should have been included from the initial planning stage – I find this simply deplorable.

It can be readily ascertained from the RC England and Wales site that male victims have yet to achieve recognition at all in some areas, let alone anything nearing equality of provision – this constitutes a significant barrier for male victims in accessing support and justice and certainly does not facilitate intelligence gathering in this area. This regrettable state of affairs clearly reflects an entrenched gendering of rape as female, and in no small part sends the message that men are marginal if not irrelevant; that this could pass Stern (2010) by is a clear indictment of the competence of that review for male victims. Given that a Survivors Trust (2010) review of third-sector provision noted limited provision for males across the board, disparity for males in RC England and Wales is not redressed by provision in other agencies. For some male rape victims, there is simply nowhere to turn.

Gender discrimination for victims should not be acceptable. I would argue that it is only through latent reliance on male rape myths, and the ideal victim construct in particular, that this situation is tolerated. Through such glaring de-prioritization and flagrant omission the overwhelming message is that male victims are not important and that male rape is not real rape. It's certainly not considered to be Rape Crisis England and Wales's problem, which of course is precisely the problem – this is a 'postcode lottery' that RC does not decry, but enables and perpetuates.

All rape crisis organizations are not equal

Still navigating from the RC England and Wales website, using the links provided at the left hand side of the pane, I sought to ascertain whether this scarcity of provision is the norm. Links to Scotland, Ireland and the EU were all used. The findings were surprising – England and Wales is by no means the worst offender, with both Scotland and the EU having a paucity of provision for men, whilst Ireland, in contrast, is utterly exemplary and clearly demonstrates that exclusion of male victims is not inevitable and can be easily remedied.

Following the link for RC Scotland brings up a web page where the predominant image (at the top of the page) is of a woman, the only other image (at the foot of the page) is a cartoon drawing of a female – possibly a young girl. The sole quote is: 'women working with women to end rape and sexual abuse'. Their only statement about expanding their services is: 'We are working towards ensuring our services can be accessed by all women and girls including women from black and ethnic minority communities, lesbians and disabled women' – this statement is clearly intended to be progressive and inclusive and yet they manage to overlook an entire victim group purely by virtue of gender. The only mention of men is: 'There is also a very useful new resource which was recently published by the Scottish Government for women and men (over 16) who have been raped or sexually assaulted.' Importantly there is no recognition outside of this legal document, nor is there any link to other agencies which might provide such support for men in this region. This site is quite literally a dead end for male victims.

RC Ireland[56] is significantly better at inclusivity than England, Wales or Scotland. It is worth examining their provision in depth as it is quite simply exemplary and clearly demonstrates what can be done. Their initial page is not gendered at all, requiring a choice between information on support and information on the organization. Clicking onto support takes you to a page that is constructed with four choices: 'Find a rape crisis centre'; 'I have just been raped'; 'Male survivors'; and finally, 'Supporters of survivors'. It is commendable that they give clear provision here for men, but it seemed somewhat pernicious that they are singled out so clearly from utilizing the other choices. However, my initial reservations about what this might indicate were quickly dispelled. Clicking onto 'male survivors' takes the user to a page that explicitly recognizes male victims of rape and sexual assault – including victims of females (this is extraordinarily progressive and I have not seen this repeated elsewhere). Here it is clarified that 'All Rape Crisis Centres support or/and offer counselling to male survivors or refer them to the appropriate local service', which goes some way to improving on the lack of clarity and/or outright exclusion in English and Welsh provision and their providers stipulated remits.

Clicking onto the option 'find an RCC' brings up an interactive map that helps victims find a RC centre in their area. In line with my analysis of other RC sites, I accessed all regions to perform a close reading of their profiles – just as any prospective client might do. I did note variations in how male victims were included across the various providers. However, the difference was not between those organizations who did, against those who did not, provide recognition of men; nor of those who did, against those who did not, provide services for men. Rather, the key difference here was in how the substantive inclusivity – which all providers made – was expressed.

For some, gender neutrality and/or express inclusivity were not maintained in their blurb. However, for the vast majority no such criticism can be made. Whilst such limitation may be significant, the fact remains that this is small criticism indeed in comparison with the above in relation to England, Wales and Scotland. There does remain some discrepancy in service provision for males compared with females (for example home visits restricted to female victims only), but again, in comparison with the experience of the rest of the UK, this is still far more egalitarian.

Having looked at best practice, we now turn to worst. In comparison with RC Ireland – which is a clear example of best practice at the moment – and alarmingly even in comparison with RC Scotland, RC Network Europe[57] is quite simply a travesty of exclusivity. The initial page does not appear to be gendered, however, nor is it clear how to use this website to seek counselling or crisis services. At the top of the page are the RCNE logo and the statement: 'Help is there for you, no matter where you are'. Three sub-headings in bold are 'what can men do?', 'consciousness raising' and 'group initiative'. Making the reasonable assumption that the link 'what can men do?' may be similar to the link on the Irish site, which is provided to explicitly recognize male victims and clarify inclusivity of all providers in their group, I duly clicked on this. So far, this site appeared to be gender neutral in scope and to clearly include the male. However, this assumption is not borne out in actual content.

Under the main heading 'what can men do?', comes the response:

> it is a known fact that the participation of men in the movement against violence against women is of fundamental importance. As

sexual violence is overwhelmingly male violence meaning it is the result of men's behaviour, it can only be solved by men in the long run

A male victim seeking any validation – let alone support – would find none whatsoever here. Men are clearly ascribed only the role of perpetrators or colluders. The potentiality of victimhood is not broached at all.

Under the sub-heading 'consciousness raising' comes advice that can be summarized thus: men wanting to combat violence against women need to stop perpetrating it and help other men to cease. Whilst the final sub-heading, 'group initiative', contains material that advises men – essentially – that if they want to help rape victims they should stop sexually assaulting women themselves and cease attitudes and behaviour that condone the sexual assault of women by others.

After the profoundly inclusive approach of RC Ireland, this site comes as rather a shock. I had not been prepared to see such blatant gendered responsibilization, vilification, stereotyping and exclusion. There is simply no space here for a male victim to achieve any recognition, let alone support. Their slogan states: 'Help is there for you, no matter where you are'; but clearly, the unspoken rider to this is that it is solely dependent on who you are.

6.4 Conclusion

It is clear that legislative change does not necessarily impact on either policy or provision. As such, those analyses that foreground legislative inclusion and then pose the 'problem' as being victim reluctance to report, do a considerable disservice to male rape victims. As illustrated here, it may well be the case that male victims of rape and sexual violence cannot access support services that are widely accepted as vital in facilitating formal reports to statutory agencies such as the police. They are quite simply disenfranchised and, as such, their access to justice is titular only.

Part III
Concluding Thoughts

7
Feminism and Male Rape – Ironies and Governmentality

Foucault highlights the significance of ironies to the circulation of power within the social body, stating that 'people know what they do; they frequently know why they do what they do; but what they don't know is what what they do does' (Foucault, personal communication cited in Dreyfus and Rabinow, 1982, p. 187). This is not just a casual criticism of those operating in ignorance; it is also a blistering condemnation of those operating from positions of 'expertise'. Thus, the generation and promulgation of unintended, deleterious consequences has been a recurrent thematic in this book. In this way, ironies are regarded as key to governmentality and, in this way, I have argued that the gendering of rape and the continued legitimization of the ideal victim binary as a rationale should not be regarded as indicative of any failure, per se; but instead should be taken to illustrate the success of governmentality in the deployment of gender. This necessitates that we 'think differently', not just about the 'evidence' produced nor about the 'knowledge' generated but moreover about the role and function of polemical debate in this area, lest we persist in producing knowledge in this well-worn vein that continues to bear traces of the 'dust in [our] eyes and dust on [our] fingers' (Foucault, 1997, p. 50).

Some of the trends of note in relation to male rape excavated in this book have included: tokenistic inclusion; marginalization; redaction; valorization of rape; eroticization; didacticism; minimization of harm; hierarchies of harm; and exclusions. I argue that all of these either draw from or contribute to the notion of the ideal victim – or rather, the male's exemption from legitimate victimhood. Allowing individuals to be designated as undeserving of victim status due to factors intrinsic to them, as opposed to aspects of the offence itself, is pernicious and dangerous, but, of course, the logics around male rape are not quite so straightforward as to pivot solely nor explicitly on gender.

In order to make sense of rape of the male, whilst simultaneously eliding him as a victim of rape, we have seen the systematic and pervasive resurrection of various orthodox myths and conflations set up in contrast, or at least in relation, to the female, which enable the understanding of male victimhood as similar yet different – with a range of caveats and conditions, prescriptions and proscriptions imposed as necessary to be deserving of victimhood; the implications and impact of which cannot possibly be contained by gender delineation. After all, as demonstrated in the triangulation chapters, our gendered dimensions are fluid and permeable: in the information media and policy section, it was noted that there is slippage so that when we talk about rape we think about women; as illustrated in the entertainment media and the audience section there is also surrogacy, so that when we depict male rape we feminize our male characters. Wherever our male rape victim is constructed, it is as contiguous to the female – this then is the single archive relating to rape, and is where the potential for recursion lies.

In the genealogy it was illustrated that rape was not always gendered. Historically the male victim was obfuscated, whilst the female victim was highlighted. Significantly this process of apocrypha for the male predates feminism. Likewise, it is important to recognize that the male rape victim precedes modern legislative constructs. The rhetorical journey for the male rape victim in academic discourse was noted to closely resemble that of the orthodox understanding of female rape, but lacking the female's exculpation. The feminist model of rape and activist feminism can be regarded as implicated in this stasis for the male.

The first stage of this triangulation addressed the media as one of the means by which we 'know' victimhood. In information media, rape is implicitly gendered with a profound neglect of the male victim; in entertainment media male rape is valorized as revenge and/or redemption, with precipitative elements of the ideal victim construct clearly intact. At the very least that chapter illustrates that male victims are not considered worthy of the victim mantle. It was postulated that the male victim has supplanted the female as a target for and vehicle of rape myths, with pro-feminist depictions functioning ultimately as anti-feminist.

The second stage of the triangulation looked at the 'active' audience, with slash fiction used as a means by which to examine the 'imagining' of victimhood and the 'ethics' of the fan. In the material examined, the male rape victim was clearly used as a female surrogate, with sexual violence against him/her eroticized and various myths utilized as explanatory devices. The precipitative elements of the ideal victim construct were again credibilized. Once more, supposedly pro-feminist was revealed to be anti-feminist.

In the third and final stage of the triangulation, law, policy and provision were examined in respect of the male rape victim in order to ascertain how we 'act' on victimhood. The construct of the male can be traced over its journey from formal inclusion in law to grudging and token inclusion in policy to omission in practice. The male is effectively 'redacted' from the criminal justice and Rape Crisis agenda. Such omission credibilizes a hierarchy of victimhood, whilst gendered priorities and exceptions legitimize notions of rape/sex/gender conflation and deserving versus undeserving victim. As such, privileging of the female rape victim, either in the supposed interests of female victims or of feminism, is counter-productive and misguided. Again, pro-feminism is anti-feminist in its effects.

It has been illustrated that various stereotypes and myths that were effectively deconstructed under the feminist gaze regarding women's victimization have been effectively resurrected in respect of male victimization. These myths have at their core a number of assumptions that directly undermine feminist theorizing. Of key concern here are: reciprocity, rape as sex, constancy, and affirmations of gender/sexuality/ identity. These conspire to resuscitate patriarchal notions of culpability by lending weight to the rationalization of rape through victim precipitation and the distorted lens of the ideal victim. These myths, particularly that of the conflation of rape/sex, in gaining legitimacy within rape scripting, come to be transcribed back onto our understanding of the rape of the female, 'writing-back' to ironically preserve normative gender roles and thus undermine rather than preserve feminism.

I am sensitized to the fact that it is perfectly possible to read the findings presented in each of my chapters as fitting comfortably within the established debate, be that interpreted as in defence of feminism or as an indictment of feminism – but we must negotiate this terrain with care. The core issues raised in my discussion stem from the historical gendering of rape that has proved so persistent and resilient, a gendering that surely bears no small relationship to the 'discovery' of sex and sexuality that underlies (patriarchal) modernity. So we must exercise caution. Whilst we can assert with confidence that rape is not just a women's issue, we cannot move from this to denying the significance or relevance of feminism. After all, if we accept that the apocrypha of the male rape victim correlates with patriarchal modernity then the male rape victim might be regarded as of import to patriarchy, which of course then in itself renders it significant for feminism. This must not be overlooked.

What needs to be revealed here is what Foucault terms the 'truth that functions as a weapon', and I would argue that this is not the explicit and combative truth claims posited by the opposing camps, it is instead the 'truth' to which these camps are blinded and yet continue to endorse with each exchange, the 'truth' to which both camps subscribe, and of which each camp perpetuates: natural, normalized, embodied gender – tethered irreducibly to hegemonic masculinity and to patriarchy. This is the value of this otherwise apparently futile exchange, and is of course where a gendered notion of rape – and the particularization of 'male' rape – becomes a strategic site for governmentality.

8
Excavating the Gendered/ing Dimensions of Male Rape

In constructing the 'truth' of male rape, what is preserved over the course of its historical narrative is a definitive specialism and expertise – separate to and distinct from rape of the female. Of particular note here is the emergence of enclaves within the academic body that are locating male rape within psychopathology, masculinities and special victim populations. Despite claims to the contrary, such trends persist in marginalizing, segregating and obfuscating this phenomenon. Not only are they key to Othering the male rape victim, they are central in normalizing the female rape victim – gendered particularizations that are key to gendering.

The gendered perception of this phenomenon, and the perceived centrality of this to feminist credibility in terms of theory and activism, is enormously problematic. Fundamentally, the notion of gender-exclusive sexual victimization emerging in research and pressure groups, in the face of conflicting lived experience, has become (or at least is being presented as) the Achilles heel of the feminist stance and movement. The central irony here of course is that this gendering of rape has become a central tenet of, and is staunchly and vehemently defended by the very movement concerned to dismantle patriarchy as a system of oppression. This can be seen in the dispute around moves to truly gender neutral legislation,[1] in the reluctance to broaden Rape Crisis provision to all victims and in the continued privileging of the feminist model of sexual violence. It is also the driver behind feminist derogation of works and provision in respect of male sexual victimization as being somehow indicative of, or commensurate with, 'backlash'.

Let us note then that the reluctance to embrace male rape within the feminist rape model, as popularly conceived, is a result of the reluctance to adapt it, not an inability to do so. But this reluctance is understandable when the model itself is presented as so enmeshed with the legitimacy of the theoretical stance. One cannot revisit the feminist rape model without supposedly impinging on the feminist paradigm as a whole. This being the case, feminism becomes caught up in a self-defeating and tautological rationale – to either simplistically blame feminism or defend it is to overlook the function of this discursive exchange within governmentality.

What is problematic is that at present feminism is commonly regarded as being a problem for male rape, and indeed male rape is presented as a problem both for and of feminism. Both of which are entirely plausible, but rather miss the point – which of course is precisely the point. Let us remember that the preservation and privileging of gender difference in the understanding of rape rests largely on the supposed centrality of female rape to feminism, but that this in itself is erroneous. Not least because the legitimacy of feminism does not, and should not, rest on female sexual victimhood. Rape (whether understood as a harm or a crime) pre-exists both feminism and patriarchy and was adopted by early women's movements pre-feminism, whilst being also recognized by anti-slavery and children's rights movements. Indeed, it was only adopted by feminism as a women's issue by second wave feminists, in the 1960s and 1970s.[2] Thus, whilst the contributions of feminism to rape theory, legislation and provision cannot be overstated, the significance of female sexual victimization to feminism can.

As Bevacqua (2000) has so readily noted, rape was most certainly of strategic value to feminism, not least because it enabled the negotiation of class and racial difference necessary to galvanize collective action in second wave feminism. However, I would argue that the continued retention and preservation of rape as a simplistically gendered issue is misplaced, and is actually self-defeating. Where feminism's reluctance to engage with male rape has been noted, apologists frequently defensively attribute this to logics around protectionism of activist feminism and fear over competition for resources.[3] But such strategies are ill-advised, as the exclusion of the male can be utilized in rhetorical scapegoating of the feminist movement as discriminatory, whilst gendering provision of services necessarily divides already limited funding. Thus, precisely what is feared is facilitated.

The ultimate irony, however, is recursion. Whilst male rape discourse is superficially a separate repertoire, and an ostensibly oppositional one at that, it does draw from repertoires of sexual violence more generally, and rape discourse about women in particular. In doing so it opens up the possibility of 'writing back' from one repertoire to another, becoming intersecting components in a single archive through which rape is 'known' and is reified. These discourses cannot be regarded as mutually exclusive or diametrically opposed, but rather should be regarded as interdependent, complex and confounding practices, which, in providing a superficial discontinuity, elide a continuity of governmentality that is oriented – in this instance – around gender. At the very least, such an understanding might go some way to explaining the stubborn persistence of low rates of reporting and the attrition of offences that are reported, including: no-criming,[4] discontinuance[5] and acquittal[6] that continue to plague the criminal justice system for all complaints of rape. At worst, such an understanding places feminism centre stage in the deployment of gender.

Let us not forget though that what this best illustrates, in a Foucauldian sense, is the 'tyranny' of (gendered) discourse – this will be discussed in the sections that follow and illustrated in reference to Foucauldian feminism – in particular Gavey (2005).

8.1   Foucauldian feminism and male rape: the tyranny of the model

The apparent feminist protectionism – and indeed, the supposed chivalric protectionism of feminism performed by other defenders – around the gendered specificity of rape as a female experience, and indeed oppression, pivots on a number of problematic assumptions: that male victims are statistically insignificant or 'rare' when compared with female victims; that the history of rape is a feminist history; and that rape has strategic value to feminism. The first can be readily countered through standard critique of official statistics and reference to inhibitors to reporting behaviours, such as originally detailed by Warshaw (1994) in her classic text *I Never Called it Rape*. The second cannot be so readily rejected, but our understanding of the credence of this needs to be problematized and complexified in relation to a more lengthy genealogy of rape per se. The third falters as a consequence of critique in relation to the other two.

As previously indicated, I approached Foucauldian feminism with a view to remedying the problems I saw unfolding in other areas of the Academy. I was aware that both feminism and Foucault recognize the importance of disruption to circulations of power, and understood that there are differences in how that is conceived; nevertheless, I anticipated this body of work to be vital to breaching the impasse in relation to the gendered exclusions within 'rape', and to be a site in itself for disruption. However, the body of works identified as 'Foucauldian feminism' is not quite the Foucauldian project I expected it to be.

I anticipated this to draw from Foucault's later works and, in so doing, to liberate 'rape' from its sexualized and gendered forms. Neither is the case. Instead I found such works to draw selectively from Foucault's oeuvre, and to steadfastly defend and advocate gendered and sexualized specificities and hierarchies of harm. Given that I argue the particularization of male rape to function within an archive that relates to rape proper and to surreptitiously revalidate the ideal victim and its myths for all victims of rape – I did not find a site for disruption here; I found a key site for promulgation. A perturbing discovery and one I am not content to let stand without more considered inquiry.

I was struck by the fact that many authors wholly lacked insight as to the ironic consequences that might be enabled through their work, even as mere potentialities; but perhaps even more surprising is that this ignorance cannot be said of all. Some, such as Gavey (2005), acknowledge the opportunity for disruption of gendered binaries inherent in including the male, which to my mind implies recognition that his exclusion functions counter to this, yet thereafter make a concerted effort to disabuse their analysis of its ramifications. For those authors, defence of the orthodox feminist stance and its gendered model of rape becomes consciously promoted and prioritized. This is to say that a clear choice is made to prefer the model at the ultimate expense of any and all victims. Worse still, such authors articulate this strategy in terms of success, and in so doing raucously celebrate their pyrrhic victory.

Feminism's (mis)perceived role in the 'battle' over the male rape victim as 'the front-line' is not so much in defence of feminism per se as it is the feminist model of rape. What rapidly became apparent to me is the struggle faced by these authors in attempting inclusion of the male rape victim, which then – seemingly – 'must' be denied in order to protect and defend the feminist model. This is a functional imperative that I will illustrate through more detailed critical reading of Gavey (2005).

Gavey (2005) is of particular interest as she does not just utilize Foucauldian tools, she explicitly presents her thesis as an avowedly Foucauldian feminist analysis of rape. In actuality, her stance is not all that it seems[7] – a criticism echoed by reviewers of her text, for example, Adam and Ryan (2008, p.894), who noted this as 'not completely Foucauldian'. Indeed, I would present this as a clear example of a feminist-Foucauldian analysis that, despite the author's stated desire to challenge orthodox feminism and reject non-complexity, actually works diligently to preserve both.

The overarching aim of her work is stated on the back jacket as: to 'examine the convergences of gender, power and sexuality, in order to critique the cultural conditions of the possibility for rape', and her thesis is lauded there as 'a valuable contribution to feminist and social constructionist work on rape and sexuality' – and I can certainly agree with both statements, but only in so much as the identifier 'feminist' privileges (and therefore prescribes) certain omissions and exclusions, such that: 'gender' is understood to be female; 'power' is an orthodox patriarchal model that privileges and benefits all men, subjugating and exploiting all women; 'rape' is understood as that of male-on-female; and finally, 'sexuality' refers to heterosexuality. So long as one is attuned with all these assumptions, this is indeed a valuable piece. However, anyone looking for a truly inclusive or assuredly critical piece will struggle to find satisfaction here – despite (and perhaps even because of) all pretensions to the contrary.

For me, it is those very pretensions that make this work so fascinating. Unlike other authors, Gavey (2005) goes to great lengths to pre-empt criticism for exclusion of the male victim from her thesis, and consequently acknowledges the male to a far greater extent than many of her contemporaries.[8] Yet, despite Gavey's (2005) efforts, her form of 'inclusion' is expressly reluctant and at times apologetic, and sees her, therefore, conscientiously toeing the invisibilization line.

In her discussion, Gavey (2005) appears to accept the validity of hegemonic masculinity and male sexual drive discourse as affecting normative male behaviour resulting in the victimization of women. These constructs are retained in her thesis in order to critique men as advantaged in being aggressors, with the constructs themselves accepted therefore as 'real' without question. This is despite the fact that she extensively critiques the patriarchal construct (and homogenizing) of femininity as false, and surely if we are to deconstruct one we must deconstruct both. But herein lies the sticking point – for Gavey (2005), gender-neutrality is misguided and 'gender-equivalency' is explicitly denounced as backlash. This is a technique of de-legitimization utilized several times where exclusion of the male might otherwise seem indefensible.

Her concerns about dealing with this issue at all are candidly conveyed in her introduction to Chapter 7 of her book, where she asserts that she is unable to conceive or validate notions of heterosexual aggression that postulate similarity in this experience between the genders. She clarifies that such gender-neutrality leaves her suspicious, and highlights that the principle reservation for her is what she regards as an inherent danger: that 'there is always the potential for male victims of gendered violence to usurp female victims as the more interesting side of the coin: the sexy issue' (Gavey, 2005, p. 194).

To justify this, she falls back on official statistics and self-report data that indicate such victimization as 'extremely rare' (p. 195) – a common enough belief in the wider academic literature for sure, but in this case it reveals a double-standard given that her preceding chapters deal sensitively with the myriad of ways that rape for women can go unacknowledged, unreported and unrecorded and yet assert that the rape is no less 'real' for it.

Her thesis is astute, compelling and insightful for sure, but it remains resolutely gendered. Indeed, in a startling move for a piece informed by Foucault, Gavey (2005) predicates her gendered notion of rape on an uncritical acceptance of official statistics and even 'official' estimates that support rape as being a gendered crime, with no consideration given to these as cultural constructs that are themselves a part of discourse (rather than existing outside of it). What is particularly revealing is that she does indeed recognize cultural constructions in mediating understanding and even in affecting behaviour, in point of fact this is the crux of her thesis, but this is only so for the feminist model of rape – with the gendered binary of offender and victim intractably vaunted, protected and preserved.

The traditional gendered roles of women as victims/men as offenders are immediately apparent in her introduction to this work. The two chapters that comprise this introduction: 'Rape as a social problem' (p. 17) and 'The discovery of a rape epidemic' (p. 50), despite covering almost a century's development in rape research and legislation, manage to contain only two brief acknowledgements of men as rape victims. In both instances, following the aside, the male is immediately redacted to be supplanted by female pronouns only. It must also be noted that major legal reforms, which included the formal recognition of males as victims, are not indicated in these contextualizing chapters nor later ones; nor any research relating to manifold environments for male sexual victimization; nor does she make any effort to include classic research into this (for example, by Scacco, 1982; McMullen, 1990; Scarce, 1997; or Mezey and King, 1992, 2000) either for these chapters nor the book as a whole – this is despite the fact that all of these were published at the time of her own research.[9] This demonstrates considerable bias in her selection. I understand that she might not consider male rape to be central to her thesis (as she has preferentially delineated it), but to simply omit it is unjustifiable, as this forms a concrete part of the academic, legal and criminal justice landscape for the period she covers.

Her dedicated chapter regarding male rape victims is oriented to the issue of women raping men, with the only value accorded for recognizing female-on-male rape presented as a decidedly abstract, academic one – expressed as a need to 'imagine' the 'possibility' of these inverted roles, stating that to do so might then disrupt the binaries that perpetuate women's victimhood and men's offending. This is a valuable insight for sure and, caveats aside, is one I wholeheartedly concur with; but it must be noted that the male rape victim is deftly dismissed here and denied any substance. In this same chapter, she goes on to de-legitimize a gender-neutral notion of 'rape' as wholly problematic and postulated in ways that present this as commensurate with 'backlash' – this is an astonishing sleight of hand that allows her to simultaneously acknowledge and disavow, seemingly include but then efface.

Gavey (2005, pp. 141–142) convincingly postulates that women subject themselves to self-surveillance in an attempt to conform to the cultural norm in respect of a 'sexual imperative' or obligation borne from patriarchal hegemonic femininity within the stereotyped discourse of actively/passively gendered heterosexuality, a notion that I would suggest draws implicitly from 'ethics'; but there is no recognition that men are also constrained and subject to self-regulation oriented to this same construct. For her, the only 'oppression' resulting from patriarchal normative gender constructs is experienced by women. Obviating the male in this way allows Gavey to draw on and preserve the orthodox feminist model, with the overriding assumption being that rape-supportive discourse benefits all men (presumably in their fixed role as potential rapists), but she proffers no recognition that this self-same discourse, drawing as it does on hegemonic masculinities, also facilitates the victimization of men – for example, in contributing to the construction of the ideal victim that underlies various male rape myths. But, of course, this is facilitated by the exclusion of works relating to male rape from her research.

For Gavey (2005) my attempt at 'equivalency' here negates my argument, so allow me to illustrate other techniques utilized herein: she acknowledges sexual victimization of men only within the parameters of 'unwanted' sex – where 'psychologically pressured' or 'encouraged'; this allows her to deduce that 'unwanted sex' for men is a crime of low-harm and little consequence, something she supports through reference to interview data, without acknowledging at this point in her discussion the problems inherent in asking a male victim to articulate his victimhood.

In an effort to illustrate female offending/male victimhood and the fundamental differences she perceives between this and 'the more common and systemic forms of male coercion of women' (Gavey, 2005, p. 196) she includes data drawn from research around 'women's "active" sexuality on film' (Doherty, 2000, cited in Gavey, 2005, p. 198), specifically a screening of a film that contains a scene 'where there is a question mark over the man's consent', something she then equates as a woman's 'initiation of sex with a man' (p. 198). Note, then, that she moves quickly from questioning the consent of the male character, to negating its necessity – within the same paragraph. In leading into the analysis, she does assert the possibility that the female character's actions 'could constitute sexual aggression', but then moves to query this by denoting the issue via her sub-title as one of 'rape or seduction', with the former interpretation postulated as only conceivable 'in the interests of moral consistency' (p. 199). At this point, it must be noted that the scene in question can be deduced from Gavey's (2005) own description to involve clearly articulated non-consent by the male to an older female, who proceeds to perform fellatio on him whilst he is sleeping; an act that progresses to full intercourse on his awakening. Note too that a similar scenario, albeit male-on-female, was raised by Gavey (2005) in a preceding chapter and clearly denounced as rape. For Gavey (2005) then, the more meaningful aspect of these two scenarios is clearly not the behaviour, nor the articulation of non-consent, but the gender of the individuals involved in relation to the roles ascribed.

Gavey (2005) notes that for the audience to whom she screened this, the behaviour could only be understood as rape through the 'lens' of gender-reversal (only by talking about the experience of the male as if he was a female could the act be understood as rape) and interprets this as indicating that such interactions fall 'outside of dominant understanding of heterosexuality [such] that we need to work to make sense of them, and to place them in a proper moral order' (p. 201). I strongly agree with this observation, but she and I disagree fundamentally on what this means – for her this 'struggle' indicates that gender has a substantive reality and, therefore, it is in this moment that 'the rhetoric of gender-reversal deconstructs itself' (p. 201). This is an ingenious move in preservation of her thesis and the feminist model, but such a rapid and wholesale dismissal of the male rape victim is rather troubling – particularly from an analysis informed by Foucault. After all, the most basic interpretation of Foucault's truth/power can allow that: just because we struggle to comprehend does not mean there is no veracity, where we have no measure does not mean that it is not happening and where we fail to recognize it does not mean it is not real. She does acknowledge such potentialities later in the chapter (p. 204), but it comes rather late to her analysis, and indeed, that acknowledgement is fleeting and not sustained. In examining that same data, as she presents it, I am inclined to interpret this need to 'make sense' as arising from the immutable discourse of gender rather than revealing the truth of gender.

This notion of gender as a concrete 'lived' difference underlies her assertion that rape is experienced differently for men compared with women. Unfortunately, although she draws on the process of meaning-making in reference to gender-norms here, specifically postulating that the impact of the behaviour is mediated by gender, she does so to minimize harm caused to men and emphasize harm caused to women. I can see that this might be plausible, but – had she consulted it – she would find that there is robust challenge to this in the literature around male rape;[10] however, of greater concern to me is her subsequent move which smacks of rape-denial.

Gavey (2005) confidently states that for men 'the very experience of what could be characterized as "rape" by a woman may be experienced in a way that is positive' (p. 203). Let us be clear here, this is not merely asserting that our general understanding may be to rationalize male rape as positive, instead she is explicitly stating that an individual man's experience of coerced sex may in itself be understood by him as positive; going on to state that 'this renders men unrapeable – especially, perhaps, heterosexual men by a women' (p. 204). The notion that men cannot be raped is indeed significant, but only in as much as it persists as a myth, though this is left unacknowledged.

Having previously asserted that male rape can only be understood through the (inherently delegitimizing) logic of gender-reversal, she includes an analysis of a transcript from her research that shows some of her participants moving beyond mere gender-reversal to using objective measures drawn from legislation and debates around 'consent', although this is not something she notes. One of her participants[11] indicates her outrage at the film scene in question and notes that the male character did not articulate consent. Of interest to me, is that she moves to draw on gender-reversal logics only when challenged on her interpretation by another participant, and still persists in clearly categorizing this as rape in her final response, as cited by Gavey (2005, p. 206). Clearly then, this participant did not need to draw on gender-reversal to understand this as rape herself, and only did so when it became necessary to persuade another. To my mind, this stands counter to the point Gavey (2005) made in asserting that male rape could only be understood through gender-reversal logics. This does not draw any attention from the author, however, and instead this segment is used as an illustration of 'the risk' to feminism arising from what she implies is the misappropriation of feminist tools for understanding rape. In particular, she dismisses as 'nonsensical' that this participant draws on the feminist understanding of rape/power/aggression to explain female-on-male sexual offending.

For Gavey (2005) the film scene in question cannot be rape, given that there is no 'aggression' (something left undefined), and is not what she regards as an 'improper assault' (again, undefined). In regards to the former statement, this is surely dependent on a very narrow understanding of what constitutes aggression if it does not include being sexually assaulted in one's sleep (especially given that consent had previously been sought and denied); as to the latter, she seems to be suggesting in her subsequent explication that because she interprets that the male in question 'chose to change his mind' (p. 206) he was thus transformed into a willing sexual partner, and that this nullifies any assault. Such a deduction bears the hallmarks of various rape myths, such as: rape is sex, no means yes, rape can unlock desire, rapists are insightful and noble – to see these given any credence in an avowedly feminist analysis is startling.

Ultimately, violence towards men by women in the course of sexual relations is only recognized in Gavey's text as consensual sadomasochism; men are only unreservedly validated as 'true' victims where in same-sex relationships (2005, p. 226). For her, victimhood is reserved for the homosexual male assaulted by a homosexual male, with no room here for the male victimized either by another man or woman, irrespective of sexuality. The sustained focus on what she regards as 'heterosexual rape' is foundational to her thesis and is especially problematic in the face of her claims to Foucauldian positioning, and indeed in validating myths that have 'sex' and 'sexuality' as their core; I would rather she problematize perceptions of rape as having any congruence at all with these constructs.

The most pressing issue for Gavey (2005) is presented as the difficulties in recognizing female sexual agency: bemoaning that because female-on-male sexual offending cannot be easily countenanced, this serves to bolster the feminine gender norm of passivity that contributes to women's sexual victimization by men; but what of the denial of men as victims? This is simply not a 'worthy' issue.

One might be tempted to ask how work informed by both Foucault and feminism can fail to perceive such dynamics, but this is to misunderstand the 'problem' – or rather, the lack of a problem so far as such authors are concerned. We must recall that this is the 'front-line' in the battle over 'male' rape; that the validity of feminism is (mis)understood as inextricably tied to the feminist model of rape and that this model is gendered. Such authors then do not fail; they succeed in providing a defence – as they perceive it. We should also understand that, for such authors, this defence extends to protectionism of feminism against Foucault, and of Foucauldian feminism against feminism. This is a body of work attempting to perform an incredible balancing act in the face of precarious theoretical and political positioning. This should not diminish the importance of this approach – after all, for Foucault, ambivalence and resistance go hand in hand.

8.2   Foucauldian feminism and male rape: ambivalence and resistance

Despite cautions from feminist authors and others along the lines that 'if feminism clings to an emancipatory project for female victims of power, it will "preserve the old dichotomies of power in spite of itself"' (Jenkins, 2002, p. 6, citing Aladjem), Foucauldian feminism overwhelmingly appropriates Foucault strategically, much in line with Sawicki's assertion that 'attending to the exigencies of feminist practice will sometimes require that we either ignore Foucault or move beyond him' (1991, p. 109). Consequently many authors leave the mainstay of orthodox feminism intact; particularly that relating to identity politics and to the gendered particularization that underscores activism and intervention. In so doing, they draw ostensibly from Foucault's 'care of the self', although this actually presents a significant problem in Foucauldian terms, as 'care of the self' was never intended to be liberationist or emancipatory of any 'inner' or 'deep' self, and certainly not of an essentialist self. Certainly, where that notion of self is regarded as fundamentally gendered – and the practices based on such are delineated by gender – this cannot be regarded as anything other than folly in Foucauldian terms. Appropriating the language of Foucault cannot disguise the disciplinary effects here.

The temptation, as ever, is to responsibilize that ever-culpable figure of feminism, but I must reiterate that we should recognize the relational importance of 'feminist' knowledge and practices to the circulation of power associated with current discourse without singularly responsibilizing feminism. Thus, whilst it can be said that the present construct of male rape risks becoming 'the emperor's new clothes' of feminist theorizing of sexual violence, across its various incarnations; that failure to adequately include male rape is undermining feminism by challenging the integrity and credibility of feminist explanations of rape; that this in itself is ironic as male rape can actually be regarded as illustrative of many feminist assertions; and finally, that present strategies of inclusion and exclusion are surreptitiously resuscitating conventional rape myths in service of patriarchy, despite all of this, it must be understood that it is the dynamic that is important and that, therefore, to 'blame feminism' is to be deflected from the transactions at play here and to once again be caught up in existing deployments. The more Foucauldian task at this point is to seek opportunities for disruption.

Clinging to a gendered and universalist notion of 'woman' in feminist theory and practice has long garnered criticism – not least from critical feminists, post-modern feminists, third world feminists, critical race theorists and queer theorists, precisely because of its inherent exclusions and privileging. To see this not only as enduring but now actually advocated within feminist works influenced by Foucault or supposedly 'Foucauldian feminism' is astonishing. However, this should not be used to diminish the importance of this approach – after all, if we can understand feminist practices as disciplinary, then this is also clearly where the potential for transgression could be fostered.

Foucault is largely silent on gender, preferring instead to focus on sex and sexuality, and has been criticized for this apparent oversight by many. But in his work we can negotiate and mediate this silence, as Bell notes, where Foucault talks of sexuality 'he is necessarily talking about the creation of gender' (1993, p. 27). I would argue that whilst he neglects to address sexed *as* gendered individuals, his conception of 'asymmetric' power relations and 'transactional' notions of power provides a means by which this silence can be modulated. After all, what Foucault does offer us is the capacity to recognize complexity in power and its productivity, rather than monolith oppression. This in itself is valuable.[12]

Ways forward have been posited from within Foucauldian feminism, for example, in recognising the value of situated selves and difference that contribute to a complex 'weaving' of self (see Qin, 2004) and/or unifying around not any notion of self-hood per se but of experience, what Jenkins (2002) calls 'common interest'. We can understand 'rape' then, as a de-gendered lived not embodied experience, as having the capacity to facilitate this.

Many other authors[13] agree that including male rape victims in various ways has potential as a strategy for resistance in various forms – albeit frequently with reservations and caveats asserted. I argue instead that we need to recognize a sexualized aggression and a gendering aggression without reifying it as sexual and gendered. In incorporating male rape victims, the gendered dimensions of sexual violence – tethered irreducibly to the gendered truth claims that prop up patriarchy – can be destabilized. This is particularly plausible if we remind ourselves of the apocrypha of male rape as corresponding with the rise of patriarchy. Recognition of the male, then, enables a site of transgression in respect of gendered identity and experience – so that, in a Foucauldian sense, we might become 'other than we are'.

In closing though, a caution must be issued: we must beware the 'theoretical crown' so derided by Foucault as part of the tyranny of discourse. What is not needed here is a unitary theory or model of sexual violence, nor a homogenized Foucauldian feminism. Indeed, I would argue instead that the value of male rape lies precisely in the challenge, the difficulty, the struggle towards inclusion, and not its triumphant achievement.

Thus, it is the disruption of existing discursive exchange that is important, not substitution; fragility and tentativeness, not absolutes and certainties; the foiling of existing relays of power-effects, as opposed to their replacement – perhaps in so doing, we might then exercise what Foucault expressed simply as 'the will not to be governed thus' (Foucault, 1978, cited in Gordon, 2001, p. xxxix).

9
Epilogue – Male Rape is a Feminist Issue/Male Rape is a Feminist Issue!/Male Rape is a Feminist Issue?

Over the course of this book, the proposition that 'male rape is a feminist issue' has been illustrated in various ways: existing concerns in the literature can be seen to posit that male rape is an issue deserving of feminism's attention and/or that 'male' rape is a by-product of feminism. These are predicated on concerns that male rape is both a problem for feminism and a problem of feminism, and as such they are oriented around combative exchange between opposing camps. But we must not neglect the alternative reading of this work's proposition: the problematization of male rape as a feminist issue. This approach attempts to shift the focus from the camps themselves to the exchange between them. In this way the fact that existing discourse functions to posit male rape as a problem for and of feminism is of concern, as is the emergence of a particularized and distinct understanding of the male rape victim in relation to a normalized female.

Thus, it is the orientation to feminism, and the stubborn persistence of the ideal victim binary that is important. In this way, it can be argued that discourse around male rape entangles feminism in the deployment of gender within governmentality; thus, we may understand the particularized and recursive knowledge around male rape – and the ironies associated with 'feminist' practices – not as indicative of the failure of feminism, but as indicative of the success of governmentality. Indeed, popularizing understanding of this issue as relational to feminism forms a core component in present circulations of power – an irony inherent in this present work that does not escape me.

Above all, this work was an experiment in and conversation with Foucauldian thought. Its primary aim was simply to problematize the existing debate in this area, satisfying the Foucauldian imperative to 'think differently' and, in so doing, illustrate the value of Foucault to this field. For this author, utilizing Foucault in this manner has lent a valuable perspective to this area that ultimately proves more than a little troubling and troublesome.

Notes

1 Introduction – Feminism, Governmentality and 'Male' Rape

1. This book is based on a sole-author paper I presented at the 2007 British Society of Criminology conference (18–20 September, London School of Economics, London, UK), entitled 'Feminism, Governmentality and the Political Economy of Male Rape: Why Male Rape is a Feminist Issue'.
2. See Bevacqua (2000), Sielke (2002) and Bourke (2007), amongst others, for a detailed examination of the history of feminism and rape.
3.. Issues around the construct of male rape and the male rape victim have been raised by other authors. Graham's (2006) article discusses the construction of the male rape victim, and ostensibly adopts a critical stance in seeking to engage with the emerging knowledge as discourse, but hers is a notion of social constructionism and discourse in the thinnest sense (rather than the Foucauldian usage I adopt). It is also important to recognize that her work contains a number of flaws, many of which are readily noted by Rumney and Jamel (2009). However, their criticism seems predicated on a cynical rejection of what they appear to dismiss as 'blue-sky' theorizing, whilst I would argue conversely that Graham's analysis remains far too enmeshed in a pragmatically mired administrative and 'rights'-based agenda.
4. Updated in the 2003 Act to include oral penile-penetration as rape, and create a new offence of Assault by Penetration, which can be committed by either a male or female using any body part or object.
5. Andrew Richards, who was 26 years old, was sentenced to 10 years imprisonment on the 9 June 1995 for the attempted rape, indecent assault and actual bodily harm of an 18-year-old male.
6. Despite including reference to the Criminal Justice and Public Order Act 1994, Barnett (1997) neglects the provision therein regarding the male victim, preferring instead to focus on the aspects relating to marital rape in respect of female spouses.
7. For example, Home Office data reveal that in 2008/2009 police-recorded rapes of a female increased by 5 per cent (on the previous year) to 12,165 offences, whilst sexual assaults on a female fell by 4 per cent to 19,740 offences. Rape of a male decreased by 4 per cent to 968 offences, whilst sexual assaults on a male fell by 12 per cent to 2,323 offences (Walker et al., 2009).
8. Notions of 'common sense' include: the 'stereotypes of everyday life' (Becker, 1974, cited in Tierney, 2006, p. 8); the 'philosophy of nonphilosophers' (Gramsci, 1971, cited in Jewkes, 2004, p. 12); and 'public image' (Hall, cited in Jewkes and Letherby, 2002, p. 117).
9. Foucault specifically explicates this for us in his works; for example, see his introductory chapter in *The Use of Pleasure* (1984), pp. 8–13.
10. For example, in the 2008 British Crime Survey the self-completion module on intimate violence reveals that approximately 3 per cent of women aged

16 to 59 and less than 1 per cent of men (of the same age) had experienced a sexual assault (including attempts) in the previous 12 months. The majority of these are accounted for by less serious sexual assaults. Significantly, fewer than 1 per cent of *both* women and men reported having experienced a serious sexual assault, which would include rape (Walker et al., 2009).

11. Discussed at length in 'Questions of Method' in Faubion (2001).

12. This is not to say that resistance is ineffective, but rather that it is necessary. Freedom after all is a precondition for power and is itself held within power relations, the transactional nature of which means that breach or disruption – rather than revolution – should be the goal of what Couzens Hoy (cited in Kelly, 2009) terms 'emancipatory resistance'.

13. 'Irony' is the term coined by Jock Young to characterize what is commonly regarded as the 'post-modern turn' in criminology; see Young (n.d.).

14. 'Writing back' is a term I've borrowed from post-colonial studies, and in my usage it is more akin to what Sielke (2002, p. 5) describes as 'refiguration'. However, whilst it shares Seilke's (2002) concern with 'rhetorical processes' it also bears post-colonialism's concern with counter-discourse's potential for unintentional affirmation of the canonic discourse (for a detailed discussion of this, see Thieme, 2001).

15. 'Rape myths' refers to misconceptions around rape, and thus what constitutes a genuine or 'real' rape and likewise a 'real' victim. Their function is to shift culpability from offender to victim. For a detailed discussion of male rape myths and perceptions thereof, see Chapleau, Oswald and Russell (2008).

16. Example of which relate to attrition in general but low conviction rates in particular – thus it is noteworthy that the conviction rate has reduced from 1 in 3 in the 1970s to 1 in 18 at present, see Kelly, Lovett and Regan (2005). Myths are recognized as constraints on reporting and recording, and on prosecution and conviction practices; see, for example, Du Mont, Miller and Myhr (2003), and the classic feminist research by Warshaw (1994).

17. 'Hegemonic masculinities' was coined by Connell (1987) to refer to the culturally idealized patterns (norms, forms and practices) of masculinity that privilege men and support patriarchal society – in essence, it is the model or ideal of masculinity. For a concise overview of this concept, see Spade and Valentine (2008).

18. For a discussion and clarification of 'the subject' in Foucault's works, see 'The Subject and Power' in Foucault (2001).

19. In this instance, and as a regime of truth, one must note the interrelationship between knowledge and the creation of objects and subjectivities in the social body.

20. 'Regime of truth' is understood here as an asymmetrical power-effect t^i the existing apparatus of sexuality and predicated on gender.

21. 'Victimology' is a subset of criminology; for a critical introductio' (1996).

22. See Soyland and Kendall (1997) for a discussion of the u^c Foucault.

23. See L.G. Graham (2005) and Kendell and Wickham (2 $^{0'}$

24. See Foucault, 2001, p. 338.

25. In other words, to make real. Similar, therefore, $^+$ 'social facts'.

2 Problematization – A Critical Ontology of the Present

1. For the tracing and situating of 'scholarly knowledge and disqualified knowledges', see Foucault, (1997, pp. 8–11).
2. I performed a rudimentary critical discourse analysis (CDA). This methodology is explained in greater detail in the following chapter.
3. For a discussion of this concept, see Connell and Messerschmidt (2005).
4. Feminist explications thus seek to rationalize masculine vulnerabilities, and in doing so such discourse makes male victims 'feminine'.
5. I use rape-able to indicate his being sexually violable – able to be raped. This is converse to the usage by feminist authors who use this to mean his proclivity for rape – able to rape. My perversion of this is deliberate and intended to be disruptive.
6. The ideal victim is also known as the symbolic victim, credible victim, legitimate victim, blameless victim, the key to the binaries of deserving versus undeserving victim. This will be explicated in Chapter 3.
7. Feminist models are overviewed in Martin et al. (2006).
8. See Newburn and Stanko (2002); Nathanson and Young (2006).
9. See Cressey (1992); Elias (1994).
10. See Farrell (1993); Thomas (1993); Synnott (2009).
11. See Paglia (1991, 1992); Roiphe (1994); Hoff Sommers (1994, 2001).
12. For example, Gillespie (1996); Dworkin (1997); MacKinnon (2006).
13. See Scacco (1982); McMullen (1990); Scarce (1997).
14. Landrum (1993) identified six texts of significance at that time from the major publishers' lists, and from books used in his own courses. The texts listed here were all recommended reading on my own modules and/or modules within my former department (Department of Law and Criminal Justice Studies, Canterbury Christ Church University).
15. See Hannon and Dufour (1998).
16. For example, Hogben and Waterman (1997).
17. Specialist texts include: Scacco (1982); McMullen (1990); Scarce (1997); Mezey and King (1992, 2000); Abdullah-Khan (2008).
18. I searched for the specialist texts that have been published in this field – availability/accessibility being necessary for dissemination. World Catalogue (http://www.worldcat.org/) was used to check holdings in the UK as at 3 November 2010. I found: Abdullah-Khan (2008) held by five UK universities, indicated by region (Cambridge, Essex, Glasgow, Leicester, Oxford); Scarce (1997) held by three (Manchester, Essex, Leicester); McMullen (1990) not held in the UK – closest holding listed in Germany; Scacco (1982), held by two (Essex and London); Mezey and King (2000) held by 12 (Cambridge, Cardiff, London, Swansea, Manchester, Glasgow, Leicester, Newcastle, Nottingham, Oxford, Bangor, Wolverhampton).
19. I followed Rentoul and Applebloom's (1997) literature search, which used various databases and the Internet to demonstrate clearly the limited available number of studies at the time.
    As is the case with McMullen (1990) – only three second-hand copies available worldwide via Amazon (as at April 2009).
    Scacco (1982).

22. In particular, some authors go to great lengths to rebut the notion 'homosexual rape', see Struckman-Johnson (1988); Canter and Hodge (1998); Chapleau et al. (2008).

23. For correlations in victim sexual orientation and attribution of blame, see Daugherty and Esper (1998) and Davies and McCartney (2003).

24. Who states that 'since most of this research entails feminist assumptions, attitudinal correlates of blame have never been previously discussed in relation to male victims' (ibid., p. 210).

25. Foucauldian feminism is perhaps something of a misnomer as this stance does not adopt a Foucauldian positioning as might be implied. Note that Alcoff (1997), cited in Howe (2008), asserts her position as feminist Foucauldian to designate her work as having such inherent prioritization, but that her usage of this identifier as described therein is not the same as my own in respect of existing 'feminist Foucauldian' scholarship.

26. These are discussed in greater depth in Part III.

27. Bourke (2007) does include male-on-male rape, but only for incarcerated/institutionalized populations.

28. Discussed in more detail in subsequent chapters.

29. Not gender-neutral though as the assailant must penetrate using his penis.

30. Consider for instance the phenomenon of rape within marriage.

31. An adaptation that Rape Crisis struggles to accomplish. This organization still resists the inclusion of male victims and victims of women. See the discussion in Chapter 6.

32. For example Koss and Cook (1993), cited in Bevacqua (2000).

33. Abdullah-Khan's (2008) text is a clear attempt to redress this, but is empirically driven with a pragmatic agenda.

34. The allegation that feminism has ignored male rape is directly rebutted in the response piece by Rumney and Jamel (2009).

35. For example, Tong (1984); Hall (1988); MacKinnon (1990); Rush (1990); Naffine (1994); Rumney and Morgan-Taylor (1997a, b); Novotny (2003).

36. For example, Gillespie (1996).

37. For example, Lees (1997); Gregory and Lees (1999).

38. Funk (1993); Scarce (1997); Allen (2002); Davies and Rogers (2006).

39. For example, Butler (1990); Stanko and Hobdell (1993); Newburn and Stanko (2002); Walklate (2007a, b).

40. Heterosexual masculinity as hierarchical has been raised in the literature that purports to explain male rape, albeit limited to institutional settings (prison, armed forces etc.) – ostensibly explaining rape of the male in the absence of the female and thus still within evolutionary and heterosexual masculine imperatives, whereas my explicit focus is most assuredly not institutional settings, it is community settings.

41. Feminists have in fact been at the forefront of masculinities research that has enabled recognition of male victimhood. The reality therefore is a little more complex.

42. For a specific discussion of historical depictions of male rape.

43. Documented as encompassed in legislative form during the Qing period in China, albeit interpreted as homosexual by modern day authors.

44. But note that, once again, this is interpreted as homosexuality.

45. Where sexual assault was recognized for both males and females.

46. The latter interpretations have led to examples being positively reconfigured and appropriated as key to queer theory – including examples in Foucault's own works.
47. Or Caeneus.
48. See Lefkowitz (2002) for a discussion about predatory goddesses in ancient Greek mythology.
49. For 'the crime of Laius', he and his people were cursed – he was killed by Oedipus, his own son. Significantly, this is an aspect of the myth much neglected by Freud in the analysis he undertook to develop his theory of the Oedipus complex. For a discussion of how acknowledgement of Laius would undermine Freud's theory or, to put it another way, how this omission was necessary to preserve the plausibility of his theory, see Gilman et al. (1994, pp. 29–37). Interestingly, these authors interpret Laius as homosexual rather than a rapist.
50. For example, Gillespie (1996); DeKeseredy (1999).
51. See Bevacqua (2000); Sielke (2002); Bourke (2007), amongst others, for a detailed examination of the history of feminism and rape.

3   Investigation – A Foucauldian Triangulation?

1. For a concise discussion of the development of the notion of victim blame in Amir's work, see Cuklanz (1996, pp. 23–27).
2. For an overview of the development of 'victim blame' and its interrelationship with the birth of victimology and specifically the study of rape, see Cole (2007, pp. 123–134).
3. Von Hentig first coined the term 'victim precipitation' in the 1940s, building on work performed in the 1930s by Mendelsohn. It was later adopted and developed by Wolfgang (1958) in respect of murder, or what he termed 'victim precipitated homicide'.
4. 'Just-world theory', coined by Lerner and Mathews (1967).
5. See Kelly (2000) and Kelly et al. (2005).
6. Still detected though – see criminal injuries compensation decision to reduce awards to women who had consumed alcohol, as noted by Williams (2008a).
7. See Lamb (1999). Interestingly, this is a text that at the same time is critical of the feminization of victimhood, but in overlooking the male it privileges a gendered notion of the victim. This gendering is replicated in Newburn and Stanko's (2002) chapter, 'When men are victims: the failure of victimology', about the failure of victimology to recognize male victims, where they criticize that criminology prefers to cast males solely as offenders and yet they themselves repeat this by overlooking females as offenders (only recognizing men as victims of other men).
8. As seen with studies conceptualizing male rape (victim and perpetrator) as oriented around homosexuality (be that as within same-sex relationships, homophobic behaviour or as repressed desire/psychoanalytic conflict in sexual identity). For example, see Toolis (1995), Stermac et al., (1996), Scarce (1997), Wallace (2007).
9. For example, young people – adolescents or children.

10. Ways of organizing 'knowledge', though by no means limited to this – see 'The Will to Knowledge' in Foucault (2000).
11. Principally the 'sciences' where such knowledge is generated, though by no means limited to this – see 'The Will to Knowledge' in Foucault (2000).
12. Mechanism of power that regulates individuals.
13. CDA is discussed in more detail in the following chapter. See Wodak and Meyer (2001) for an overview of methods within the umbrella of CDA.
14. Foucault suggests using theory as a 'tool-kit' or 'toolbox'– in the sense of an instrument, rather than a system. See Packer (2003, p. 28).
15. For example, Bratich et al. (2003); Miller and Rose (2008); Nadeson (2008); Dean (2010).
16. Especially regarding the focus on so-called 'mentalities' of governing, for example work by Pavlich (2005), Miller and Rose (1990) and Rose and Miller (1992). However, for a discussion that supports this interpretation, see Dean (2010, pp. 24–29).
17. 'Where the principles associated with working in business and industry in a market economy have been incorporated into the public sector' (Skelton and Francis, 2005, p. 5), the emphasis on measurable outputs is summed up in the mantra of the late 1980s Audit Commission, 'economy, efficiency and effectiveness' (cited in Clarke et al., 2000, p. 260). For a concise definition of managerialism, see Wakefield and Fleming (2009, pp. 196–198).
18. See Foucault (2000) for a collection of his works in this area, and Luxon (2008) for a specific discussion of ethics and subjectivity.
19. Especially in the legitimization of hierarchies of victimization and the resurrection of victim binaries that together underscore a notion of the ideal victim and thus the privileged accord of victimhood – to recognize and exclude.
20. À la Jock Young (nd).

4 Representations – Knowing Victimhood

1. For a detailed discussion see Chapleau et al. (2008).
2. For example in the case of Boyle (2005, p. 142) and Demirkan-Martin (2009, pp. 128–162).
3. A prolific and highly productive area of study and one that Lamb (1999) notes as achieving ever greater prominence whilst theorizing rape stagnated, an observation supported by Mardorossian (2002) who states that rape has become 'undertheorized' and 'untheorizable', thus neglected in preference for more 'ambivalent' areas such as the media.
4. For example Boyle (2005) dedicates all of a quarter of a page to male rape in her *Media and Violence* text.
5. The mass media is far more diverse than this, as is its audience. I did consider organizing this chapter in terms of 'infotainment' and 'critical literacy' in order to try to more clearly indicate this, but this became far too unwieldy because reflecting the multiplicity of formats available within the media creates a barrier to discussion by rendering it far too stilted. Unfortunately, it is beyond the scope of this present project to more clearly

illustrate complexity and contingency, though they will be explicitly raised in discussion.

6. Fan-authored fictional pieces that draw on and extend the myths and tropes of the 'official' source of fandom.
7. Whilst Cohen and Young (1973, p. 339) contend, 'This influence is not monolithic ... the audience can perhaps shop around within this framework, but they can rarely escape it.'
8. The work of Jock Young exemplifies this.
9. See Ferrell, Hayward and Young (2008).
10. See Altheide (2003, p.16).
11. Also conceived of as a culture of fear. See works by Furedi (for example, 2005 and 2006).
12. For a general discussion of the gendered dimensions of fear of crime, see Goodey (1997).
13. Not LexisNexis or any other source only available by subscription.
14. *The Guardian, The Mirror, The Daily Mail, The Times* (UK).
15. *The Los Angeles Times, New York Daily News, USA Today.*
16. *China Daily.*
17. *The Globe and Mail.*
18. Specific problems were encountered in usage of the UK publication *The Daily Mail* and the US publication the *LA Times*. In the former, the search engine gave constant false positives in respect of their running banner advertising their coverage of a high-profile rape case, which combined with their own fixed limit of 50 hits as a restricted maximum actually produced very few relevant results. In the latter, there was a large number of false positives due to their search engine automatically bringing up related terms such as 'assault' and 'violation'. In neither case could the errors be remedied.
19. Bajwa (2009); Kelaway (2009); Mullan (2009).
20. Levy (2009).
21. Dodd (2009a); Fletcher (2009, note that this article was repeated in a later search and so counted twice); Homayoun (2009); Leeder (2009); Smith, D (2009b); The Associated Press (2009).
22. Armario (2009).
23. Gibb (2009).
24. Daily Mail Reporter (2008).
25. http://www.guardian.co.uk/society/rape.
26. And their sister publication, the *Observer*.
27. Baird (2009); Canning (2009); Harvey (2009); Smith, D. (2009a); *The Guardian* (2009); Williams (2008a).
28. Barrett (2008); Bindel (2008a, 2008b, 2008c, 2009a, 2009b); Brooks (2008, 2009); Cochrane (2008); Conroy (2009); Dodd (2009b); Dustin (2008); Elliott (2008a, 2008b); Gentleman (2009); Laville (2009a, 2009b); Lister (2009); Longstaff (2009); McEwan (2009); Mulholland (2009a, 2009b); Russell (2009); Ryan (2008); Smith, J (2009a, 2009b); Travis (2009); Williams (2008b, 2008c, 2009a); Williams and Hirsch (2008); Williams (2009b, 2009c, 2009d); Yates (2009).
29. Katy Price.
30. The Internet Movie Database, http://www.imdb.com/.

31. See Projansky (2001); Wlodarz (2001); and Demirkan-Martin (2009).
32. For example, US produced certificate-12 films *Liar, Liar* (1997) and *Bruce Almighty* (2003); Hong Kong Cinema released *Dummy Mommy Without a Baby* (2001); US daytime television series *Malcolm in the Middle* (2000).
33. *Liar, Liar* (1997); *Audition* (1999); *Deep in the Woods* (2000); *Ginger Snaps* (2000); *Me, Myself and Irene* (2000); *Road Trip* (2000); *Scary Movie* (2000); *Battle Royale* (2001); *Dummy Mommy Without A Baby* (2001); *Scary Movie 2* (2001); *The Hot Chick* (2002); *Bruce Almighty* (2003); *Euro Trip* (2004); *Without a Paddle* (2004); *The Spirit of Jeet Kune Do: Once Upon a Time in High School* (2004); *Scary Movie 4* (2006); *I Now Pronounce You Chuck and Larry* (2007); Rush Hour 3 (2007); *Harold and Kumar Escape Guantanamo Bay* (2008); *Mum and Dad* (2008); *You Don't Mess with the Zohan* (2008).
34. Once again I deliberately attempted to challenge my own assumptions, and endeavoured to include material that I did not anticipate would be useful.
35. *Malcolm in the Middle* (2000); *The World Stands Up* (2004); *Never Mind the Buzzcocks* (2005); *Supernatural* (2005); *Two Pints of Lager and a Packet of Crisps* (2005); *Mock The Week* (2007); *My Name is Earl* (2007); *Supernatural* (2007a, 2007b); *Commercial Breakdown with Jimmy Carr* (2008); *My Name is Earl* (2008); *Dollhouse* (2009); *Jack Dee, Live at the Apollo* (2009); *Michael Macintyre's Comedy Road Show* (2009); *Mock the Week* (2009); *The Kevin Bishop Show* (2009).
36. See Mellencamp, 1995, pp. 147–151.
37. This is something Projansky (2001, pp. 146–153) argues of *Thelma and Louise* – reviewing feminist analyses of this film she asserts that to read this film as pro-feminist is far too simplistic.
38. This cannot be regarded as fulfilling the legal definition of rape, as despite the use of overt force to achieve congress, the penetration is done *to* Ginger. The legal definition pivots on penetration by a penis of a victim, and therefore precludes a female being a rapist (except in the case of certain transgender populations). Suffice to say that in the audience's mind this scene – whilst literally constituting sexual assault – does in fact connote rape.
39. Clover (1992, p. 226) states that 'the capacity for sadistic violence is what finally distinguishes male from female'.
40. Chapter 6 on the DVD root menu.
41. He does not regard it as conventional, but I do – given that his examples all involve male-on-male rape as homosexualized and in orthodox and stereotypical settings, namely institutions, prison, children's homes, etc. His analysis does not involve male rape in the community, or in heterosexual or desexualized contexts.
42. A scene where miscommunication between Ginger and her sister results in the sister assuming Ginger was raped, and leads the viewer to think Ginger has killed the boyfriend.
43. I have deliberately excluded reference to homophobic themes that also occur throughout Korn's back catalogue, not because I do not believe them to be important, but because I believe such a focus would function as deflection. The homophobia that is notable is used for many of the same purposes

as described above – to make the male violable, weak, demeaned and feminized. It is significant for this reason, not as homophobia per se.

5   Biopolitics – Imagining Victimhood

1. Sellnow (2010, p. 4) defines artifacts as 'a sign or series of signs that is socially grounded ... its meaning shared by some identifiable community or cultural group'.
2. 'there is a tendency (even in the best of us) to see fan studies as a somewhat specialized, narrowly defined body of research that operates on the fringes of contemporary media studies' (Jenkins, 2007, p. 363).
3. The competing notions of the fan, and their relevance for biopower, are discussed in more detail below.
4. Which is guilty of a simplistic celebration of Otherness that reifies the fan's placement in a binary, rather than challenging the binaried construct itself.
5. As Bley (2009, p. 56) asserts, slash 'makes up a significant portion – if not the majority of many media fandoms' fan fiction, fan art and fan vids'.
6. Not to be confused with fem-slash which is female/female.
7. For a list of terminology and definitions, see Hellekson and Busse (2006, pp. 9–12).
8. Often in terms of awakening a sexual identity or unleashing a repressed desire, thus drawing on common male rape myths.
9. A wealth of feminist analyses of female authored male on male (m/m) slash has been performed, focussing on 'romance' and interpreted in ways that comply with this as subversion, resistance or 'empowerment' (see Hellekson and Busse, 2006, p. 17). But there is no similar wealth of attention regarding m/m non-con (non-consensual sex – i.e. rape) and women's role in re-inscribing hegemonic masculinity. Convention here is to interpret m/m as erotic fiction, with female authors subverting traditional gender roles. I believe it is limited and indeed dangerously short-sighted to apply this to non-con.
10. That this medium is dominated by heterosexual contributors is supported by the research of many of the authors cited in this chapter. Although, interestingly, Scodari (2007, p. 51) asserts this medium is wholly non-heterosexual, 'slash is homoerotic fiction that can be composed by gay, bisexual, or lesbian fans about characters of their own sex'. She cites no evidence for this assumption and one must wonder then why she supposed this.
11. For example see Tosenberger (2008a).
12. For example: Keft-Kennedy (2008); Kustritz (2008); Tosenberger (2008b); Chan (2010).
13. A sentiment echoed by authors such as Jung (2006), amongst others contributing to Hellekson and Busse's (2006) text.
14. In this instance comprised of active fans, which is significant as many authors laud these as exercising resistance.
15. For example, see Kirby-Diaz (2009); and Gray et al. (2007).
16. In the material I identified, the rapes were frequently associated with: gang-rape scenarios involving multiple and simultaneous aggressors; coercion involving threats of or actual violence, including the presence of weaponry

such as guns or knives, and the use of these and other objects for the purpose of penetration; the explicit and elaborate infliction of pain and degradation.

17. Similar to gratuitous depictions of female rape predominant in 1970s and 1980s.

18. For complexities in the definition of fandom, see essays by contributors to Kirby-Diaz (2009) and Gray et al. (2007), as well as the classic text by Jenkins (1997). Kirby-Diaz (2009, p. 197) defines fandom as 'A fan culture that develops around a specific entertainment phenomenon'. For my purposes I am merely pointing to those groups/communities, their spaces and artifacts that involve production of novel text etc. by fans that in themselves become exclusive. In this sense a fandom – whilst it may be based on canon – may move beyond it.

19. Canon refers to the original, 'official' or copy-written text.

20. Google ranks search results by 'popularity' so that those sites that have been selected more often will rank higher in the search results that each subsequent user is presented with (Somers, 2005).

21. LiveJournal is a host site that allows users to create personal blogs and other ephemera, and link with other users to form a 'virtual community'. For a discussion of the significance of LiveJournal to fans and fandoms, see Busse (2006). Suffice to say that this specific social networking medium has become an important site for fandom in terms of production, consumption and communality.

22. On the 20 December, 2009 there were 451,000 hits for 'Supernatural Slash' on Google; 45,300 hits for 'SPN slash' (SPN being a fandom contraction of 'Supernatural'); 287,000 for 'spn slash non-con' with multiple groups and lists on LiveJournal, each recommending multiple pieces of work

23. Nominations for which are a significant indicator of esteem, being voted for by the LiveJournal SPN community, see http://community.livejournal.com/spn_oscars

24. In the sense of a psychosexual disorder or 'abnormality'.

25. Darkestangel (2009a, 2009b, 2005–2009); Starbright73 (2009).

26. Authors known only by their pseudonyms: 'Darkestangel', award winner on Slash Oscars, highly recommended via LiveJournal and who hosts her own site which itself appeared top on a Google search for 'spn non-con slash' (http://supernaturalfic.darknessprevails.com/); and 'Starbright73', award winner on Slash Oscars and highly recommended via LiveJournal, where she presents her blog, discussion board and fiction (http://starbright73.livejournal.com/profile).

27. Not including the accompanying blogs and discussion board posts.

28. Indicating not only an invested fan, but an investment in this sole work.

29. Some authors preferring simply 'the conduct of conduct'.

30. He explicitly states that 'In most of the rest of the present text I shall discuss practices concerned to conduct the conduct of others rather than those concerned to conduct one's own conduct. I shall thus deal with "practices of government" in a narrower sense than that encompassed by the phrase "conduct of conduct"' (Dean, 2010, p. 21) but doesn't explain his reasoning here. He doesn't apply this to a social 'problem' as such, but simply seeks to illustrate the principles through reference to various examples.

31. For an overview of UK, US and Australian variations in Foucauldian informed scholarship, see Packer (2003, pp. 25–26) – this outlines different interpretations and 'paradigms' of Foucault and governmentality, concerned with micropolitics (Britain) versus the philosophical (Australia). Bratich et al. (2003) provide a useful introduction to the different ways of 'doing' Foucault and assert that, certainly at the time of writing their text, the British version of Foucault was not at all concerned with 'the provenance of culture', and instead, exemplified in the works of Nikolas Rose, is focused on state government. This of course accounts for the preoccupation with structures, institutions and policy – continuing the Marxist legacy. Criminology also has this preoccupation: if it isn't crime science, it's political economy.

32. Where Nadeson (2008) refers to the American public's 'self-assessment and knowledge' as rooted in and known through the principles of mental hygiene, particularly in the form of child-guidance literature and expertise, and early advertising.

33. Deployment in this instance can also be understood as dispositifs, those 'structures', relations, etc. that perpetuate and maintain power in the social body (see O'Farrell, 2007).

34. For example, in the works of Starbright73, such as (2009) 'Faces of Evil' [online] http://starbright73.livejournal.com/223010.html#cutid1 (accessed 12/11/2009); and other winners of the 2008 Slash Oscars (http://community. livejournal.com/spn_oscars accessed 22/12/2009), especially those under the categories of Erotica and Angst/Drama; and those on the recommended list 'Hurt! Sam: because we care' at http://community.livejournal.com/hurt_sam (accessed 26/11/2009) such as those by Nebula, eg 'Touch Lightly Lest I Break' at http://community.livejournal.com/hurt_sam (accessed 12/11/2009).

35. Youssef (2004) cites Bacon-Smith (1992), Jenkins (1992) and Penley (1991) in supporting her assertion that most authors of slash are female. The prevalence of women authoring such fan fiction online is mirrored by the production of specific 'boys love' manga for females that also draw from the same genre; this is borne out in several other studies, such as Rebaza (2009, p. 155), who notes that it tends to be women who produce and consume fan fiction, saying that 'If one is a female in this fandom, there is only a 7 percent chance that she has never tried reading any fanfic'. Hill (2009, p. 174) states that for vidders (those slashing video or other visual media) 'the most common type of vids are "slash" vids'.

36. Rebaza (2009, p. 155) notes that – in general – fan-fiction writers and consumers tend to be young, with over 34 per cent of writers being 18–24, the highest proportion in her study; she also notes that 90 per cent of women in this bracket have read fan fiction, a far higher rate than the 25–35 age group, but one that her survey revealed was matched by the over 50s. What can be said from her results is that the younger fans are more likely to both consume *and* produce in this fandom. One must consider the significance here for socialization and indoctrination into normative gender roles. We must also question how many of those identifying as 18 are in reality younger. LiveJournal enforces age-appropriate content, effectively prohibiting under-age slashers, with many accounts historically blocked or deleted in purges, and content restricted to only those users whose profiles comply.

As a consequence 'new' users ensure their profiles comply, irrespective of reality.

37. This type of sentiment was a recurring feature in discussion boards around individual pieces of non-con slash expressed by authors and readers.

38. Such as: the attributes of key characters – their physical appearance, personalities, manner and mode of expression; their mythologies – backgrounds, experiences and histories contained in official story arcs; the foci of the show itself – a focus on the paranormal, supernatural, religious and urban legends; its genre – drama, horror, buddy/family, road-trip; its locations – small American towns, motel rooms, bars, diners; props – the make and model of their car, preferred weapons etc; and soundtrack (stipulated by the author, not provided for download) – classic rock.

39. Alternate Universe designates the slasher deliberately progressing their story outside of canon.

40. Please note that page numbers are not necessarily stable in this medium.

41. This also intertwines with feminization, as the notion of such is stereotypically that of the sensitive and unstable female, thus the author makes reference to Dean's: 'intuition', 'sixth sense' and 'mood swings'.

42. This doesn't necessarily satisfy legal definitions of rape any more than Ginger's assault (in the previous chapter) does. It is no less significant for its literal position as a serious sexual assault given that it is unequivocally an act of sexual aggression that incorporates penetration.

43. The phrase 'slut! Dean' acts as a classification denoting a particular type of characterization within the slash genre.

44. See posts on http://www.squidge.org/peja~/cgi-bin/reviews.php?sid=19819 [accessed 26/11/2009].

45. As the author states through Dean: 'great, I get to be an abused housewife for the rest of eternity' (p. 288).

46. A strong case being one that – unsurprisingly – best conforms to anticipated jury prejudice in favour of the ideal victim. See Rumney and Morgan-Taylor (2004) for a detailed examination of how rape myths are utilized to discredit victims as witnesses.

47. Research with community and college samples reveals a prejudice in favour of 'typical' (see above) male rape, wherein the ideal victim binary is very much in operation, see literature review by Davies and Rogers (2006). For a case study examining this bias in action in the courtroom, see Rumney and Morgan-Taylor (2004).

48. See Tewkesbury (2007) for a good overview here. Note the correlation between demonstrable 'submissive injuries' and signs of 'excessive violence' with reporting/help-seeking behaviours. Whilst these may make up the majority of officially recorded male rapes, they are not necessarily 'typical' of male rape. This is an important distinction.

49. See Gavey and Gow (2001) for a good introduction and overview of this issue in respect of female victims, using New Zealand as a case study.

50. See Pineau (1989) for a classic feminist analysis of the construct of 'date' or 'acquaintance' rape.

51. Especially in respect of intoxication, see Struckman-Johnson and Struckman-Johnson (1992)

52. It is worth recalling here that non-consensual oral penetration by a penis (being made to perform fellatio) does satisfy the legal definition of rape in the UK, whilst being made to endure fellatio (having this performed on you against your will) does not – it is demoted in seriousness.

6 Individuation – Acting on Victimhood

1. Deleuze (1992) prefers to use the terms 'apparatus' or 'social apparatus', but warns that these are not synonyms for 'dispositif' and indeed goes on to caution that there is simply no direct translation of this term.
2. Literally 'edited out'.
3. Expression borrowed from Margarey (1978, p. 120).
4. Term coined by Best (1997).
5. Not a circular argument (à la philosophy and logic), more akin to a circular narrative (as it is used in media studies); although in my usage it is certainly my intention to disrupt the former through the latter. Foucault advocated and utilized this strategy himself, as described by Davidson in his introduction to Foucault's (1997) text.
6. It is important to note the wider context here, see, for example, the WHO (2005) *Multi-Country Study on Women's Health and Domestic Violence against Women*. Funding is also a relevant issue, for example, DAPHNE; and Government grants, for example, the victims fund from the Ministry of Justice; however, it is beyond the scope of this endeavour to examine these in full.
7. For relevant, albeit general, discussions on the victimology/victimization industry, see Elias (1994) and Best (1997)
8. See Abdullah-Khan (2008).
9. Exceptions here include works by Rumney and Morgan-Taylor regarding the issue of gender neutrality in rape law, see, for example, Rumney and Morgan-Taylor, 1997 a, b; Rumney, 2007.
10. See vignette on p. 31.
11. See Sarrel and Masters (1982); Anderson and Struckman-Johnson (1998); Fiebert and Tucci (1998); although more frequently in respect of child abuse, for example, Johnson and Shrier (1987); Oliver (2007); and Duncan (2010).
12. See Steinmetz (1978); Flynn (1990); Dobash et al. (1992); George (1994); Gadd et al. (2002); Belknap and Melton (2003); Kelly (2003); Dobash and Emerson (2004).
13. See the paper by Novotny (2003), and the response piece by Rumney (2007).
14. Suffice to say that injustice for one group facilitates and legitimizes injustice for all.
15. Davies et al. (2005, p. 83) caution that policy making is not the sole preserve of Whitehall or Westminster – there are a wealth of agencies, including professional and voluntary bodies, that together constitute the criminal justice system. 'Other influential players in the process of consultation are professional groups, pressure groups and lay participants' – this puts feminism and 'knowledge' centre stage – or rather the feminist knowledge of rape that underscores current male rape myths.

16. Research indicates that for many women, voluntary agencies, rather than the police, are their first point of contact post-rape. These agencies play a significant role in referring victims to the police. Likewise, the police will ensure victims are referred to them if they have not been already been referred (for example, the *Haven* and project *Sapphire* in London).

17. In the main body of the review, it should be noted that male victims are given some separate attention (pp. 30–31), which is seemingly well intentioned though not without problems; but the following section titled 'effects of rape' should be inclusive, and certainly commences as such – using 'victim' in its supposedly neutral sense, but a female example is quickly foregrounded and sustained.

18. In fact it comprises one of the earliest 'accepted' forms of male rape in the community. See Groth and Burgess (1980); Scacco (1982); and Scarce (1997).

19. Regarding female-on-female sexual violence in prison, see Struckman-Johnson et al. (1996); for female-on-male sexual violence in general see Sarrel and Masters (1982); Smith et al. (1988); Fiebert and Tucci (1998); and Oliver (2007).

20. Hereafter IGR.

21. Hereafter RC.

22. http://www.rapecrisis.org.uk/news_show.php?id=41 (accessed 26/04/2010).

23. Despite research indicating that myths around male rape persist in this sector, for example, classic work by Donnelly and Kenyon (1996) and more recent investigation by Kassing and Prierto (2003).

24. A failure plausibly underwritten by their continued identification – overt or covert – as 'feminist' organizations, see Maier (2008).

25. See statistical data on provision published by the Fawcett Society (2008).

26. By RC but not exclusive to RC – the most recent report by the Survivors Trust (2010) states that across the sector as a whole only 67 per cent of respondents to their survey make provision for males and that this is 'consistently less' (p. 40) than for females.

27. (http://www.rapecrisis.org.uk/centres.php, accessed 26/04/2010) which covers England and Wales.

28. This is not to say that there is no such support available in those areas, but that RC provides neither support themselves nor indication of support provided by others.

29. Rape and Sexual Abuse Centre (Merseyside) (RASA); Cheshire and Merseyside RASASC; Chester Sexual Violence Support Service (CSVSS); Manchester Rape Crisis (MRC); West Cumbria Rape Crisis (WCRC).

30. West Cumbria Rape Crisis (WCRC); Cheshire and Merseyside RASASC.

31. Barnsley Sexual Abuse and Rape Crisis Helpline (BSARCH); Bradford Rape Crisis and Sexual Abuse Survivors Service (BRCandSASS); Doncaster Rape and Sexual Abuse Counselling Service (DRASACS); Kirklees Rape and Sexual Abuse Counselling Centre (KRASACC); Sheffield Rape and Sexual Abuse Counselling Service (SRASACS); Support After Rape and Sexual Violence Leeds (SARSVL).

32. Doncaster Rape and Sexual Abuse Counselling Service (DRASACS); Kirklees Rape and Sexual Abuse Counselling Centre (KRASACC).

33. Sexual Abuse and Incest Line (SAIL); Derbyshire Rape Crisis (DRC); Northamptonshire Rape and Incest Crisis Centre (NRICC); Nottingham Rape Crisis Centre (NRCC); Jasmine House, Leicester Rape Crisis.
34. Northamptonshire Rape and Incest Crisis Centre (NRICC) and Derbyshire Rape Crisis (DRC).
35. Coventry Rape and Sexual Abuse Centre Ltd (CRASAC); Savana; Worcestershire Rape and Sexual Abuse Support Centre (WRSASC).
36. Savana.
37. Cambridge Rape Crisis Centre (CRCC); Centre for Action on Rape and Abuse (CARA); Herts Area Rape Crisis and Sexual Abuse Centre (HARCSAC); Peterborough Rape Crisis Counselling Group (PRCCG); South Essex Rape and Incest Crisis Centre (SERICC); Sexual Violence Alliance (SeVA); Watford Rape Crisis and Sexual Abuse Helpline (WRC).
38. Centre for Action on Rape and Abuse (CARA); Sexual Violence Alliance (SeVA).
39. Aylesbury Vale Rape Crisis (AVRC); Oxford Sexual Abuse and Rape Crisis Centre (OSARCC); Southampton Rape Crisis and Sexual Abuse Counselling Service; Rape Crisis (Wycombe, Chiltern and South Bucks); East Kent Rapeline (EKRL); Survivors Network (SN).
40. Southampton Rape Crisis and Sexual Abuse Counselling Service.
41. North Wales Rape and Sexual Abuse Support Centre.
42. http://www.mankindcounselling.org.uk
43. http://www.thesurvivorstrust.org
44. Free phone from the UK: 08088029999.
45. Based in the North West.
46. Based in the East Midlands.
47. Based in the West Midlands.
48. Based in the North West.
49. Based in the East of England.
50. Based in the East of England.
51. Based in the South East.
52. Based in the West Midlands.
53. Based in the South East.
54. Based in the North West.
55. Based in the Yorkshire and Humber region.
56. http://www.rcni.ie
57. http://www.rcne.com

8 Excavating the Gendered/ing Dimensions of Male Rape

1. See Cahill (2000); Rumney (2008); Bonthuys (2008); and Loizidou (2000) for an overview of relevant issues.
2. See Bevacqua (2000).
3. See Abdullah-Khan (2008, p. 70).
4. Where the police decide there is not enough evidence to record the offence as a crime; this can include assessment of the 'reliability' of their witness – who it is worth remembering is also the victim. Dyer (2007) cites an independent report that found 'of a sample of 752 rape reports in 2005 looked

at by the inspection team, 179 were "no-crimed", of which 57 should have been recorded as crimes. Among the eight police areas studied, the rate of no-criming varied hugely – from 4% to 47%.'

5. Where the CPS decide not to take a case to court as the expectation of conviction is low; according to research by Kelly, Lovett and Regan (2005) some 26 per cent of all reported and recorded rapes are affected.

6. Where the prosecution is unsuccessful and the defendant is found not guilty. In 2002, 79 per cent of all prosecutions for rape ended in acquittal. See Kelly, Lovett and Regan (2005).

7. Not least in respect of her methodology, which utilizes traditional discourse analysis rather than a Foucauldian CDA.

8. For example, Howe (2008) mentions male rape only on page 194 of a 219-page monograph dealing with sexual violence; Cahill (2001) acknowledges only the possibility of male rape in a curious aside on page 23 of her 217 page monograph about rape; and Bevacqua (2000) mentions the male as a possibility on page 98 of her 240 page text concerned with the history of rape.

9. By which I mean both material in her book (2005) that was previously published as journal articles or chapters in other textbooks, as well as new material written specifically for her book (2005).

10. Where sexual victimization is frequently regarded as traumatic precisely because it is dissonant to hegemonic masculinity.

11. W6, a female.

12. For a discussion of some of these issues see Phelan (1990); classic works by feminists around the value of Foucault include Diamond and Quinby (1988), Nicholson, (1990), Sawicki (1991), McNay (1992), and Ramazanoglu (1993); more recent works include Taylor and Vintges (2004) and Howe (2008).

13. For example, Gavey (2005), Scarce (1997), and McMullen (1990) amongst others.

References

Abdullah-Khan, N. (2008) *Male Rape: The Emergence of a Social and Legal Issue*, Hampshire: Palgrave Macmillan.

Abercrombie, N. and Longhurst, B. (1998) *Audiences: A Sociological Theory of Performance and Imagination*, London: Sage.

Adam, N.M. and Ryan, K.M. (2008) 'The grey area of heterosexual sex' *Sex Roles*, 58(11–12): 894–895.

Ainsworth, P.B. (2000) *Psychology and Crime: Myths and Reality*, Harlow: Longman.

Allen, S. (2002) 'Male victims of rape: responses to a perceived threat to masculinity' in Hoyle, C. and Young, R. (eds.) *New Visions of Crime Victims*, Oxford: Hart.

Altheide, D. (2003) 'Notes towards a politics of fear' *Journal for Crime, Conflict and the Media*, 1 (1): 37–54.

Amir, M. (1967) 'Victim precipitated forcible rape' *Journal of Criminal Law, Criminology and Police Science*, 58 (4): 493–502.

Amir, M. (1971) *Patterns in Forcible Rape*, Chicago: University of Chicago Press.

Anderson, C.L. (1982) 'Males as sexual assault victims: multiple levels of trauma' *Journal of Homosexuality*, 7 (2–3): 145–162.

Anderson, L. (1999) 'Characterological and behavioural blame in conversations about male and female rape' *Journal of Language and Social Psychology* 18 (4): 377–394.

Anderson, I. and Doherty, K. (2008) *Accounting for Rape: Psychology, Feminism and Discourse Analysis in the Study of Sexual Violence*, London: Routledge.

Anderson, I. and Struckman-Johnson, C. (eds.) (1998) *Sexually Aggressive Women: Current Perspectives and Controversies*, New York: The Guilford Press.

Anderson, I. and Swainson, V. (2001) 'Perceived motivation for rape: gender differences in beliefs about female and male rape' *Social Psychology*, 6 (4): 1–12.

Antoniou, A. (2004) 'Batoru Rowaiaru/Battle Royale' in Bowyer, J. (ed.) *The Cinema of Japan and Korea*, London: Wallflower Press.

Armario, C. (2009) 'School bullying grows from silent battle to crime' *USA Today*, 7 September.

Atmore, C. (1999) 'Victims, backlash, and radical feminist theory (or, the morning after they stole feminism's fire)' in, Lamb, S. (ed.) *New Versions of Victims: Feminists Struggle with the Concept*, London: New York University Press.

Audition (1999) [film] Dir. Takashi Miike, Japan: Shout Factory.

Bacon-Smith, C. (1992) *Enterprising Women: Television Fandom and the Creation of Popular Myth*, Philadelphia, PA: University of Pennsylvania Press.

Baird, V. (2009) 'Sustainable support for rape victims' *The Guardian*, 12 August.

Bajwa, S. (2009) 'Why you don't get ... Hollyoaks' *The Guardian*, 17 September.

Balmain, C. (2008) *Introduction to Japanese Horror Film*, Edinburgh: Edinburgh University Press.

Barkan, S.E. (2006) *Criminology: A Sociological Understanding*, Upper Saddle River, NJ: Pearson Prentice Hall.

Barker, M., Mathijs, E. and Mendik, X. (2006) 'Menstrual monsters: the reception of the Ginger Snaps cult horror franchise' *Film International* 21, 4 (3): 68–77.

Barnett, H. (1997) *Sourcebook on Feminist Jurisprudence*, London: Cavendish.

Barrett, D. (2008) 'Convictions for rape a postcode lottery, says equality group' *The Guardian*, 7 July.

Bart, P.B. (1979) 'Rape as a paradigm of sexism in society – victimization and its discontents' *Women's Studies International Quarterly*, 2: 347–357.

Bartol, C.R. and Bartol, A.M. (eds.) (2006) *Current Perspectives in Forensic Psychology and Criminal Justice*, Thousand Oaks, CA: Sage.

Battle Royale (2001) [film] Dir. Kinji Fukasaku, UK: Tartan.

BBC News (2009) [TV], 'At one', BBC, BBC1, original air date 22 Sept 2009, UK.

Belknap, J. and Melton, H.C. (2003) 'He hits, she hits: assessing gender differences and similarities in officially reported intimate partner violence' *Journal of Criminal Justice and Behaviour*, 30 (3): 328–348.

Bell, V. (1993) *Interrogating Incest: Feminism, Foucault and the Law*, London: Routledge.

Berrill, K.T. (1990) 'Anti-gay violence and victimization in the United States: an overview' *Journal of Interpersonal Violence*, 5 (3): 274–294.

Best, J. (1997) 'Victimization and the victim industry' *Society*, 34 (4): 9–17.

Bevacqua, M. (2000) *Rape on the Public Agenda: Feminism and the Politics of Sexual Assault*, Boston: Northeastern University Press.

Bhattacharyya, G. (2000) 'Black skin/white boards' in Back, L. and Solomos, J. (eds.) *Theories of Race and Racism: A Reader*, London: Routledge.

Bindel, J. (2008a) 'A rape campaigner runs for office' *The Guardian*, 2 July.

Bindel, J. (2008b) 'Rape victims nationwide need this support' *The Guardian*, 16 July.

Bindel, J. (2008c) 'There is no excuse' *The Guardian*, 28 July.

Bindel, J. (2009a) 'Just another week of rapes' *The Guardian*, 29 May.

Bindel, J. (2009b) 'Mirran's twisted logic' *The Guardian*, 2 September.

Bley, R. (2009) 'RL on LJ: fandom and the presentation of self in online life' in Kirby-Diaz, M. (ed.) *Buffy and Angel Conquer the Internet: Essays in Online Fandom*, Jefferson, NC: McFarland and Company.

Blumberg, R.L. (2007) 'Gender bias in textbooks: a hidden obstacle on the road to gender equality in education', Paper commissioned for the EFA Global Monitoring Report 2008, *Education for All by 2015: Will We Make it*, UNESCO [online] http://unesdoc.unesco.org/images/0015/001555/155509e.pdf [accessed 31 July 2013].

Bonthuys, E. (2008) 'Putting gender into the definition of rape or taking it out? Masia v Director of Public Prosecutions (Pretoria) and others, 2007 (8) BCLR 827 (CC)' *Feminist Legal Studies*, 16: 249–260.

Bourke, J. (2007) *Rape: A History from 1860 to the Present*, London: Virago.

Bowyer, J. (2004) (ed.) *The Cinema of Japan and Korea*, London: Wallflower Press.

Boyle, K. (2005) *Media and Violence*, London: Sage.

Bratich, J.Z. (2003) 'Making politics reasonable: conspiricism, subjectification, and governing through styles of thought' in Bratich, J.Z., Packer, J. and McCarthy, C. (eds.) *Foucault, Cultural Studies and Governmentality*, Albany, NY: State University of New York Press.

Bratich, J.Z., Packer, J. and McCarthy, C. (2003) 'Governing the present' in Bratich, J.Z., Packer, J. and McCarthy, C. (eds.) *Foucault, Cultural Studies and Governmentality*, Albany, NY: State University of New York Press.

Brochman, S. (1991) 'Silent victims: bringing male rape out of the closet' *The Advocate*, 582: 38–43.

Brooks, L. (2008) 'This debate on rape should focus on rapists, not victims' *The Guardian*, 17 July.

Brooks, L. (2009) 'It is a national disgrace that in 2009 rape almost always goes unpunished' *The Guardian*, 15 April.

Brownmiller, S. (1975) *Against Our Will: Men, Women and Rape*, Penguin: London.

Bruce Almighty (2003) [film] Dir. Tom Shadyac, US: Universal Studios.

Budrionis, R. and Jongsma, A.E. Jr (2003) *The Sexual Abuse Victim and Sexual Offender: Treatment Planner*, Hoboken, NJ: Wiley.

Bumiller, K. (2008) *In an Abusive State: How Neoliberalism Appropriated the Feminist Movement Against Sexual Violence*, Durham, NC: Duke University Press.

Burchell, G. (1991) 'Peculiar interests: civil society and governing 'the system of natural liberty' in Burchell, G., Gordon, C. and Miller, P. (eds.) *The Foucault Effect: Studies in Governmentality*, Chicago: University of Chicago Press.

Burchell, G., Gordon, C. and Miller, P. (eds.) (1991) *The Foucault Effect: Studies in Governmentality*, Chicago: University of Chicago Press.

Busse, K. (2006) 'My life is a WIP on my LJ: slashing the slasher and the reality of celebrity and internet performances' in Hellekson, K. and Busse, K. (eds.) *Fan Fiction and Fan Communities in the Age of the Internet: New Essays*, Jefferson, NC: McFarland and Company.

Butler, J. (1990) *Gender Trouble: Feminism and the subversion of identity*, New York: Routledge.

Cahill, A.J. (2000) 'Foucault, rape and the construction of the feminine body' *Hypatia*, 15 (1): 43–63.

Cahill, A.J. (2001) *Rethinking Rape*, Ithaca, NY: Cornell University Press.

Calderwood, D. (1987) 'The male rape victim' *Medical Aspects of Human Sexuality*, 21 (5): 53–55.

Canning, L. (2009) 'We need a targeted attack on rape' *The Guardian*, 18 March.

Canter, D. and Hodge, S. (1998) 'Victims and perpetrators of male sexual assault' *Journal of Interpersonal Violence*, 13: 222.

Carrabine, E., Iganski, P., Lee, M., Plummer, K. and South, N. (2004) *Criminology: A Sociological Introduction*, London: Routledge.

Chapleau, K.M., Oswald, D.L. and Russell, B.L. (2008) 'Male rape myths: the role of gender, violence and sexism' *Journal of Interpersonal Violence*, 23 (5): 600–617.

Chan, S. (2010) 'Supernatural bodies: writing subjugation and resistance onto Sam and Dean Winchester' *Transformative Works and Cultures*, 4 [online] http://dx.doi.org/10.3983/twc.2010.0179 [accessed 31 July 2013].

Chin, B. (2007) 'Beyond kung fu and violence: locating east Asian cinema fandom' in Gray, J., Sandvoss, C. and Harrington, C.L. (eds.) *Fandom: Identities and Communities in a Mediated World*, New York: New York University Press.

Choi, J. (2008) 'Sentimentality and the cinema of the extreme' *Jump Cut: A Review of Contemporary Media* No. 50, spring [online] http://www.ejumpcut.org/archive/jc50.2008/sentiment-Extreme/text.html [accessed 31 July 2013].

Clarke, J., Gerwitz, S., Hughes, G. and Humphry, J. (2000) 'Guarding the public interest? Auditing the public services' in Clarke, J., Gerwitz, S. and McLaughlin, E. (eds.) *New Managerialism, New Welfare?*, London: Sage.

Clover, C. (1987) 'Her body, himself: gender in the slasher film' *Representations*, 20: 187–228.

Clover, C. (1992) *Men, Women and Chainsaws: Gender in the Modern Horror Film*, London: BFI Publishing.

Cochrane, K. (2008) 'Now, the backlash' *The Guardian*, 1 July.

Cohen, S. and Young, J. (eds.) (1973) *The Manufacture of News: Social Problems, Deviance and the Mass Media*, London: Constable.

Cole, A.M. (2007) *The Cult of True Victimhood: From the War on Welfare to the War on Terror*, Stanford, CA: Stanford University Press.

Commercial Breakdown with Jimmy Carr (2008) [TV], Series 11, Danielle Lux, Celador/BBC, BBC1, original air date 13 July 2008, UK.

Conklin, J.E. (2007) *Criminology*, Boston, MA: Pearson.

Connell, R.W. (1987) *Gender and Power*, Stanford, CA: Stanford University Press.

Connell, R.W. and Messerschmidt, J.W. (2005) 'Hegemonic masculinity: rethinking the concept' *Gender and Society*, 19 (6): 829–859.

Connelly, W. (1998) 'Beyond good and evil: the ethical sensibility of Michel Foucault' in Moss, J. (ed.) *The Later Foucault: Politics and Philosophy*, London: Sage.

Conroy, A. (2009) 'Police still dismiss rape victims' *The Guardian*, 10 June.

Coxell, A., King, M., Mezey, G. and Gordon, D. (1999) 'Lifetime prevalence, characteristics, and associated problems of non-consensual sex in men: cross sectional survey' *British Medical Journal*, 318: 846–850.

Cressey, D. (1992) 'Research implications of conflicting conceptions of victimology' in Fattah, E.A. (ed.) *Towards a Critical Victimology*, New York: St Martin's Press.

Crome, S. (2006) 'Male survivors of sexual assault and rape' Australian Centre for the Study of Sexual Assault: ACSSA wrap no.2, Melbourne, Australia: Australian Institute of Family Studies [online] http://www.aifs.gov.au/acssa/pubs/wrap/acssa_wrap2.pdf [accessed 31 July 2013].

Crome, S.A., McCabe, M.P. and Ford, L. (1999) 'Male rape victims: fact and fiction' *The Law Institute Journal*, 73 (1): 60–65.

Cuklanz, L.M. (1996) *Rape on Trial: How the Mass Media Construct Legal Reform and Social Change*, Philadelphia, PA: University of Pennsylvania Press.

Daily Mail Reporter (2008) 'My cry rape hell: wrongly accused man tells of his 11 month nightmare' *The Daily Mail*, 17 September.

Darkestangel (2005–2009) *Deadly Temptation* [online] http://deadlytemptation.darknessprevails.com/ [accessed 31 July 2013].

Darkestangel (2009a) *Just Another Day in the Life of Dean Winchester* [online] http://supernaturalfic.darknessprevails.com/Another%20Day%20in%20the%20Life%20of%20Dean%20Winchester%20Nov%202009.htm [accessed 31 July 2013].

Darkestangel (2009b) *My One Good Deed* [online] http://supernaturalfic.darknessprevails.com/My%20One%20Good%20Deed%20Oct%202009.htm [accessed 31 July 2013].

Das, V. (2008) 'Violence, gender and subjectivity' *Annual Review of Anthropology*, 37: 283–299.

Daugherty, T.K. and Esper, J.A. (1998) 'Victim characteristics and attributions of blame in male rape' *Traumatology*, 4 (2): 22–39.

Davies, M. (2002) 'Male sexual assault victims: a selective review of the literature and implications for support services' *Aggression and Violent Behaviour*, 7: 203–204.

Davies, M., Croall, H. and Tyrer, J. (2005) *Criminal Justice: An introduction to the Criminal Justice System of England and Wales*, Third Edition, London: Longman.

Davies, M. and McCartney, S. (2003) 'Effects of gender and sexuality on judgements of victim blame and rape myth acceptance in a depicted male rape' *Journal of Community and Applied Social Psychology*, 13 (3): 391–398.

Davies, M., Pollard, P. and Archer, J. (2006) 'Effects of perpetrator gender and victim sexuality on blame towards male victims of sexual assault' *The Journal of Social Psychology*, 146: 3.

Davies, M. and Rogers, P. (2006) 'Perceptions of male victims in depicted sexual assaults: a review of the literature' *Aggression and Violent Behaviour*, 11: 367–377.

Davies, P., Francis, P. and Greer, C. (eds.) (2007) *Victims, Crime and Society*, London: Sage.

Dean, M. (2010) *Governmentality: Power and Rule in Modern Society*, 2nd Edition, London: Sage.

Deep in the Woods (2000) [film] Dir. Lionel Delplanque, France: Lions Gate.

DeKeseredy, W.S. (1999) 'Tactics of the anti-feminist backlash against Canadian national women abuse surveys' *Violence Against Women*, 5: 1258–1276.

Deleuze, G. (1992) 'What Is a dispositif?' in Armstrong, T.J. (ed.) *Michel Foucault, Philosopher*, New York: Harvester Wheatsheaf.

Deliverance (1972) [film] Dir. John Boorman, US: Warner Brothers.

Demirkan-Martin, V.V. (2009) 'Queerable spaces: homosexualities and homophobias in contemporary film', unpublished PhD thesis, Canterbury, NZ: University of Canterbury.

Diamond, I. and Quinby, L. (eds.) (1988) *Feminism and Foucault: Reflections on Resistance*, Boston, MA: Northeastern University Press.

Dispatches: 'Male Rape' (1995) in Gregory, J. and Lees, S. (1999) *Policing Sexual Assault*, London: Routledge.

Dispatches: Rape in the City (2009) [TV], Karen Edwards, Wall to Wall Media, Channel 4, original air date 22 June 2009, UK.

Dobash, R.P., Dobash, E.R., Wilson, M. and Daley, M. (1992) 'The myth of sexual symmetry in marital violence' *Social Problems*, 39 (1): 71–91.

Dobash, R. and Emerson, D. (2004) 'Women's violence against men in intimate relationships' *The British Journal of Criminology*, 44: 324–349.

Dodd, V. (2009a) 'British soldiers accused of raping Iraqi man' *The Guardian*, 14 September.

Dodd, V. (2009b) 'Trigger for lasting change' *The Guardian*, 13 March.

Dollhouse (2009) [TV programme], Dir. Joss Whedon, Twentieth Century Fox, FX, Original air date February–July, 2009, US.

Donnelly, D.A. and Kenyon, S. (1996) 'Honey, we don't do men: gender stereotypes and the provision of services to sexually assaulted males' *Journal of Interpersonal Violence* 11 (3): 441–448.

Dreyfus, H.L. and Rabinow, P. (1982) *Michel Foucault: Beyond Structuralism and Hermeneutics*, Chicago, IL: University of Chicago Press.

Dummy Mommy Without a Baby (2001) [film] Dirs. Joe Ma and Albert Kai-kwong Mak, Hong Kong: Mei Ah.

Du Mont, J., Miller, K. and Myhr, T. (2003) 'The role of "real rape" and "real victim" stereotypes in the police reporting practices of sexually assaulted women' *Violence Against Women*, 9 (4): 466–486.

Duncan, K. (2010) *Female Sexual Predators: Understanding Them to Protect our Children and Youths*, Santa Barbara, CA: Praeger Publishers.

Dustin, H. (2008) 'What Joe Biden can teach the British' *The Guardian*, 11 September.

Dworkin, A. (1997) *Life and Death: Unapologetic Writings on the Continuing War Against Women*, New York: The Free Press.

Dyer, C. (2007) 'Third of dropped rape cases should have been pursued, says report' *The Guardian*, 31 January.

Elias, R. (1994) 'Has victimology outlived its usefulness?' *Critical Criminology*, 6 (1): 4–25.

Elias, R. (1996) 'Paradigms and paradoxes of victimology' in Sumner, C., Israel, M., O'Connell, M. and Sarre, R. (eds.), *International Victimology: Selected Papers from the 8th International Symposium*, Canberra: Australian Institute of Criminology [online] http://www.aic.gov.au/media_library/publications/proceedings/27/elias.pdf [accessed 11 September 2013].

Elliott, C. (2008a) 'Blaming the innocent', *The Guardian*, 30 October.

Elliott, C. (2008b) 'Rape victims deserve better', *The Guardian*, 13 August.

Ellis, L. and Beattie, C. (1983) 'The feminist explanation for rape: an empirical test' *Journal of Sex Research*, 19 (1): 74–93.

Etherington, K. (1995) *Adult Male Survivors of Childhood Sexual Abuse*, London: Pitman.

Euro Trip (2004) [film] Dir. Jeff Schaffer, US: DreamWorks.

Farrell, W. (1993) *The Myth of Male Power: Why Men are the Disposable Sex*, London: Fourth Estate.

Faubion, J.D. (2001) 'Introduction' in Foucault, M., Faubion, J.D. (ed.) *Michel Foucault, Power: Essential Works of Foucault 1954–1984*, volume 3, Hurley, R. (trans.), London: Penguin.

Fawcett Society (2008) 'Not either/or but both/and: why we need Rape Crisis Centres and Sexual Assault Referral Centres: A briefing' *End Violence Against Women, Rape Crisis* (England and Wales), the Child and Woman Abuse Studies Unit and Fawcett, England: End Violence Against Women, Rape Crisis (England and Wales), the Child and Woman Abuse Studies Unit and Fawcett Society [online] http://www.sericc.org.uk/pdf/rapecrisis_sarc.pdf [accessed 11 September 2013].

Ferrell, J. (1999) 'Cultural criminology' *Annual Review of Sociology*, 25: 395–418.

Ferrell, J., Hayward, K. and Young, J. (2008) *Cultural Criminology*, London: Sage.

Fiebert, M.S. and Tucci, L.M. (1998), 'Sexual coercion: men victimized by women' *Journal of Men's Studies* 6 (2): 127–133.

Fletcher, M. (2009) 'Raped and beaten for daring to question President Ahmadinejad's election' *The Times*, 11 September.

Flynn, C.P. (1990) 'Relationship violence by women: issues and implications' *Family Relations*, 39 (2): 194–198.

Forman, B.D. (1982) 'Reported male rape' *Victimology: An International Journal*, 7: 235–236.

Foucault, M. (1984) *The Use of Pleasure: The History of Sexuality Volume 2*, Hurley, R. (trans.), London: Penguin.

Foucault, M. (1997) in Bertani, M. and Fontana, A. (eds.) *Society Must Be Defended: Lectures at the Collège de France, 1975–1976*, Macey, D (Trans.) Penguin: London.

Foucault, M. (2000) in Rabinow, P. (ed.) *Foucault, Ethics: Essential Works of Foucault 1954–1984*, volume 1, Hurley, R. (trans.), Penguin: London.

Foucault, M. (2001) in Faubion, J.D. (ed.) *Michel Foucault, Power: Essential Works of Foucault 1954–1984*, volume 3, Hurley, R. (trans.), Penguin: London.

Frazier, P.A. (1993) 'A comparative study of male and female rape victims seen at a hospital-based Rape Crisis programme' *Journal of Interpersonal Violence*, 8 (1): 64–76.

Funk, R.I. (1993) *Stopping Rape: A Challenge for Men*, Philadelphia: New Society Publishers.

Funk, R.I. (1997) 'Men who are raped: a pro-feminist perspective' in Scarce, M. *Male on Male Rape: The Hidden Toll of Stigma and Shame*, Cambridge, MA: Perseus.

Furedi, F. (2005) *Politics of Fear: Beyond Left and Right*, London: Continuum.

Furedi, F. (2006) *Culture of Fear Revisited: Risk Taking and the Morality of Low Expectation*, London: Continuum.

Gadd, D., Farall, S., Dallimore, D. and Lombard, N. (2002) 'Domestic abuse against men in Scotland' *Scottish Executive Central Research Unit* [online] http://www.scotland.gov.uk/Resource/Doc/46737/0030602.pdf [accessed 31 July 2013].

Gavey, N. (2005), *Just Sex? The Cultural Scaffolding of Rape*, London: Routledge.

Gavey, N. and Gow, V. (2001) '"Cry wolf", cried the wolf: constructing the issue of false rape allegations in New Zealand media texts' *Feminism and Psychology*, 11 (3): 341–360.

Gentleman, A. (2009) 'Government rape review fails to convince women's groups' *The Guardian*, 22 September.

George, M.J. (1994) 'Riding the donkey backwards: men as the unacceptable victims of marital violence' *Journal of Men's Studies*, 3 (2): 137–159.

Gibb, F. (2009) 'Transsexual killer wins battle to serve life sentence in a women's jail' *The Times*, 5 September.

Gilchrist, H., Smith, K., Magee, C.A. and Jones, S. (2012) 'A hangover and a one-night stand: alcohol and risky sexual behaviour among female students at an Australian University' *Youth Studies Australia*, 31(2): 35–43 [online] http://ro.uow.edu.au/cgi/viewcontent.cgi?article=3378&context=hbspapers [accessed 31 July 2013].

Gillespie, T. (1996) 'Rape Crisis Centres and "male rape": a face of the backlash' in Hester, M., Kelly, L. and Radford, J. (eds.) *Women, Violence and Male Power*, Buckinghamshire: Open University Press.

Gilman, S., Birmele, J., Gellar, J. and Greenberg, V. (1994) *Reading Freud's Reading*, New York: New York University Press.

Ginger Snaps (2000) [film] Dir. John Fawcett, Canada: Millennium Entertainment.

Gonsiorek, J.C., Bera, W.H. and LeTourneau, D. (1994) *Male Sexual Abuse: A Trilogy of Intervention Strategies*, London: Sage.

Goodey, J. (1997) 'Boys don't cry: masculinity, fear of crime and fearlessness' *British Journal of Criminology*, 37 (3): 401–408.

Goodey, J. (2005) *Victims and Victimology: Research, Policy and Practice*, Harlow: Longman.

Gordon, C. (1991) 'Governmental rationality: an introduction' in Burchell, G., Gordon, C. and Miller, P. (eds.) *The Foucault Effect: Studies in Governmentality*, Chicago: The University of Chicago Press.

Gordon, C. (2001) 'Introduction' in Faubion, J.D. (ed.) *Michel Foucault, Power: Essential Works of Foucault 1954–1984*, volume 3, Hurley, R. (trans.), London: Penguin.

Goyer, P.F. and Eddleman, H.C. (1984) 'Same sex rape of nonincarcerated men' *American Journal of Psychiatry*, 141 (4): 577–579.

Graham, L.J. (2005) 'Discourse analysis and the critical use of foucault' in Conference Proceedings for *The Australian Association for Research in Education: Annual Conference*, Sydney, Australia, 27 November–1 December [online] http://eprints.qut.edu.au/2689/1/2689.pdf [accessed 31 July 2013].

Graham, R. (2006) 'Male rape and the careful construction of the male victim' *Social Legal Studies*, 15 (2): 187–208.

Gray, J. (2007) 'The news: you gotta love it' in Gray, J., Sandvoss, C. and Harrington, C.L. (eds.) *Fandom: Identities and Communities in a Mediated World*, New York: New York University Press.

Gray, J., Sandvoss, C. and Harrington, C.L. (2007) 'Introduction: why study fans?' in Gray, J., Sandvoss, C. and Harrington, C.L. (eds.) *Fandom: Identities and Communities in a Mediated World*, New York: New York University Press.

Gregory, J. and Lees, S. (1999) *Policing Sexual Assault*, London: Routledge.

Groth, A.N. and Burgess, A.W. (1980) 'Male rape: offenders and victims' *American Journal of Psychiatry*, July, 137 (7): 806–810.

Guettel-Cole, S. (1984) 'Greek sanctions against sexual assault' Classical Philology, 79 (2): 97–113.

Hall, C. (1988) 'Rape: the politics of definition' *South African Law Journal*, 105: 67–82.

Hannon, L. and Dufour, L.R. (1998) 'Still just the study of men and crime? A content analysis' *Sex Roles*, 38 (1–2): 63–71.

Hansell, J. and Damour, L. (2005) *Abnormal Psychology*, Hoboken, NJ: Wiley.

Harold and Kumar Escape Guantanimo Bay (2008) [film] Dirs. John Hurwitz and Hayden Schlossberg, US: Warner Bros.

Harper, J. (2009) *Flowers from Hell: The Modern Japanese Horror Film*, Hereford: Noir Publishing.

Harvey, H. (2009) 'Rape: the unprosecuted war crime' *The Guardian*, 30 September.

Hassan, R. and Thomas, J. (eds.) (2006) *New Media Theory Reader*, Berkshire: Open University Press.

Hay, J. (2003) 'Unaided virtues: the (neo)liberalization of the domestic sphere and the new architecture of community' in Bratich, J.Z., Packer, J. and McCarthy, C. (eds.) *Foucault, Cultural Studies and Governmentality*, New York: State University of New York Press.

Hellekson, K. and Busse, K. (eds.) (2006) *Fan Fiction and Fan Communities in the Age of the Internet: New Essays*, Jefferson, NC: McFarland and Company.

Hickson, F.C.I., Davies, P.M., Hunt, A.J., Weatherburn, P., McManus, T.J. and Coxon, A.P.M. (1994) 'Gay men as victims of nonconsensual sex' *Archives of Sexual Behaviour*, 3 (3): 281–294.

Hill, K. (2009) '"Easy to associate angsty lyrics with Buffy": an introduction to participatory fan culture: *Buffy The Vampire Slayer*, vidders, popular music and the internet' in Kirby-Diaz, M. (ed.) *Buffy and Angel Conquer the Internet: Essays in Online Fandom*, Jefferson, NC: McFarland and Company.

Hillman, R.J., Tomlinson, D., McMillan, A., French, P.D. and Harris, J.R.W. (1990) 'Sexual assault of men: a series' *Genitourinary Medicine*, 66: 247–250.

Hoff Sommers, C. (1994) *Who Stole Feminism? How Women Have Betrayed Women*, New York: Simon and Schuster.

Hoff Sommers, C. (2001) *The War Against Boys: How Misguided Feminism is Harming our Young Men*, New York: Touchstone.

Hogben, M. and Waterman, C.K. (1997) 'Are all of your students represented in their textbooks? A content analysis of coverage of diversity issues in introductory psychology textbooks' *Teaching of Psychology*, 24 (2): 95–100.

Homayoun, H. (2009) 'Iranian boy who defied Tehran hardliners tells of prison rape ordeal' *The Times*, 22 August.

Home Office (2010) *Interim Government Response to the Stern Review*, London: Government Equalities Office, Home Office [online] http://webarchive.nationalarchives.gov.uk/20100418065537/http://equalities.gov.uk/pdf/Response_to_Stern_finalWeb.pdf [accessed 11 September 2013].

Hopkins-Burke, R. (2003) *An Introduction to Criminological Theory*, Devon: Willan.

Horvath, M. and Brown, J. (eds.) (2009) *Rape: Challenging Contemporary Thinking*, Devon: Willan.

Howe, A. (2008) *Sex, Violence and Crime: Foucault and the 'Man' Question*, Oxon: Routledge-Cavendish.

Howitt, D. (2006) *Introduction to Forensic and Criminal Psychology*, 2nd edition, Harlow: Pearson.

Huckle, P.L. (1995) 'Male rape victims referred to a forensic psychology service' *Medicine, Science, Law* 35 (3): 187–192.

Hunter, M. (1990) *The Sexually Abused Male: Prevalence, Impact and Treatment. Volumes 1 & 2*. Lexington, MA: Lexington Books.

I Know What You Did Last Summer (1997) [film] Dir. Jim Gillespie, US: Sony Pictures.

I Now Pronounce You Chuck and Larry (2007) [film] Dir. Dennis Dugan, US: NBC Universal.

Isely, P.J. and Gehrenbeck-Shim, D. (1997) 'Sexual assault of men in the community' *Journal of Community Psychology* 25 (2): 159–166.

Island, D. and Letellier, P. (1991) *Men Who Beat the Men Who Love Them: Battered Gay Men and Domestic Violence*, London: Routledge.

Ivison, D. (1998) 'The disciplinary moment: Foucault, law and the reinscription of rights' in Moss, J. (ed.) *The Later Foucault: Politics and Philosophy*, London: Sage.

Jack Dee, Live at the Apollo (2009) [TV programme], 'featuring Jason Manford and Russell Howard', BBC, BBC1, original air date 21 March 2009, UK.

Jaworski, A. and Pritchard, A. (eds.) (2005) *Discourse, Communication and Tourism*, Clevedon: Channel View Publications.

Jenkins, H. (1992) *Textual Poachers: Television Fans and Participatory Culture*, New York: Routledge.

Jenkins, H. (2007) 'Afterword' in Gray, J., Sandvoss, C. and Harrington, C.L. (eds.) *Fandon: Identities and Communities in a Mediated World*, New York: New York University Press.

Jenkins, S. (2002) 'Foucault and feminism: reevaluating traditional criticisms' *Agora*, 3 (1) [online] http://www.scribd.com/doc/6567521/Foucault-Feminism [accessed 31 July 2013].

Jewkes, Y. (2004) *Media and Crime: Key Approaches to Critical Criminology*, London: Sage.

Jewkes, Y. and Letherby, G. (eds.) (2002) *Criminology: A Reader*, London: Sage.

Johnson, R.L. and Shrier, D. (1987) 'Post-sexual victimization by females of male patients in an adolescent medicine clinic population' *American Journal of Psychiatry*, 144 (5): 650–652.

Jones, A. (2009) *Gender Inclusive: Essays on Violence, Men and Feminist International Relations*, Oxon: Routledge.

Jones, I.H. (2000) 'Cultural and historical aspects of male sexual assault' in Mezey and King (eds.) *Male Victims of Sexual Assault*, 2nd edition, Oxford: Oxford University Press.

Jung, S. (2006) 'Queering popular culture: female spectators and the appeal of writing slash fan fiction' in Hellekson, K. and Busse, K. (eds.) *Fan Fiction and Fan Communities in the Age of the Internet: New Essays*, Jefferson, NC: McFarland and Company.

Kassing, L. and Prierto, L. (2003) 'The rape myth and blame-based beliefs of counsellors-in-training toward male victims of rape' *Journal of Counselling and Development*, 81: 455–461.

Kaszniak, A.W. and Nassbaum, P.D. (1988) 'Amnesia as a consequence of male rape: a case report' *Journal of Abnormal Psychology*, 97 (1): 100–104.

Kaufman, A., Divasto, P., Jackson, R., Voorhees, D. and Christy, J. (1980) 'Male rape victims: non-institutionalised assault' *American Journal of Psychiatry*, 137 (2): 221–223.

Keft-Kennedy, V. (2008) 'Fantasising masculinity in Buffyverse slash fiction: sexuality, violence and the vampire' *Nordic Journal of English Studies*, 7 (1): 49–80.

Kelaway, K. (2009) 'The Shawl, The Shawshank Redemption, Othello' *The Observer*, 20 September.

Kelly, L. (2000) 'A war of attrition: recent research on rape' *Trouble and Strife*, 40: 9–16.

Kelly, L. (2003) 'Disabusing the definition of domestic violence: how women batter men and the role of the feminist state' *Florida State University Law Review*, 30 (4): 791–856.

Kelly, L., Lovett, J. and Regan, L. (2005) 'A gap or a chasm? Attrition in reported rape cases' *Home Office Research Study* 293, London: Home Office.

Kelly, M.G.E. (2009) *The Political Philosophy of Michel Foucault*, Oxford: Routledge.

Kendell, G. and Wickham, G. (2003) *Using Foucault's Methods*, London: Sage.

Kern, M., Just, M. and Norris, P. (2003) 'The lessons of framing terrorism' in Norris, P., Kern, M. and Just, M. (eds.) *Framing Terrorism: The News Media, the Government and the Public*, New York: Routledge.

Kershaw, C., Nicholas, S. and Walker, A. (2008) *Crime in England and Wales: Findings from the British Crime Survey and Police Recorded Crimes*, Londoon: Home Office.

Kibby, M. (2001) 'Women and sex entertainment on the Internet: discourses of gender and power' Mots Pluriels, number 19 [online] http://motspluriels.arts. uwa.edu.au/MP1901mk.html [accessed 31 July 2013].

Kidd-Hewitt, D. (2002) *'Crime and the media: a criminological perspective' in* Jewkes, Y. and Letherby, G. (eds.) *Criminology: A Reader*, London: Sage.

Kiessling, N. (1975) 'Doctor Faustus and the sin of demonality' *Studies in English Literature 1500–1900*, 15 (2): 205–211.

Kimmel, M.S. (1994) 'Masculinity as homophobia' in Brod, H. and Kaufman, M. (eds.) *Theorising Masculinities*, London: Sage.

King, M.B. (1992) 'Male rape in institutional settings' in Mezey, G.C. and King, M.B. (eds.) *Male Victims of Sexual Assault*, Oxford: Oxford University Press.

King, M.B., Coxell, A. and Mezey, G. (2000) 'The prevalence and characteristics of male sexual assault' in Mezey, G.C. and King, M.B. (eds.) *Male Victims of Sexual Assault*, 2nd edition, Oxford: Oxford University Press.

King, M.B., Coxell, A. and Mezey, G. (2002) 'Sexual molestation of males: associations with psychological disturbance' *British Journal of Psychiatry*, 181: 153–157.

King, M. and Woollett, E. (1997) 'Sexually assaulted males: 115 men consulting a counselling service' *Archives of Sexual Behavior* 26 (6): 579–588.

Kirby-Diaz, M. (2009) 'Buffy, Angel and the creation of virtual communities' in Kirby-Diaz, M. (ed.) *Buffy and Angel Conquer the Internet: Essays in Online Fandom*, Jefferson, NC: McFarland and Company.

Korn (1994), 'Ball Tongue', written by Korn, *Korn*, produced by Weintraub, L. and Robinson, R. [Audio CD], Epic/Immortal: US.

Korn (1994), 'Daddy', written by Korn, *Korn*, produced by Weintraub, L. and Robinson, R. [Audio CD], Epic/Immortal: US.

Korn (1994), 'Faget', written by Korn, *Korn*, produced by Weintraub, L. and Robinson, R. [Audio CD], Epic/Immortal: US.

Korn (1994) *Korn*, produced by Weintraub, L. and Robinson, R. [Audio CD], Epic/Immortal: US.

Korn (1996) *Life is Peachy*, produced by Robinson, R. [Audio CD] Epic/Immortal: US.

Korn (1996) 'No place to hide', written by Korn, *Life is Peachy*, produced by Robinson, R. [Audio CD] Epic/Immortal: US.

Korn (1998) 'All in the family', written by Korn and Durst, F., *Follow the Leader*, produced by Thompson, S., Wright, T. and Korn [Audio CD] Epic/Immortal: US.

Korn (1998) *Follow the Leader*, produced by Thompson, S., Wright, T. and Korn [Audio CD] Epic/Immortal: US.

Korn (1998) 'Freak on a leash', written by Korn, *Follow the Leader*, produced by Thompson, S., Wright, T. and Korn [Audio CD] Epic/Immortal: US.

Korn (1999) *Issues*, Produced by O'Brien, B. [Audio CD] Epic/Immortal: US.

Korn (1999) 'Reclaim my place', written by Korn, *Issues*, produced by O'Brien, B. [Audio CD] Epic/Immortal: US.

Korn (1999) 'Wish you could be me', written by Korn, *Issues*, produced by O'Brien, B. [Audio CD] Epic/Immortal: US.

Korn (2002) 'Bottled up', written by Korn, *Untouchables*, produced by Beinhorn, M. [Audio CD] Epic/Immortal: US.

Korn (2002) 'Thoughtless', written by Korn, *Untouchables*, produced by Beinhorn, M. [Audio CD] Epic/Immortal: US.

Korn (2002) *Thoughtless* [Video], Dirs. The Hughes Brothers.

Korn (2002) *Untouchables*, produced by Beinhorn, M. [Audio CD] Epic/Immortal: US.

Korn (2003) 'Break some off', written by Korn, *Take a Look in the Mirror*, produced by Korn and Davis, J. [Audio CD] Epic/Immortal: US.

Korn (2003) *Take a Look in the Mirror*, produced by Korn and Davis, J. [Audio CD] Epic/Immortal: US.

Koss, M.P. and Harvey, M.R. (1991) *The Rape Victim: Clinical and Community Interventions*, 2nd edition, London: Sage.

Krahe, B. (2000) 'The prevalence of sexual aggression and victimization among homosexual men' *Journal of Sex Research*, 37 (2): 1–15.

Kustritz, A. (2008) 'Painful pleasures: sacrifice, consent, and the resignification of BDSM symbolism in The Story of O and the Story of Obi' *Transformative Works and Cultures*, 1 (31) [online] http://journal.transformativeworks.org/index. php/twc/article/view/31 [accessed 31 July 2013].

Lacey, H.B. and Roberts, R. (1991) 'Sexual assault on men' *International Journal of STD and Aids*, 2: 258–260.

Lamb, S. (ed.) (1999) *New Versions of Victims: Feminists Struggle with the Concept*, London: New York University Press.

Landrum, R.E. (1993) 'Identifying core concepts in introductory psychology' *Psychological Reports*, 72: 659–666.

Larimer, M.E. (1999) 'Male and female recipients of unwanted sexual contact in a college student sample: prevalence rates, alcohol use, and depression symptoms' *Sex Roles: A Journal of Research*, 40: 295–308.

La Valle, J. (1996) *Everything You Need to Know: When You are the Male Survivor of Sexual Assault*, New York: The Rosen Publishing Group.

Laville, S. (2009a) 'Grassroots attitudes obstruct search for justice' *The Guardian*, 14 March.

Laville, S. (2009b) 'Metropolitan police facing crisis after failures in Kirk Reid rape enquiry' *The Guardian*, 27 March.

Lazzarato, M. (2002) 'From biopower to biopolitics' *Pli: The Warwick Journal of Philosophy*, 13: 100–111 [online] http://cms.gold.ac.uk/media/lazzarato_ biopolitics.pdf [accessed 31 July 2013].

Lea, S.J. (2007) 'A discursive investigation into victim responsibility in rape' *Feminism Psychology* 17: 495.

Leeder, J. (2009) 'Perils of a policewoman: I know that danger is with me' *The Globe and Mail*, 23 September.

Lees, S. (1997) *Ruling Passions: Sexual Violence, Reputation and the Law*, Buckinghamshire: Open University Press.

Lefkowitz, M.R. (2002) 'Predatory goddesses' *Hesperia*, 71: 325–344.

Lehman, P. (ed.) (2001) *Masculinity: Bodies, Movies, Culture*, AFI Film Readers, New York: Routledge.

Lerner, M.J. and Matthews, J. (1967) 'Reactions to suffering of others under conditions of indirect responsibility' *Journal of Personality and Social Psychology*, 5: 319–325.

Levy, S. (2009) 'Paul Newman: a life' *The Sunday Times*, 20 September.

Liar, Liar (1997) [film] Dir. Tom Shadyac, US: Universal Studios.

Light, D. and Monk-Turner, E. (2009) 'Circumstances surrounding male sexual assault and rape: findings from the National Violence against Women Survey' *Journal of Interpersonal Violence*, 24 (11): 1849–1858.

Lister, B. (2009) 'Rape centres in crisis' *The Guardian*, 22 February.

Lockwood, D. (1980) *Prison Sexual Violence*, New York: Elsevier.

Loizidou, E. (2000) 'The trouble with rape: gender matters and legal "transformations"' *Feminist Legal Studies*, 7: 275–297.

Longstaff, L. (2009) 'Rape victims don't want tea and sympathy but protection and justice' *The Guardian*, 2 April.

Luxon, N. (2008) 'Ethics and subjectivity: practices of self-governance in the late lectures of Michel Foucault' *Political Theory*, 36: 377–402.

Lynch, M. and Bogen, D. (1997) 'Sociology's asociological "core": an examination of textbook sociology in light of the sociology of scientific knowledge' *American Sociological Review*, 62: 481–493.

Lyon, M.R. (2004) 'No means no? Withdrawal of consent during intercourse and the continuing evolution of the definition of rape' *Journal of Criminal Law and Criminology*, 95 (1): 277–313.

MacKinnon, C. (1990) 'Reflections on sex equality under law' *The Yale Law Journal*, 100 (5): 1281–1328.

MacKinnon, C. (2006) *Are Women Human? And Other International Dialogues*, Cambridge, MA: Harvard University Press.

Maguire, M., Morgan, R. and Reiner, R. (eds.) (2002) *The Oxford Handbook of Criminology*, 3rd edition, Oxford: Oxford University Press.

Maier, S.L. (2008) 'Are Rape Crisis Centres feminist organisations?' *Feminist Criminology*, 3 (2): 82–100.

Malcolm in the Middle (2000) [TV] series 2, episode 4, 'Dinner Out', Dir. Jeffrey Melman, Twentieth Century Fox, FOX, original air date 15 November 2000, US.

Mardorossian, C.M. (2002) 'Towards a new feminist theory of rape' *Signs: Journal of Women and Culture in Society*, 27 (4): 743–775.

Margarey, S. (1978) 'The invention of juvenile delinquency in early nineteenth century England' in Hughes, G., Mclaughlin, E. and Muncie, J. (eds.), (2006), *Youth Justice: Critical Readings*. 4th Edition. London: Sage Publications.

Martin, K., Vieraitis, L.M. and Britto, S. (2006) 'Gender equality and women's absolute status: a test of the feminist models of rape' *Violence Against Women*, 12 (4): 321–329.

McEwan, M. (2009) 'Misogyny, up close and personal' *The Guardian*, 26 August.

McGuire, J. (2004) *Understanding Psychology and Crime: Perspectives on Theory and Action*, Berkshire: Open University Press.

McKee, A. (2007) 'The fans of cultural theory' in Gray, J., Sandvoss, C. and Harrington, C.L. (eds.) *Fandom: Identities and Communities in a Mediated World*, New York: New York University Press.

McMullen, R.J. (1990) *Male Rape: Breaking the Silence on the Last Taboo*, London: Gay Men's Press.

McNay, L. (1992) *Foucault and Feminism: Power, Gender and the Self*, Boston, MA: Northeastern University Press.

McRoy, J. (ed.) (2005) *Japanese Horror Cinema*, Edinburgh: Edinburgh University Press.

Me, Myself and Irene (2000) [film] Dirs. Bobby Farrelly, Peter Farrelly, US: Twentieth Century Fox.

Meadows, R.J. (2007) *Understanding Violence and Victimisation*, 4th edition, New Jersey: Pearson.

Mellencamp, P. (1995) *A Fine Romance: Five Ages of Film Feminism*, Philadelphia: Temple University Press.

Memon, A., Vrij, A. and Bull, R. (2006) *Psychology and Law: Truthfulness, Accuracy and Credibility*, 2nd edition, West Sussex: Wiley.

Mendieta, E. (2002) 'To make live and let die: Foucault on racism' Paper presented at the meeting of the Foucault Circle, APA Central Division Meeting – Chicago, 25 April [online] http://www.stonybrook.edu/commcms/philosophy/people/faculty_pages/docs/foucault.pdf [accessed 11 September 2013].

Merton, R.K. (1948) 'The self-fulfilling prophecy' *The Antioch Review*, 8 (2): 193–210.

Meyer, M. (2001) 'Between theory, method and politics: positioning of the approaches to CDA' in Wodak, R. and Meyer, M. (eds.), *Methods of Critical Discourse Analysis*, London: Sage.

Mezey, G.C. and King, M.B. (1989) 'The effects of sexual assault on men: a survey of 22 victims' *Psychological Medicine*, 19 (1): 205–209.

Mezey, G.C. and King, M.B. (eds.) (1992) *Male Victims of Sexual Assault*, Oxford: Oxford University Press.

Mezey, G.C. and King, M.B. (2000) *Male Victims of Sexual Assault*, Oxford: Oxford University Press.

Michael Macintyre's Comedy Road Show (2009) [TV], 'Belfast', BBC, BBC1, original air date 4 September 2009, UK.

Miller, P. and Rose, N. (1990) 'Governing economic life' *Economy and Society*, 19 (1): 1–31.

Miller, P. and Rose, N. (2008) *Governing the Present*, Cambridge: Polity Press.

Mitchell, D., Hirschman, R. and Nagayama Hall, G.C. (1999) 'Attributions of victim responsibility, pleasure and trauma in male rape' *Journal of Sex Research*, 36 (4): 369–374.

Mock The Week (2007) [TV] Season 5, 'featuring Andy Parsons, Russell Howard, Ian Stone and Mark Watson', BBC, BBC2, original air date 18 January 2007, UK.

Mock the Week (2009) [TV], Season 7, 'featuring David Mitchell and Sarah Millican', BBC, BBC2, original air date 17 September 2009, UK.

Moss, J. (ed.) (1998) *The Later Foucault: Politics and Philosophy*, London: Sage.

Mulholland, H. (2009a) 'Boris Johnson vows to "eradicate" violence against women in London' *The Guardian*, 21 April.

Mulholland, H. (2009b) 'YouTube video shows roadside ambush on mayor over lack of funding for rape crisis centres in London' *The Guardian*, 21 July.

Mullan, J. (2009) 'Ten of the best books written in prison' *The Guardian*, 19 September.

Mum and Dad (2008) [film] Dir. Steven Sheil, UK: Revolver Entertainment.

My Name is Earl (2007) [TV], season 3, episode 12, 'Early release', Dir. Jason Ensler, Twentieth Century Fox, FX, Original air date 6 December 2007, US.

My Name is Earl (2008) [TV], season 3, episode 13, 'Bad Earl', Dir. Eyal Gordin, Twentieth Century Fox, FX, Original air date 10 January 2008, US.

Nadeson, M.H. (2008) *Governmentality, Biopower and Everyday Life*, London: Routledge.

Naffine, N. (1994) 'Possession: erotic love in the law of rape' *Modern Law Review*, 57 (1): 10–37.

Nathanson, P. and Young, K.K. (2006) *Legalising Misandry: From Public Shame to Systemic Discrimination Against Men,* Canada: McGill-Queens University Press.

Never Mind the Buzzcocks (2005) [TV], season 17, episode 5, 'featuring Hard-Fi frontman Rich Archer and Claudia Winkleman, plus team captains Phil Jupitus and Bill Bailey', BBC, BBC2, original air date 28 November 2005, UK.

Newburn, T. and Stanko, E. (2002) 'When men are victims: the failure of victimology' in Jewkes, Y. and Letherby, G. (2002) *Criminology: A Reader,* London: Sage.

Ng, V.W. (1987) 'Ideology and sexuality: rape laws in Qing China' *Journal of Asian Studies,* 46 (1): 57–60.

Nicholson, D.B.L. (2000) *Feminist Perspectives on Criminal Law,* London: Cavendish.

Nicholson, D. and Bibbings, L. (2000) *Feminist Perspectives on Criminal Law,* Cavendish: London.

Nicholson, L. (ed.) (1990) *Feminism/Postmodernism,* New York: Routledge.

Norris, P., Kern, M. and Just, M. (eds.) (2003) *Framing Terrorism: The News Media, the Government and the Public,* New York: Routledge.

Novotny, P. (2003) 'Rape victims in the gender neutral zone: the assimilation of resistance?' *Seattle Journal for Social Justice,* 1: 743–746.

O'Farrell, C. (2007) *Key Concepts* [online] http://www.michel-foucault.com/ concepts/index.html [accessed 31 July 2013].

O'Grady, H. (2004) 'An ethics of the self' in Taylor, D. and Vintges, K. (eds.) *Feminism and the Final Foucault,* Urbana and Chicago: University of Illinois Press.

Oliver, B.E. (2007) 'Preventing female-perpetrated sexual abuse' *Trauma, Violence and Abuse,* 8: 19–32.

Oltmans, T.F., Martin, M.T., Neale, J.M. and Davison, G.C. (2007) *Case Studies in Abnormal Psychology,* 7th edition, Hoboken, NJ: Wiley.

O'Neill, D.V. (2012) 'Responding to college campus acquaintance rape: contextual issues and the challenge of inter-organizational collaboration' *Doctorate in Social Work (DSW) Dissertations,* Paper 24 [online] http://repository.upenn.edu/ edissertations_sp2/24 [accessed 31 July 2013].

Packer, J. (2003) 'Mapping the intersections of Foucault and cultural studies: an interview with Lawrence Grossberg and Toby Miller, October 2000' in Bratich, J.Z., Packer, J. and McCarthy, C. (eds.) *Foucault, Cultural Studies and Governmentality,* New York: State University of New York Press.

Paglia, C. (1991) *Sexual Personae: Art and Decadence from Nefertiti to Emily Dickinson,* New York: Vintage.

Paglia, C. (1992) *Sex, Art and American Culture: Essays,* New York: Vintage.

Pavlich, G.C. (2005) *Governing Paradoxes of Restorative Justice,* London: Glass House Press.

Perrott, S.B. and Webber, N. (1996) 'Attitudes towards male and female victims of sexual assault: implications for services to the male victim' *Journal of Psychology and Human Sexuality,* 8 (4): 19–38.

Peterson, S.B. and Kroner, T. (2006) 'Gender biases in textbooks for introductory psychology and human development' *Psychology of Women Quarterly,* 16 (1): 17–36.

Phelan, S. (1990) 'Foucault and feminism' *American Journal of Political Science,* 34 (2): 421–440.

Pineau, L. (1989) 'Date rape: a feminist analysis' *Law and Philosophy*, 8 (2): 217–243.

Pino, N.W. and Meier, R.F. (1999) 'Gender differences in rape reporting' *Sex Roles* 40 (11–12): 970–990.

Poole, E. (2002) *Reporting Islam: Media Representations of British Muslims*, London: I.B. Taurus.

Poropat, P. and Rosevear, W. (1992) 'Sexual assault of males' in Patricia, W.E. (ed.) *Without Consent: Confronting Adult Sexual Violence: Proceedings of a Conference*, Australian Institute of Criminology, 27–29 October [online] http://www.rhfinc.org.au/docs/males.pdf [accessed 11 September 2013].

Projansky, S. (2001) *Watching Rape: Film and Television in Postfeminist Culture*, New York: New York University Press.

Pulp Fiction (1994) [film] Dir. Quentin Tarantino, US: Miramax Films.

Qin, D. (2004) 'Toward a critical feminist perspective of culture and self' *Feminism and Psychology*, 14 (2): 297–312.

Ramazanoglu, C. (ed.) (1993) *Up Against Foucault: Explorations of Some Tensions Between Foucault and Feminism*, New York: Routledge.

Rape Crisis (2010) *Stern Review on Rape Reporting: Stern Review on Rape reporting in England and Wales* [online] http://www.rapecrisis.org.uk/news_show.php?id=41 (accessed 12 August 2013).

Ratner, P.A., Johnson, J.L., Shoveller, J.A., Chan, K., Martindale, S.L. and Schilder, A.J. (2002) 'Non-consensual sex experienced by men who have sex with men: prevalence and association with mental health' *Patient Education and Counselling*, 49: 67–74.

Rebaza, C. (2009) 'The problematic definition of "fan": a survey of fannish involvement in the Buffyverse' in Kirby-Diaz, M. (ed.) *Buffy and Angel Conquer the Internet: Essays in Online Fandom*, Jefferson, NC: McFarland and Company.

Reiner, R. (1997) 'Media made criminality: the representation of crime in the mass media' in Maguire, M., Morgan, R. and Reiner, R. (eds.) *The Oxford Handbook of Criminology*, 2nd edition, Oxford: Oxford University Press.

Rentoul, L. and Applebloom, N. (1997) 'Understanding the psychological impact of rape and serious sexual assault of men: a literature review' *Journal of Psychiatric and Mental Health Nursing*, 4 (4): 267–274.

Road Trip (2000) [film] Dir. Todd Phillips, US: DreamWorks.

Rogers, P. (1998) 'Call for research into male rape' *Mental Health Practice*, 1: 34.

Roiphe, K. (1994) *The Morning After: Fear, Sex and Feminism*, Boston, MA: Little, Brown and Company.

Rose, N. (1999) *Powers of Freedom: Reframing Political Thought*, Cambridge: Cambridge University Press.

Rose, N. and Miller, P. (1992) 'Political power beyond the state: problematic of government' *British Journal of Sociology*, 43 (2): 173–205.

Ross, J.M. (1982) 'Oedipus revisited – Laius and the Laius complex' *Psychoanalytic Study of the Child*, 37: 169–200.

Rumney, P. (2007) 'In defence of gender neutrality within rape' *Seattle Journal of Social Justice*, 6: 481–526.

Rumney, P. (2008) 'Gender neutrality: rape and trial talk' *International Journal for the Semiotics of Law*, 21 (2): 139–155.

Rumney, P. and Jamel, J. (2009) (unpublished) 'The not so carefully constructed male rape victim: a response to Ruth Graham' working paper series, *Social Sciences Research Network* [online] http://papers.ssrn.com/sol3/papers. cfm?abstract_id=1339585 [accessed 31 July 2013].

Rumney, P. and Morgan-Taylor, M. (1997a) 'Recognising the male victim: gender neutrality and the law of rape part one' *Anglo American Law Review*, 26: 198–234.

Rumney, P. and Morgan-Taylor, M. (1997b) 'Recognising the male victim: gender neutrality and the law of rape part two' *Anglo American Law Review*, 26: 330–336.

Rumney, P. and Morgan-Taylor, M. (2004) 'The construction of sexual consent in male rape and sexual assault' in Cowling, M. and Reynolds, P., *Making Sense of Sexual Consent*, Aldershot: Ashgate.

Rush, F. (1990) 'The many faces of the backlash' in Leidholdt, D. and Raymond, J.G. (eds.) *The Sexual Liberals and the Attack on Feminism*, New York: Pergamon Press.

Rush Hour 3 (2007) [film] Dir. Brett Ratner, US: New Line Home Video.

Russell, K. (2009) 'Gaps in support are failing women' *The Guardian*, 30 January.

Ryan, R. (2008) 'Met deputy demands special rape investigation units' *The Guardian*, 9 July.

Said, E.W. (1993) *Culture and Imperialism*, London: Vintage.

Said, E.W. (1997) *Covering Islam: How the Media and the Experts Determine How We See The Rest of the World*, London: Vintage.

Said, E.W. (2003) *Orientalism*, London: Penguin.

Sanders, C.R. and Lyon, E. (1995) 'Repetitive retribution: media images and the cultural construction of criminal justice' in Ferrell, J. and Sanders, C.R. (eds.) *Cultural Criminology*, Boston, MA: Northeastern University Press.

Sarrel, P.M. and Masters, W.H. (1982), 'Sexual molestation of men by women' *Archives of Sexual Behaviour* 11 (2): 117–131.

Sawicki, J. (1991) *Disciplining Foucault: Feminism, Power and the Body*, New York: Routledge.

Scacco, A.M. Jr. (ed.) (1982) *Male Rape: A Casebook of Sexual Aggressions*, New York: AMS Press.

Scarce, M. (1997) *Male on Male Rape: The Hidden Toll of Stigma and Shame*, Cambridge, MA: Perseus.

Scary Movie (2000) [film] Dir. Keenan Ivory Wayans, US: Dimension Films.

Scary Movie 2 (2001) [film] Dir. Keenan Ivory Wayans, US: Dimension Films.

Scary Movie 4 (2006) [film] Dir. David Zucker, US: Dimension Films.

Scheufele, D.A. (1999) 'Framing as a theory of media effects' *Journal of Communication*, 49: 103–122.

Scodari, C. (2007) 'Yoko in cyberspace with Beatles fans: gender and the recreation of popular mythology' in Gray, J., Sandvoss, C. and Harrington, C.L. (eds.) *Fandom: Identities and Communities in a Mediated World*, New York: New York University Press.

Seigal, J.M., Golding, J.M., Stein, J.A., Burnam, A. and Sorenson, S.B. (1990) 'Reactions to sexual assault: a community study' *Journal of Interpersonal Violence*, 5: 229.

Sellnow, D.D. (2010) *The Rhetorical Power of Popular Culture*, Thousand Oaks, CA: Sage.

Sgarzi, J.M. and McDevitt, J. (eds.) (2003) *Victimology: A Study of Crime Victims and Their Roles*, Upper Saddle River, NJ: Prentice Hall.

Shively, M. (2003) 'Percieved risks of date rape' in Sgarzi, J.M. and McDevitt, J., *Victimology: A Study of Crime Victims and Their Roles*, Upper Saddle River, NJ: Prentice Hall.

Sielke, S. (2002) *Reading Rape: The Rhetoric of Sexual Violence in American Literature and Culture, 1790–1990*, Princeton, NJ: Princeton University Press.

Sigal, P. (2002) 'Gender, male homosexuality and power in colonial Yucatan' *Latin American Perspectives*, 29, 2 (123): 24–40.

Simons, J. (2004) 'Michel Foucault (1926–84)' in Simons, J. (ed.) *Contemporary Critical Theorists: From Lacan to Said*, Edinburgh: Edinburgh University Press.

Sivakumaran, S. (2005) 'Male/male rape and the "taint" of homosexuality' *Human Rights Quarterly*, 27 (4): 1274–1306.

Skelton, C. and Francis, B. (eds.) (2005) *A Feminist Critique of Education: Fifteen Years of Gender Education*, Oxford: Routledge.

Smart, B. (1986) 'The politics of truth and the problem of hegemony' in Hoy, D. (ed.) *Foucault: A Critical Reader*, Oxford: Blackwell.

Smith, D. (2009a) 'Crime fears grow as South Africa readies for football World Cup' *The Guardian*, 22 September.

Smith, D. (2009b) 'Quarter of men in South Africa admit rape, survey finds' *The Guardian*, 17 June.

Smith, J. (2009a) 'Soft on rape, soft on the causes of rape' *The Observer*, 15 March.

Smith, J (2009b) 'Britons warned over rise in Greek holiday "binge-drinking" rapes' *The Observer*, 14 June.

Smith, R.E., Pine, C.J. and Hawley, M.E. (1988) 'Social cognitions about adult male victims of female sexual assault' *Journal of Sex Research*, 24: 101–112.

Somers, B. (2005) *Search Rank Facts*, KWB Entertainment, US: Cafe Press.

Sorenson, S., Stein, J., Seigal, J., Golding, J. and Burnam, A. (1987) 'The prevalence of adult sexual assault: the Los Angeles epidemiologic catchment area project' *American Journal of Epidemiology*, 126: 1154–1164.

Soyland, A.J. and Kendall, G. (1997) 'Abusing Foucault: methodology, critique and subversion' *History, Philosophy and Psychology Newsletter*, 25: 9–17.

Spade, J.Z. and Valentine, C.G. (2008) *The Kaleidoscope of Gender: Prisms, Patterns and Possibilities*, Thousand Oaks, CA: Pine Forge Press.

Stanko, E. and Hobdell, K. (1993) 'Assault on men: masculinity and male victimization' *British Journal of Criminology*, 33 (3): 400–415.

Starbright73 (2009) *Faces of Evil* [online] http://starbright73.livejournal.com/222828.html [accessed 31 July 2013].

Steinmetz, S.K. (1978) 'The battered husband syndrome?' *Victimology: An International Journal*, 2: 499–509.

Stermac, L., Sheridan, P.M., Davies, A. and Dunn, S. (1996) 'Sexual assault of adult males' *Journal of Interpersonal Violence*, 11 (1): 52–64.

Stermac, L., del Bove, G. and Addison, M. (2004) 'Stranger and acquaintance sexual assault of adult males' *Journal of Interpersonal Violence*, 19: 901–915.

Stern, V. (2010), *The Stern Review*, Government Equalities Office, Home Office: London [online] http://webarchive.nationalarchives.gov.uk/20110608160754/http:/www.equalities.gov.uk/PDF/Stern_Review_acc_FINAL.pdf [accessed 11 September 2013].

Struckman-Johnson, C. (1988) 'Forced sex on dates: it happens to men too' *The Journal of Sex Research*, 24: 234–241.

Struckman-Johnson C.J. (1991) 'Male victims of acquaintance rape' in Parrot, A.L. and Bechhofer, L. (eds.) *Acquaintance Rape: The Hidden Crime*, New York: Wiley.

Struckman-Johnson, C. and Struckman-Johnson, D. (1992) 'Acceptance of male rape myths among college men and women' *Sex Roles*, 27 (3–4): 85–100.

Struckman-Johnson, C. and Struckman Johnson, D. (1994) 'Men pressured and forced into sexual experience' *Archives of Sexual Behaviour* 23 (1): 93–114.

Struckman-Johnson C; Struckman-Johnson D; Rucker, L; Bumby, K and Donaldson, S (1996) 'Sexual coercion reported by men and women in prison' *The Journal of Sex Research*, 33 (1): 67–76.

Supernatural (2005) [TV], season 1, episode 1, 'Pilot episode', Dir. David Nutter, Warner Bros, WB, original air date 13 September, 2005, US.

Supernatural (2007a) [TV], season 2, episode 19, 'Folsom prison blues', Dir. Mike Rohl, Warner Bros, WB, original air date 26 April 2007, US.

Supernatural (2007b) [TV], season 2, episode 15, 'Tall tales', Dir. Bradford May, Warner Bros, WB, original air date 15 February 2007, US.

Survivors Trust (2010) 'Developing stability, sustainability and capacity for specialist third sector rape, sexual violence and abuse services', *Consult Trust* [online] http://www.thesurvivorstrust.org/info/research.aspx#developing [accessed 11 September 2013].

Suzuki, K. (1998) 'Pornography or therapy? Japanese girls creating the Yaoi phenomenon' in Inness, S.A. (ed.) *Millennium Girls: Today's Girls Around the World*, Lanham, MD: Rowman and Littlefield.

Synnott, A. (2009) *Re-Thinking Men: Heroes, Villains and Victims*, Surrey: Ashgate.

Taylor, D. and Vintges, K. (eds.) (2004) *Feminism and the Final Foucault*, Urbana, IL: University of Illinois Press.

Tewkesbury, R. (2007) 'Effects of sexual assaults on men: physical, mental and sexual consequences' *International Journal of Men's Health*, 6 (1): 22–35.

The Associated Press (2009) 'Report: Iraq prisoner abuse photos depict torture, rape', *USA Today*, 28 May.

The Guardian (2009) 'Rape and the media: your responses' *The Guardian*, 5 June.

The Hot Chick (2002) [film] Dir. Tom Brady, US: Walt Disney Video.

The Kevin Bishop Show (2009) [TV], series 2, episode 1, Objective Productions, Channel 4, original air date 10pm, 7 September, UK.

Thelma and Louise (1991) [film] Dir. Ridley Scott, US: Twentieth Century Fox.

The Rape of Richard Beck (1985) [film] Dir. Karen Arthur, US: American Broadcasting Company.

The Shawshank Redemption (1995) [film] Dir. Frank Darabont, US: Warner Brothers.

The Spirit of Jeet Kune Do: Once Upon a Time in High School (2004) [film] Dir. Ha Yu, South Korea: Sidus Pictures.

The World Stands Up (2004) [TV], 'featuring Chris Wainhouse, Rod Man, Dan Naturman and Howard Read', IMWP, transmitted 1:45am April 14 2009 on Comedy Central Extra UK.

The Wright Stuff (2009) [TV], season 10, Princess Productions, Channel 5, original air date 16 September 2009, UK.

Thieme, J. (2001) *Post-Colonial Con-Texts: Writing Back to the Canon*, Continuum: New York.

Thomas, D. (1993) *Not Guilty: In Defence of Modern Man*, Weidenfeld and Nicolson: London.

Tierney, J. (2006) *Criminology: Theory and Context*, 2nd edition, Harlow: Pearson.

Tomb Raider: The Cradle of Life (2003) [film] Dir. Jan De Bont, US: Paramount Pictures.

Tong, R. (1984) *Women, Sex and the Law*, New Jersey: Rowman and Allanheld.

Toolis, K. (1995) 'A queer verdict' *The Guardian*, 25 November.

Tosenberger, C. (2008a) 'Homosexuality at the online Hogwarts: Harry Potter slash fanfiction' *Childrens Literature*, 36: 185–207.

Tosenberger, C. (2008b) '"The epic love story of Sam and Dean": supernatural, queer readings, and the romance of incestuous fan fiction' *Transformative Works and Cultures*, 1 (30) [online] http://journal.transformativeworks.org/index.php/twc/article/view/30 [accessed 31 July 2013].

Travis, A. (2009) 'Cabinet rift delays rape law review' *The Guardian*, 5 August.

Two Pints of Lager and a Packet of Crisps (2005) [TV], season 5, episode 14, 'Near, far', Dirs. Carrivick, G. and Wood, N., original air date 5 April 2005, BBC, BBC 2, UK.

Van de Veer, G. (1998) *Counselling and Therapy with Refugees and Victims of Trauma*, 2nd edition, Chichester: Wiley.

Van Zoonen, L. (2005), *Entertaining the Citizen: When Politics and Popular Culture Converge*, Oxford: Rowman and Littlefield Publishers.

Viswanathan, G. (2004) (ed.) *Power, Politics and Culture: Interviews with Edward W. Said*, London: Bloomsbury.

Wakefield, A. and Fleming, J. (2009) *The Sage Dictionary of Policing*, London: Sage.

Wakelin, A. and Long, K.M. (2003) 'Effects of victim gender and sexuality on attributions of blame to rape victims' *Sex Roles* 49 (9–10): 477–487.

Walker, A., Flatley, J., Kershaw, C. and Moon, D. (eds.) (2009) 'Crime in England and Wales 2008/09' *Volume 1: Findings from the British Crime Survey and Police Recorded Crime*, Home Office Statistical Bulletin, Home Office: London.

Walker, J., Archer, J. and Davies, M. (2005) 'Effects of rape on men: a descriptive analysis' *Archives of Sexual Behaviour*, 34 (1): 69–80.

Walklate, S. (2007a) 'Men, victims and crime' in Davies, P., Francis, P. and Greer, C. (eds.) *Victims, Crime and Society*, London: Sage.

Walklate, S. (ed.) (2007b) *Handbook on Victims and Victimology*, Devon: Willan.

Wallace, H. (2007) *Victimology: Legal, Psychological and Social Perspectives*, 2nd edition, London: Pearson.

Walters, B. (1999) 'Jonathan Davis, public freak on a leash, lashes back' *The Village Voice* [online] http://www.villagevoice.com/1999-11-30/music/jonathan-davis-public-freak-on-a-leash-lashes-back/ [accessed 31 July 2013].

Warshaw, R. (1994) *I Never Called it Rape: The Ms. Report on Recognizing, Fighting and Surviving Date and Acquaintance Rape*, London: Harper Perennial.

Waterman, C.K., Dawson, D.A. and Bologna, J. (1989) 'Sexual coercion in gay male and lesbian relationships: predictors and implications for support services' *Journal of Sex* Research, 1: 118–124.

Watts, R., Bessant, J. and Hil, R. (2008) *International Criminology: A Critical Introduction*, Oxford: Routledge.

Wells, P. (2000) *The Horror Genre: From Beelzebub to Blair Witch*, London: Wallflower Press.

White, B.H. and Kurpius, S. E. R. (2002) 'Effects of victim sex and sexual orientation on perceptions of rape' *Sex Roles: A Journal of Research*, 46 (5–6): 191–200.

WHO (2005) *Multi-Country Study on Women's Health and Domestic Violence against Women*, WHO: Geneva [online] http://www.who.int/gender/violence/who_multicountry_study/summary_report/en/ [accessed 31 July 2013].

Williams, P. and Chrisman, L. (eds.) (1994) *Colonial Discourse and Post-Colonial Theory*, London: Harvester Wheatsheaf.

Williams, K. (2004) *Textbook on Criminology*, 5th edition, Oxford: Oxford University Press.

Williams, R. (2008a) 'Rape victims told alcohol consumption may cost them compensation' *The Guardian*, 12 August.

Williams, R. (2008b) 'Payout review in drink-related cases ruled out' *The Guardian*, 13 August.

Williams, R. (2008c) 'Sex assaults: police accused of adopting 'life on mars' attitude' *The Guardian*, 16 August.

Williams, R. (2009a) 'This crime ruins people's lives' *The Guardian*, 27 March.

Williams, R. (2009b) 'Police targets "meant car crime was given higher priority than rape'" *The Guardian*, 17 March.

Williams, R. (2009c) 'Conviction rates for rape remain alarmingly low' *The Guardian*, 27 March.

Williams, R. (2009d) 'Postcode lottery in rape convictions "getting worse"' *The Guardian*, 10 June.

Williams, R. and Hirsch, A. (2008) 'Court ruling hailed as refuting "rape myth"' *The Guardian*, 25 October.

Without a Paddle (2004) [film] Dir. Steven Brill, US: Paramount Pictures.

Wlodarz, J. (2001) 'Rape fantasies: Hollywood and homophobia' in Lehman, P. (ed.) *Masculinity: Bodies, Movies, Culture*, New York: Routledge.

Wodak, R. and Meyer, M. (eds.) (2001) *Methods of Critical Discourse Analysis*, London: Sage.

Wolfgang, M.E. (1958) *Patterns in Criminal Homicide*, Philadelphia: University of Pennsylvania Press.

Xu, M., Chia, L.T. and Jin, J. (2005) 'Affective content analysis in comedy and horror videos by audio emotional event detection' in Conference Proceedings for *IEEE International Conference on Multimedia and Expo*, Amsterdam, Netherlands, 6–9 July [online] http://cemnet.ntu.edu.sg/home/asltchia/publication/AudioAnalysisUnderstanding/Conference/Affective%20Content%20Analysis%20in%20Comedy%20and%20Horror%20Videos%20by%20Audio%20Emotional%20Event%20Detection.pdf [accessed 31 July 2013].

Yates, J. (2009) 'My wish list for Met rape case investigation' *The Guardian*, 26 March.

You Don't Mess with the Zohan (2008) [film] Dirs. Dennis Dugan, Judd Apatow, US: Sony Pictures Home Entertainment.

Young, J. (nd) *Critical Criminology for the Twenty-First Century: Critique, Irony and Always Unfinished* [online] http://www.malcolmread.co.uk/JockYoung/Critical.htm [accessed 31 July 2013].

Youssef, S. (2004) (unpublished) 'Girls who like Boys who like Boys – Ethnography of Online Slash/Yaoi Fans' BA (hons) thesis, MA, US: Mount Hollyoke College [online] http://www.yuuyami.com/luce/thesis.pdf [accessed 31 July 2013].

Zizek, S. (2002) *Welcome to the Desert of the Real*, London: Verso.

Index

Printed and bound in Great Britain by
CPI Group (UK) Ltd, Croydon, CR0 4YY